THE MICROPOLITICS OF
INCLUSIVE EDUCATION

INCLUSIVE EDUCATION

Series Editors:

Gary Thomas, Professor Education, Oxford Brookes University, and Christine O'Hanlon, School of Education, University of East Anglia

The movement towards inclusive education is gathering momentum throughout the world. But how is it realized in practice? The volumes within this series will examine the arguments for inclusive schools and the evidence for the success of inclusion. The intention behind the series is to fuse a discussion about the ideals behind inclusion with pictures of inclusion in practice. The aim is to straddle the theory/practice divide, keeping in mind the strong social and political principles behind the move to inclusion while observing and noting the practical challenges to be met.

Current and forthcoming titles:

THE MICROPOLITICS OF INCLUSIVE EDUCATION

An ethnography

Shereen Benjamin

Open University Press
Buckingham · Philadelphia

Open University Press
Celtic Court
22 Ballmoor
Buckingham
MK18 1XW

email: enquiries@openup.co.uk
world wide web: www.openup.co.uk

and
325 Chestnut Street
Philadelphia, PA 19106, USA

First Published 2002

A catalogue record of this book is available from the British Library

ISBN   0 335 21048 1 (pb)   0 335 21049 X (hb)

Library of Congress Cataloging-in-Publication Data
Benjamin, Shereen, 1965–
    The micropolitics of inclusive education : an ethnography / Shereen Benjamin.
        p. cm. – (Inclusive education)
    Includes bibliographical references (p.) and index.
    ISBN 0-335-21049-X – ISBN 0-335-21048-1 (pbk.)
    1. Inclusive education – Great Britain – Case studies. 2. Educational sociology
    – Great Britain – Case studies. 3. Feminism and education – Great Britain – Case
    studies. I. Title. II. Series.
    LC1203.G7 B46 2002
    371.9′046–dc21   2002023856

Typeset by Graphicraft Limited, Hong Kong
Printed in Great Britain by St Edmundsbury Press Limited,
Bury St Edmunds, Suffolk

Contents

Series editors' preface

'Inclusion' has become something of an international buzz-word. It is difficult to trace its provenance or the growth in its use over the last two decades, but what is certain is that it is now *de rigeur* for policy documents, mission statements and political speeches. It has become a slogan – almost obligatory in the discourse of all right-thinking people.

The problem about the sloganizing of 'inclusion' is that the word has become often merely a filler in the conversation. People can talk about 'inclusion' without really thinking about what they mean, merely to add a progressive gloss to what they are saying. Politicians who talk casually about the need for a more inclusive society know that they will be seen as open-minded and enlightened, and will be confident in the knowledge that all sorts of difficult practical questions can be circumvented. If this happens and if there is insufficient thought about the nitty-gritty mechanics, those who do work hard for inclusion can easily be dismissed as peddling empty promises.

This series is dedicated to examining in detail some of the ideas lying behind inclusive education. Inclusion, much more than 'integration' or 'mainstreaming', is embedded in a range of contexts – political and social as well as psychological and educational – and our aim in this series is to make some examination of these contexts. In providing a forum for discussion and critique we hope to help provide the basis for a wider intellectual and practical foundation for more inclusive practice in schools and elsewhere.

In noting that inclusive education is about more than simply 'integration', it is important to stress that inclusive education is really about extending the comprehensive ideal in education. Those who talk about it are therefore less concerned with children's supposed 'special educational needs' (and it is becoming increasingly difficult meaningfully to define what such needs are) and more concerned with developing an education system in which tolerance, diversity and equity are striven for. To aim for such developments is surely uncontentious; what is more controversial is the means by which this is done. There are many and varied ways of helping to develop more inclusive schools and the authors of this series look at some of these. While one focus in this has to be on the place and role of the special school, it is by no means the only focus: the thinking and practice which go on inside and outside schools may do much to exclude or marginalize children and the authors of this series try to give serious attention to such thinking and practice.

The books in this series therefore examine a range of matters: the knowledge of special education; the frames of analysis which have given legitimacy to such knowledge; the changing political mood which inspires a move to inclusion. In the context of all this, they also examine some new developments in inclusive thinking and practice inside and outside schools.

In *The Micropolitics of Inclusive Education*, Shereen Benjamin opens up some of the spaces closed down by the sloganizing of 'inclusion'. We are invited to glimpse the real educational world as experienced by a group of comprehensive school students – girls and young women who would, until a short time ago, have been educated in segregated special schools. The students' negotiation of their 'inclusion' in a mainstream environment draws our attention to the complexities, and sometimes the contradictions, that are often obscured by political rhetoric.

The stories told in this book are deeply personal ones, but they are embedded in a much larger set of political contexts. The school in question is an active player in a world of league tables, performance management and, above all, of measurable results in examinations that determine, to a large extent, the future options of its students. Like schools in many parts of the world, its public face, and its own survival, is contingent on how 'effective' it is perceived to be. In their day-to-day schooling experience, students of all levels of academic proficiency have to negotiate this context. For students for whom success in examinations is not on the agenda, this negotiation is fraught with problems. They are welcomed into the school, but are they really full members of the community? Do they, and can they, participate on the same terms as everybody else?

The answers to these questions are complex, and not easily reduced to once-and-for-all answers or to one-size-fits-all prescriptions. Inclusive education must be seen to have a long-term agenda. The crucial point Shereen Benjamin makes here is that inclusion depends less on method and more on sensitivity – sensitivity to difference – and if we want to start thinking about the kinds of changes that will be sustainable in the long term, we need to consider how schools produce 'insiders' and 'outsiders'. Perceived academic competence, gender/sexuality, ethnicity, nationality, social class, access to resources, physical appearance, religion, and many other factors shape students' experiences of schooling. If we want to make schools more inclusive, we cannot afford to write these differences out of the picture.

Gary Thomas
Christine O'Hanlon

Acknowledgements

My thanks go first of all to the girls and young women who shared their thoughts and experiences with me. Their generosity and openness made the research, and this book, possible. I would also like to thank very warmly the staff at Newbrook School – my former colleagues – for welcoming me into their classrooms, and for making time in their over-stretched working schedules to talk to me. Numerous friends and colleagues at the University of London Institute of Education thought with me about this work as it progressed, and read and commented on drafts. For this I would especially like to thank my two PhD supervisors, Debbie Epstein and Valerie Hey, and also Suki Ali, Anne Gold, Claudia Lapping, Diana Leonard, Ingrid Lunt, Gretar Marinossen and Sarah O'Flynn.

The ethnographic research on which this book is based was funded by the award of a research studentship from the Economic and Social Research Council (ESRC), held at the University of London Institute of Education. I would particularly like to thank the staff involved in the administration of this award, especially Teresa Tucker of the ESRC and Patricia Kelly, Nicola Blaxill, Wendy Barber, Julia Bacon and Jenny Philips of the Institute of Education. Finally, neither this book, nor the PhD thesis from which it is drawn, would have seen the light of day without the constant encouragement and support of many people, foremost among them, Cynthia Cockburn, Liz Khan and Hilary Prentice. My deepest thanks go to them.

Introduction

Meera: If you go for a job, and you've got a really good brain
          then they give you it, they give you the job.
Ambrine: Yeah, and if you didn't get to a high level they
          wouldn't give you the job, they'd, they'd give it to
          a person who had the higher level, who had good
          GCSEs.

Ambrine and Meera are 11 years old, and in their first year of secondary education at Newbrook School for Girls (not its real name) in a UK inner city. When they were at primary school, they were identified as having 'special educational needs' (SEN), and this is a designation that has followed them into their secondary school careers. At the end of their primary schooling, both girls took the statutory tests for 11-year-olds and failed to reach the 'expected standard for their age' (Department for Education and Employment (DfEE) 1999b). They are caught in a policy contradiction. On the one hand, the standards agenda – the drive to improve perceived educational 'standards' as measured through test and examination results – constructs them as failing. Normative examination results, including National Curriculum level 4 in the national tests they have just taken and the benchmark 'C' grade in General Certificate of Secondary Education (GCSE) examinations, are not accessible to Ambrine and Meera. On the other hand, they are positioned as the recipients of 'inclusive education' and of the impetus towards educating all students within mainstream schooling (Department for Education and Skills (DfES) 2001). Schools and teachers are required to make their curricula accessible to Ambrine and Meera, and are exhorted to reduce barriers to their learning.

This book is primarily concerned with the sense that Ambrine and Meera, and students in similar positions, make of this policy contradiction. Its argument is that the standards agenda and its impact on schooling policy is itself one of the most insurmountable barriers to learning for these students. To examine the production of this particular barrier, we need to examine, in considerable depth, the politics and micropolitics of schooling. This examination is a process of teasing out the many and varied linkages between national policy (often in international contexts), formal school policy, and the informal microcultures of those who inhabit schools. These interact with and map onto each other throughout the interpersonal world of the school, to form an overlapping set of school cultures. Study of school cultures is increasingly finding its way onto the research and policy map (Epstein and Johnson 1998; Carrington 1999; Corbett 1999; Zollers et al. 1999; Alton-Lee et al. 2000). However, this book is framed not in terms of school cultures but in terms of micropolitics: the intersection of personal, institutional and global politics. Viewing inclusive education through a micropolitical lens highlights the struggle and contestation inherent in cultural processes, foregrounds their link with prevailing social and political contexts, and draws attention to issues of power and privilege.

The research in this book grew out of my own experiences as a learning support teacher in Newbrook School. I worked there, initially on a full-time and later on a part-time basis, with students on the school's 'special needs register' (see Chapter 3). I enjoyed much of my work there: teaching and non-teaching colleagues were mostly positive about working towards inclusive education (though Newbrook, rightly, does not call itself a fully inclusive school), and I very much enjoyed the company of the girls and young women with whom I spent most of my days. But I always felt a vague dissatisfaction. Somehow, in spite of all my well-intentioned attempts to enable these students to participate alongside their higher-achieving peers, I always felt complicit in the very dubious act of turning out the 'losers' required by a normative, competitive system. Pleased as I would always be when a young woman with whom I had worked scored an 'F' grade at GCSE when a 'G' at best had been expected, I also felt that nagging sense of disappointment that, in a larger context, such grades would not be recognized as 'success'. As Ambrine and Meera point out, a low grade counts for very little in the labour market. Was I somehow letting these young women down? This book tells the story of how I tried to answer that question.

What's in a name? Representing 'special needs students'

A notice attached to a machine in the computer room at Newbrook reads 'Priority Use for Special Needs Students'. This grammatically imperfect notice indicates many problems with the available language, its deployment and the meanings that underpin it. When the language of 'special educational needs' replaced the language of subnormality and handicap in the UK in the early 1980s, it was intended to bring about an attitudinal shift in which failure to make progress at school would be constructed as occurring in the interplay between the pupil and the educational experience provided for that pupil. Special needs were no longer to be understood as intrinsic deficiency (Warnock 1978; Gipps et al. 1987; Welton et al. 1990). But, as signs such as the one in the computer room at Newbrook reflect, there has been a certain amount of slippage here, and, in many instances, the student with 'special educational needs' has become the 'special needs student', a distinct subject position that designated students are required to inhabit (see Chapter 1).

The well-documented problems with 'special needs' terminology (Corbett 1996; Dyson 1999; Goodley 2001) raised several problems for me, both in my research and in my work as a learning support teacher at Newbrook. I would want to distance myself from a model which produces students as inherently deficient, in the way the categories that predated the Education Act 1981 undoubtedly did. But, equally, I would not want to claim that intellectual impairment (the term preferred in disability theory) is nothing but a social construction, although its attendant meanings and practices assuredly *are* socially and politically constructed. The language of SEN is unequal to the challenge of engaging with this problem, and does not have sufficient explanatory purchase to begin to illuminate the inequalities and oppression in which it is both embedded and implicated. Corbett (1996) remarks that:

> There is the sentimental language of 'special need' which is embodied in the imagery of protection, care, tenderness and love . . . This language needs to be examined and revealed for the sugar-coated poison that it is. Secondly . . . there is hate. The language of 'special needs' has always been composed of words and images which foster mistrust, loathing and hostility.
>
> (Corbett 1996: 3)

Each of these two strands has its own distinct discursive history (Hurt 1988; Cole 1989; Benjamin 2001) which I do not have space to explore here. For now, it is enough to note that the language of special needs presents itself as neutral, located within a liberal pluralist perspective of 'equal but different': a perspective that has come to operate, as I will show in Chapter 7, as a dangerous fiction. The special needs discourse is accordingly produced through an investment in concealing the power imbalances with which it is at the least complicit, and for which it is often responsible (Tomlinson 1982; Thomas and Loxley 2001).

The broadness and non-specificity of SEN terminology (Lunt and Norwich 1999) presents me with another problem in describing the participants of my research. My concern is not with the full range of students who have been identified as having 'special educational needs' at Newbrook: in particular, I am not concerned with those who are described as having 'behaviour as a priority concern'. Norwich examines the SEN discourse through its critics. On the one hand, there are sociologists who consider the social functions of the discourse, while on the other there are inclusive educators who attempt to 'do without difference categories' (Norwich 1993: 44). He argues that 'the concept of special educational needs is a category itself, just a broader superordinate one, rather than the more specific categories used pre-Warnock' (Norwich 1993: 45). For my purposes, this superordinate category is too broad, since it encompasses almost every way of failing to make progress at school within normative terms. Nor am I willing to make a premature attempt to do away with difference categories. As many have shown (Hall 1992; Mort 1994; Allan 1999), such premature attempts are misguided: they make it harder both to unravel the continuing repro- duction of inequalities, and to devise strategies for addressing the resultant imbalances. I need a more clearly delimited difference category in order to examine the inegalitarian meanings and practices associated with that difference.

The terminology developed from within the disability movement and associated with the social model of disability is also unsuitable here. Most of the students with whom I worked at Newbrook, and who are the subjects and participants of this research, cannot be described as 'intellectually impaired' and thereby offered a recognizable position within the disability movement. Their difference is marked and categorized only in the context of schooling. In the mid-1980s, some of the students would have received their formal education in segregated schools for children and young people with moderate learning difficulties (MLD) while others would have been educated, as now, in mainstream classrooms. They are the students who, in terms of the National Learning Targets will not 'reach the expected standard for their age' (DfEE 1999b). They are listed on Newbrook's SEN register as students who have 'learning as a priority concern', though they are mostly not recogniz- ably disabled.

How, then, am I to describe these girls and young women without con- stantly resorting to the cumbersome 'students who have been formally iden- tified as having SEN'? As I will explore more fully later on, the students do not apply SEN terminology to themselves, usually choosing to use an appar- ently much more pejorative vernacular or none at all. Nor was it possible for me to work with them to explore alternative terminology: again a theme to which I will return. While I would not presume to invent terminology on behalf of a group who experience an oppression to which I am not person- ally subject, it has been necessary to find a way of grouping the students and, very contingently, of naming that group.

As an interim solution to this problem, I have worked with the notion of 'intellectual subordination'. The production of relations of domination and subordination is a dynamic process, enacted simultaneously across multiple social differences. Through this process individuals come to occupy – or not – leading social positions and the privileges and material advantages that accrue to such positions. Perceived intellectual ability is one of several axes of difference through which power and prestige are made differentially avail- able. The students who participated in this study, and others like them, are subordinated by understandings of intellectual 'perfomance' that value levels of attainment to which they cannot aspire, and by an economic system in which unqualified women are the poorest paid group in society (National Advisory Council for Education and Training Targets (NACETT) 2000). Dominant versions of educational success – such as the A*–C grades at GCSE valued by employers and the media – are not accessible to these students. The versions of success to which they can aspire are, as I will ex- plain in Chapters 7 and 8, subordinated ones, with far-reaching implications regarding the students' current and future social positioning and material well-being.

Intellectual subordination thus implies the inscription of school students into relations of subordination through a set of normative academic expectations that are inaccessible to them. As a piece of terminology intended to make visible an axis of systemic inequality, it is not an unproblematic solution. The notion of intellectual subordination contains within itself an ambiguity over to what extent a student's 'inability' to access these expectations is inherent, and to what extent it is socially and culturally produced. This ambiguity is, I would argue, necessary at this stage, since the means of identifying (through testing and assessing) intellectual ability are produced through socially situated instruments that are themselves part of a knowledge/power apparatus (Slee 1995; Allan 1996, 1999).

To make matters more complex still, there are instances throughout the book when I do use the terminology associated with SEN, and, in particular, the phrase 'special needs student'. Where I do this, it is in order to explore how such a subject position is produced, and how it is lived by those students who have no choice but to position themselves in relation to it.

Outline

Chapter 1 introduces the conceptual and contextual frameworks of the research. It explains those elements of theory – mostly drawn from feminist post-structural and other critical theories – which are used throughout the book. Chapter 2 introduces, in some detail, Newbrook School for Girls, the students who participated in the research and the research I carried out there. It looks at some of the complexities of carrying out research, as a learning support teacher, with students who have been designated as having 'learning difficulties' of various kinds.

Chapters 3 and 4 are mainly concerned with micropolitics at school policy level, and with how these work in the context of larger political processes. Together, they demonstrate some of the real-life implications and conundrums generated by the contradiction between the standards agenda and the move towards inclusive education. Chapter 3 examines how Newbrook is positioned as a 'successful school', with the norms and requirements of the standards agenda writ large in that production. It looks at how policy in Newbrook, in conjunction with national policy, produces the subject 'successful teacher' and 'successful student'. Chapter 4 looks at constructions of 'failure' at Newbrook, and explores the production, at school policy level, of the subject 'special needs student'.

Chapters 5 and 6 are concerned with student identity work. In Chapter 5, the accounts of a group of Year 7 students – girls in their first year at Newbrook – show how they make sense of themselves and their schooling, using the 'identity resources' (see Chapter 1) available to them as 'special needs students' at Newbrook. Chapter 6 does something similar with the accounts of a group of Year 11 students. Chapters 7 and 8 link the processes of identity work with school micropolitics, in order to understand and critique both. Chapter 7 discusses the examination process in relation to the production of consent by 'special needs students' to their ongoing intellectual subordination. It outlines two distinct and hierarchically ordered versions of success in circulation at Newbrook: the dominant version, produced in relation to the norms of the standards agenda, and the 'consolation' version, produced by well-intentioned teachers and students, as a kind of consolation prize for those to whom the dominant version is unattainable. Chapter 8 goes on to explore a third hierarchical version, the 'disabled' version of success. Through the discursive practices of this version of success, again well-intentioned, the binary difference between 'able' and 'disabled' is reinscribed, with the concept of 'valuing diversity' co-opted to do the work of reinscription.

The central theme of this book is that the problem of intellectual subordination is one of unequal relations. Most emphatically, it is not a problem of human deficiency or otherwise. The problem is not that people are infinitely varied in their intellectual capacities and that life circumstances of all kinds impact on the ways in which those capacities develop. Rather, the problem is with the social and political meanings that accrue to perceived intellectual deficiency – all too often powerlessness and subordination – and with their material and economic consequences: poverty, unemployment and 'social exclusion'.

Schooling is implicated in this construction of meaning and its consequence, and three specific discourses associated with the standards agenda have a particular part to play. First, the discursive practices of 'school effectiveness' are irreducibly linked to the production of normative versions of achievement, and thereby to the production of students to whom normative versions are inaccessible. Second, the notion of 'continuous improvement' reinscribes the perception that attaining normative levels of academic success is desirable, and that the inability to attain those levels is somehow shameful. And, third, the notion of 'valuing diversity', so benevolently intended, is being deployed to hold hierarchies in place in insidious ways. Throughout the book, these three discourses emerge as problematic. As alternatives, this book discusses three discursive shifts: from school effectiveness to school effects (Lingard et al. 1998), from continuous improvement to sustainable egalitarian change, and from valuing diversity to redistribution.

CHAPTER ONE

Producing inclusion: student identity work and the micropolitics of 'special educational needs'

Power and politics in the classroom

One afternoon, after school had finished for the day, Aqsa came to see me in the staffroom. A week earlier, I had talked to her and a number of other Year 11 students about participating in my research. She had been keen to take part. Now she arrived in the staffroom, breathless from running over from the science department. She had something she wanted to say on the tape recorder, so that I could put it in my book. We went to a nearby classroom, switched the tape machine on, and her story unfolded.

> *Aqsa*: Sir he nice teacher, only tells off bad girls, girls who not do their work, innit. Sir he nice to me, because he know if I don't get good mark is not my fault, he not shout at me. And Chantelle and Tana they go [kisses teeth and demonstrates 'adolescent flounce'] and is very very rude. Is stuff everywhere, is all over the floor, here and here and here [points]. And Sir he gets angry, his face is all red, like he very very angry, he very, very angry, and he shouts, 'Is all Year 11 doesn't care about their GCSEs' [pause]. Some teachers they say we the worst Year 11, but is not true, is some very rude girls but is not everyone, is not everyone. Sir he very angry, and he say to Chantelle, 'Is you want me to tell everyone your mark what you got in Year 10 exams? Is you want me to read out to everyone? Is it you want?' He say like that, to Chantelle he say, 'Is you want me to tell everyone? No, you not want me to do that

because is you be shamed, because is lowest mark in the class'. And, Miss, I am so, so happy, innit, because I think is me get the lowest mark in the class, first, right, I think he make mistake, he not know I am worst in the class, and I going to say, 'Sir, I get lower mark than Chantelle, is me with the lowest mark', but I not want to say because I shamed, innit. But then I think must be true, is not me is the most stupid, because Chantelle she get lower mark than me, so must be true. I'm so happy, and she was born here, is even she not have to learn new language, speak English. I'm so happy . . .

(Interview 3/11/99)

A week later, Chantelle referred to the same incident. Unsurprisingly, her account was rather different from Aqsa's.

Chantelle: So, like, we wound him up something bad, and we was bad mouthing him – *Sir* – he don't usually have to put up with that sort of thing, you could see, um, he didn't know what to do, he didn't know *what* was going on, it ain't probably happened to him before, 'Girls, girls, this is *me* you're mouthing off to' it was like. So Sir, right, he gets all red in the face, it was really funny, Miss, you had to be there to see it, to believe it, to see it and *believe* it, and we're la-la-la-la-la nothing out of the ordinary is going on here, and Sir he couldn't believe his eyes, his little red ears, and we're just la-la-la-la-la. It was *worth* it Miss. It was *well* worth it . . . So Sir he shouts and he shouts and he shouts and we're all quiet at the end, the stuff's cleaned up, we're all sitting up good like little primary children on those stools – them ones really hurt your bum – and Sir he brings it all out. He's got the weapon of destruction, yeah, 'Chantelle' he goes, 'Chantelle, do you want me to tell everyone your mark what you got in the Year 10 exam?' And I'm like, not looking at everyone, especially Tana, it was like I didn't know, what was I supposed to *do*? I mean what are you supposed to *do* when that happens? 'Cause all lesson, it was like about pretending not to be scared of Mr. Evans, 'cause it was how we was ruling the lesson, and what am I supposed to *do*? So I just sits there, and I'm not looking at Tana, right, and I'm not looking at Sir [pause]. And Sir's going chatting on and on, giving us lot all grief about the exams, making out we don't care, *as if* – I mean, as if *anyone* gets to be Year 11 in this place and don't care about their exams. *As if*. And Sir, right, he goes, 'I bet you don't want me to tell you out loud what you got in the Year 10 exam. 'Cause you got the worst mark in the whole class', well, Miss, right, I could've died, and I mean died, there in the lesson.

(Interview 10/11/99)

Aqsa and Chantelle are in their final year as students at Newbrook School. Their two differing accounts of the same Year 11 science lesson raise the questions that are at the heart of this book. Both students are 15 years old, and both have been formally identified as having 'special educational needs'. But, in their accounts of the science lesson and their relation to it, they produce themselves as very different versions of the subject 'special needs student'. Running through both accounts are issues of power, linked to questions of 'success' and 'achievement' in a specific micropolitical context. For Aqsa, the public humiliation of a 'very rude girl' by a 'nice teacher' is something to be celebrated, though a core of bitterness runs through that celebration. She rescues herself from what she understands as her own ignominious position at the bottom of the class, while simultaneously confirming her investment in dominant versions of success, here encoded through examination results. Chantelle, meanwhile, finds herself with no room for manoeuvre when what started as an enjoyable wresting of power from the hands of a customarily authoritative teacher turns into public humiliation. The teacher effectively trumps her through deploying the dominant discourse of success in his successful bid to reassert his control, and she has no way of answering back.

When Aqsa and Chantelle produce themselves as different versions of the 'special needs student', they use understandings of 'success' and 'achievement' that have been produced in a discursive field that is itself produced by its specific political and microcultural context, and which is nuanced by multiple and cross-cutting indices of difference. How do students who have been formally identified as having 'SEN' use understandings of 'success' and 'achievement' in their identity work? To answer this we need to address a number of interrelated questions:

- What understandings of 'success' and 'achievement' are explicitly and implicitly encoded into student microcultures and school micropolitics? How do these understandings interact with current schooling policy?
- How do students 'do power' in relation to (dominant and other) versions of success; how do they use notions of success and achievement in positioning themselves and each other in formal and informal microcultural work?
- How do students who have been identified as having 'SEN' describe themselves? What discourses of success and achievement do they use in positioning themselves in relation to the (academic) learning process?
- How are 'failing' positions on the ability continuum articulated with other systemic axes of difference – principally here 'race'/ethnicity, religion, nationality, social class, gender sexuality, physical appearance and command of the English language?
- How do students operate discourse and practice in 'SEN' in conjunction with the different modalities of femininity available to them?

First, though, it is important to consider what is meant by the term 'identity work', to outline its theoretical foundations and to explore its implications for research into inclusive education.

The political is personal: identities at work

> Micro-social descriptions of our commonsense practices are essential
> for those who want to take a macro-economic perspective . . . Ideological
> hegemony, as part of the actual workings of control, is not something
> one sees only on the level of macro-social behaviour and economic
> relations; nor is it something that resides merely at the top of our heads,
> so to speak. Instead, hegemony is constituted by our very day-to-day
> practices. It is our whole assemblage of commonsense meanings and
> actions that make up the social world as we know it, a world in which
> the internal curricular, teaching and evaluative characteristics of educa-
> tional institutions partake.
>
> (Apple 1995: 37)

It is tempting to read Aqsa's and Chantelle's accounts of the science lesson
and seek to apportion blame. Was it the teacher's fault? After all, he could be
said to have failed to maintain adequate control of the lesson in the first
place, and then resorted to a strategy of public humiliation of a relatively
powerless student. Or was it the fault of Chantelle and her friends? They
had pushed the teacher beyond all reasonable limits, possibly at the expense
of other students who might have wanted order to be restored so that they
could learn some science. Neither explanation is adequate, though there
is truth in both. Rather, what is going on is a much more complex and
dynamic set of processes, involving a known reservoir of resources which
exist to be drawn upon by all the participants involved in the negotiation.
It is these resources that have become so taken-for-granted as to become
common sense, but if we step back we may see them in play.

When Chantelle and her friends antagonize the teacher, they are drawing
from identity resources that have been locally produced in a much wider sociopolitical context. These resources are profoundly shaped, in this instance, by
'race' (all of the young women involved in the disruption are African Caribbean
and tend to be positioned as oppositional), by gender and sexuality and by
social class as well as by perceived academic ability. They are also generated in
the ongoing identity and microcultural work that these specific young women
have been undertaking in relation to each other and the formal school
since they joined it.[1] As they take up active or audient positions in the
unfolding drama, each person in the room performs her own identity work,
producing herself (or, in the case of the teacher, himself) in relation to the
existing discursive field, and shaping that discursive field in the process.

Post-structuralism offers an account of 'identity' as 'self-in-process': a con-
tinual and lifelong process through which individuals negotiate their sense
of self. This process involves making, modifying and resisting, the identifications made available by prevailing personal, social and political contexts.
While individuals have agency in negotiating the identity process, the conditions within which this agency is exercised are produced by existing
structures, understandings and relations. The students – and the teacher – in
the Year 11 science lesson are actively involved in identity work. In Aqsa's

account, she is not simply 'being good'. She is *doing* her identity work, inscribing her own understanding of herself as a hard-working student. But the ways she can do this are constrained by the fact that she has been categorized as having 'SEN' and is positioned as 'less able'. She cannot, then, identify as a high-achieving 'good student'. She must make use of some of the identifications available to a 'special needs student'. In the telling of her account, she is *doing*, not merely *being*, a specific version of 'special needs student'. The available versions are explored in more detail later in the book.

In exploring the dynamic nature of social identities as produced at school, I have drawn largely on a set of theories and tools associated with feminist reworkings of post-structuralism. An analysis of Chantelle's and Aqsa's accounts requires an engagement with the way a specific set of meanings around perceived academic ability is deployed in the struggle over power in the science lesson. A feminist analysis which questions taken-for-granted knowledge from a position of commitment to 'analyse the hidden and the marginal' (Gordon et al. 2000: 3) both enables and makes imperative such an engagement. Kenway and her colleagues note that 'Post-structuralism . . . is concerned with the way in which meanings are made, the way they circulate among us, the way they are struggled over, the impact they have on our identities and actions. Post-structuralism is particularly interested in the connections between meaning and power' (Kenway et al. 1997: xix).

Chantelle and her friends had been 'ruling the lesson' through, amongst other things, their refusal to recognize the teacher as authority figure, reducing his status to that of a (male) plaything, his embodied discomfort (marked by his little red ears) to be looked at and delighted in. Chantelle's retelling of the story is in itself a performance, in which she reinscribes the teacher's insertion into an embodied and sexualized discourse, with herself and her friends in predatory roles (Kehily and Nayak 1996). She thereby opposes the formal positioning of teachers within a solely intellectual, and not embodied, discourse (Epstein and Johnson 1998). But the teacher has ultimate recourse to a greater, systemically embedded power which, as a last resort, he is able to call upon. He can invoke a dominant discourse of success which produces Chantelle, as I will argue in Chapter 7, as a nothing, or a nobody. In the face of this institutionally and systemically located power, Chantelle falls silent and immobile. It is the 'weapon of destruction' which she cannot, in this instance, resist.

It is important, though, not to overstate the case of the cultural construction of power through meaning. Kenway and her colleagues note that 'the politics of discourse is often overdetermined by the power relationships which exist beyond the moment and the specific locality' (Kenway et al. 1994: 190). Power is also produced in this example, and throughout school life, through a set of institutional and societal practices which have very material locations and effects. The discourses and discursive practices around perceived achievement in circulation at Newbrook are strongly related to students' future life-chances and also have present-time material implications. As students progress up the school, to be intellectually subordinated means to take up a promised future of low-paid jobs or of no work at all. As Apple

(1995) reminds us, the inscription of common-sense meanings through everyday actions is never neutral, but is part of the production of what he terms ideological hegemony. When the science teacher falls back on an act of humiliation made possible by Chantelle's ongoing intellectual subordination as a 'special needs student', the competitive, examination-performance oriented system in which someone has to be last, is inscribed, once more, as common sense and as irrefutable. Although this teacher is not responsible for the existence of that system, nor solely responsible for Chantelle's intellectual subordination, his recourse to a discourse to which all the students in the room are subject allows him to reposition himself, once more, as the authority figure. Weedon argues that 'it is the need to regulate disparate forms of subjectivity in the interests of existing power relations that motivates the language of common-sense' (Weedon 1997: 94). And, as I will argue in more detail later, the regulation of Chantelle through this particular common sense is one of the keys to her present and future subordination in the labour market (Levitas 1998).

In order to interrogate how the disparate forms of subjectivity at play in formal and informal contexts at Newbrook are regulated, and in whose interests, it is necessary first to uncover them. Here, again, it is vital to note the embodied and spatialized nature of identity work at school (Armstrong 1999), and the ways in which bodies function as both objects and agents of practice (Bordo 1993a, 1993b; Connell 1995). Gordon et al. (2000: 4) note that 'Space is social and mental, and constrained but not determined by the physical'. Sometimes the regulation is subtle: when students are required to sit up 'like good little primary children' on stools that 'really hurt your bum'. Sometimes it is more obvious, when students are physically detained by a teacher, or sent to the 'duty room' to work under the watchful surveillant eye of a member of the senior management team. Students' (and teachers') occupation of space is, like the language they use, seldom neutral. When Chantelle and her friends make a mess in the science lesson, they are, amongst other things, extending the amount of space available for their own use, asserting their right over the physical environment. They produce themselves as 'very rude girls' as much by this appropriation of space as by their utterances. Key to the teacher's ousting them from this position of power is his ability to produce these disruptive students as 'docile bodies' (Foucault 1975), occupying space in the way he wants them to.

To sum up, then, I am using the term 'identity work' to mean a version of 'politics-in-action': the ongoing process of performing, contesting, re-producing and reconfiguring power relations in contexts contingent on prevailing micropolitical conditions, but not (necessarily) determined by them. As this might imply, I am working with a model that perceives structure and agency not as polarities, but existing in symbiotic relationship with each other. I do not have space here to rehearse in any detail the debates over structure versus agency: later in the book, I will be exploring how and where the students are produced by, and produce, the discursive and material structures in and through which they 'perform' (Butler 1990) their identity work. In attempting to theorize from such a perspective, I am necessarily trying both to interrogate and to think beyond the dominant binary system of thought.

Beyond binarisms?

Hall (1992) charts the rise to pre-eminence of a binary system of thought from its origins in Renaissance Protestantism and captialism, to its ascribed zenith in the Enlightenment. He notes that 'the Enlightenment centred on the image of rational, scientific Man, freed from dogma and intolerance, before whom the whole of human history was laid out for understanding and mastery' (Hall 1992: 282). The binarism of man/nature was (and is) reflected in other key binarisms, notably man/woman, rational/irrational and thought/matter. Crucially, these dualisms are organized hierarchically: rationality, associated with maleness, has been constituted as a site of normative power, and has constituted irrationality as its negative other (Kenway et al. 1994).

Using insights associated with feminist post-structuralism, I will briefly outline three interrelated derivations of binary thought that are of particular relevance here. First, I will look at how binarisms, and especially the opposition of rational by irrational, are implicated in the reproduction of relations of subordination and domination. Second, I will look at how the rational/irrational binarism works through schooling, and in particular, how it is deployed in standards agenda discourses of school effectiveness and school improvement. Third, I will point to some of the concepts associated with a post-structural approach that attempts to move beyond binarisms, in order to explain some of the concepts that I will be using later in the book.

Pateman (1988) usefully links the system of binary thought, in which rational Man endeavoured to use natural science to know and master the Universe, with the legislative emergence of modern patriarchy through the social (and, as she argues, sexual) contract. She traces how the 'fiction' of social contract arose from the opposition of Man with Nature. This brought in its wake a social, cultural and political system in which relations of domination and subordination were inscribed and legitimized within a discourse of (male) freedom and rights. She observes that 'the civil state and law and (patriarchal) discipline are not two forms of power but dimensions of the complex, multi-faceted structure of domination in modern patriarchy' (Pateman 1988: 16). Thus, from its inception, binary thought was linked to the production of material power. In the rational–irrational opposition, mastery was the property of educated, rich, white men. Identified with irrationality were women, children, non-European or European-derived 'races', disabled people and the working classes. Only the male elite were endowed with rationality and, through it, access to the economic, social and political capital it attracted (Cohen and Bains 1988; St Pierre 2000).

Rational Man's posited endeavour to understand and master the Universe was a uniquely individualized one. Hall explains the contribution of Descartes to the emergence of this individual, rationally developing self: 'Things must be explained, [Descartes believed], by reducing them to their essentials – the fewest possible, ultimately irreducible elements. At the centre of "mind" he placed the individual subject, constituted by its capacity to reason and think' (Hall 1992: 282). Linked to the notion of the rational (male, white, adult, able-bodied and upper- or middle-class) individual was a specific notion of freedom and democracy. In what has been called the 'democratic fantasy' (Walkerdine 1988; Walkerdine and Lucey 1989), regulation, and, through it, the enduring reproduction, over time, of relations of subordination and domination, came to be normalized. Over time, the origins of the rational, choosing self have been obscured (Giddens 1991).

When compulsory mass schooling began in the UK in the 1870s, it operated both to produce the appropriately skilled and motivated workforce needed by industrial capitalism, and to reinscribe the rational–irrational binary together with the modernist project of the incrementally developing self. Beck (2000: 166) argues that 'The expansion of nation-state produced and affirmed individualisation, with doctrines of socialisation and institutions of education to match'. Arguably, this modernist/humanist project of 'the choosing, deciding, shaping human being who aspires to be the author of his or her own life' (Beck 2000: 165) is still at the heart of schooling today. This in itself would be enough to marginalize those who are deemed to have 'SEN': learning difficulties, in particular, are constructed as oppositional to the rational, incrementally developing child of psychoeducational discourse, who progresses according to a linear, normatively produced model (Walkerdine 1988). This rich, white, male-derived discourse privileges a certain model of learning and view of schooling. A meritocratic ideal, in which those pupils of 'ability' were allowed ('irrespective' of class and later of race and gender) to progress through their own achievement and effort, was built into this model. Thus 'success' in schooling became equated with the deserved right to individual social and material advancement for a few individuals into the dominant class, an ideal still present in many of the legitimizing discourses of schooling.

Current New Labour policy brings to this humanist and meritocratic model the technicism and new managerialism now associated with the school improvement approach. The reduction of human endeavour to its essentials (as Hall 1992 notes of Cartesian philosophy) is writ large in school improvement. Underpinning the search for what 'works' in schooling, is the assumption that children's and young people's educational experience can be measured through their examination 'performance', and that schools will become more effective if the results of that performance are quantified, calibrated, mapped and used as a spur to continuous improvement. The instruments used to achieve this – inspection, league tables of results and numerical targets – together with the discourses that legitimize them – the rights/consumer entitlements of parents and children, the market principle, and the desirability and possibility of continuous improvement – are also underpinned by the rational–irrational binary (Morley and Rassool 1999).

Put crudely, the standards agenda, via school improvement discourses, works to establish the notion that education can be reduced to an indeterminate number of taxonomies, and that these taxonomies can be used to regulate 'producers' of schooling, in the interests of the rational, choosing individual. The technicist fiction of school improvement is thus a direct derivation of a much older, heavily gendered discourse, and one that is deeply implicated in the production of social and material inequalities. From Chapter 3 onwards I will examine in more detail how students and teachers live the school improvement fiction, and how it contributes to the enduring reproduction of relations of domination and subordination. What I want to highlight here is its origins within a discourse that was and continues to be derived from a gendered and 'raced', as well as classed, apparatus of control.

One aspect of the school improvement fiction does require brief exploration here. Morley and Rassool (1999) show how the discourse has borrowed, from Japan, the notion of 'kaizen': the necessity and desirability of striving for continuous improvement. In a western context, this philosophy is little short of disastrous, and may have catastrophic consequences. In the western world, and in a consumer capitalist context, improvement has come to mean ever-increasing spirals of production and consumption. Binary thought and humanist individualism (which indissolubly link knowledge with mastery), together with the capitalist competitive ethic, mean that improvement must always be at someone else's expense, since market growth is predicated on winners and losers (Kenway et al. 1997). Improvement must be demonstrable through increased volume, or speed, of production. In education, this means (amongst other things) an intensification of workload for everyone. Teachers and schools must produce better and better results, and more and more data about those results, as the competition to stay ahead of the field heats up. Children and young people must work harder and smarter to secure improvements in their performance or face 'social exclusion' in the face of 'qualification inflation'.[2] Parents are made responsible for choosing the right school, and for supporting their children in the schooling business. So, while school improvement may bring about some benefits for some groups, there are terrific costs involved.

Perhaps the best way to exemplify some of the costs of such a model of continuous improvement is by looking to the environmental movement and the concept of sustainability. Improvement, where improvement means constant growth in production and consumption, is simply unsustainable over time. The earth has finite resources, and we are all living with the reality that the misuse of those resources (or, put another way, the results of rational Man's endeavours to know, master and make use of Nature) could mean the end of human (and most other) forms of life on the planet. In some parts of the world the costs of this misuse are clear. Shiva notes that 'In a world of globalised, de-regulated commerce in which everything is tradable and economic strength is the only determinant of power and control, resources move from the poor to the rich, and pollution moves from the rich to the poor. The result is global environmental apartheid' (Shiva 2000: 112). In other words, continuous improvement for some means, in global capitalist terms, severe impoverishment for others in the short term, and ultimately destruction for all.[3] Even in the rich world, we live with the knowledge of the consequences of the systemic over-consumption in which we are (differentially) implicated. The same is true of a 'continuously improving' education system in which some pay the costs of other people's apparent gains in the short term, and in which there are long-term costs to everyone (Lucey 2000). Replacing the prevailing notion of continuous improvement with notions of sustainable change would both enable and require a move beyond the winner/loser binaries inherent in and produced by current school improvement discourses.

What has a polarized view of the rational subject left out? In examining this, I do not want necessarily to exalt the realm of the non-rational: the feeling, intuiting (female) self often posited as the binary opposite of the (male) rational self (Boler 1999). Nor do I want to be drawn into a detailed engagement with the psychic world, since my concern is primarily with meanings that are socially made and negotiated. Feminist post-structuralists have developed a number of concepts which I will be using later in the book to examine what Davies (1997) has called the 'self in process'. She argues that:

> The subject of post-structuralism, unlike the humanist subject, then, is constantly in process; it only exists as process; it is revised and (re)presented through images, metaphors, storylines and other features of language, such as pronoun grammar; it is spoken and respoken, each speaking existing in a palimpsest with the others.
>
> (Davies 1997: 276)

This self-in-process is, in the context of schooling, a rational, choosing self (since schools produce their students through discourses that privilege such a project), and much else besides. It is also a feeling, intuiting self and an embodied self. Newbrook School, like many others, is a site in which students and teachers are constantly involved in the work of positioning ourselves in relation to prevailing technicist, and older humanist and radical, understandings about learning and teaching. We do this as feeling and intuiting, as well as thinking people. The act of taking up a position in discourse, and thereby producing ourselves as specific versions of 'teacher' or 'student' is one that is thought about and is also deeply felt.

The example of Aqsa and Chantelle, cited in the opening of this chapter, can help explain how we do this. So, too, can a post-structuralist re-reading of Althuser's rather deterministic concept of 'interpellation', the process through which individuals are 'summoned' (or hailed) by ideology to become subjects of the system. In post-structural terms we might more usefully imagine a set of subject positions made available by prevailing social and political conditions, and subjectivity as a continuous, complex and contested process through which individuals negotiate their way into and out of these subject positions. Interpellation is a part of this process. The actions of other individuals and groups, and the inherited social meanings and consequences of these actions, 'call' individuals to recognize themselves as particular kinds of subjects. Such recognitions – which are contingent on but not determined by existing local and systemic power relations – are very important here, as are the feelings associated with them. Aqsa describes how the teacher of the class recognizes her as a 'good girl' by not telling her off. She constructs the teacher himself as a 'nice teacher' by recognizing his understanding of her. Through such recognitions, she is interpellated into, and takes up, a subject position as a 'sweet little girl' (see Chapters 5 to 8). She *could*, in theory, resist such a position, but such (mutual and self) recognitions make this unlikely. As she recounts the teacher's remarks to Chantelle, and her response to them, Aqsa describes and reinscribes her investment in examination success. The fact that she is not, as she had thought, at the bottom of the class, makes her happy, for the time being at least.

Chantelle describes the struggle with which power was negotiated in the lesson. She remarks that she and her friends could rule the lesson only by pretending not to be scared of the teacher. She also presents her own struggle when control had been regained by the teacher. When he humiliated her through pointing out her failure within the dominant discourse of success, she did not know how to respond, or with whom to express solidarity: should she look at her friends or at the teacher? She goes on to show how she has come to want – to desire – both examination success *and* microcultural success amongst a group of what Aqsa has positioned as 'very rude girls'. For her, such desires are contradictory, and place her in a position that she describes as unviable. Implicit in the accounts of both young women is the fear and shame engendered through their failure to achieve normative versions of success. Desire, fear and shame thus operate as key reference points through which interpellation takes place and via which students and teachers come to 'invest' in particular subject positions. As the book progresses, I will be showing how these processes are nuanced through multiple indices of systemic difference, including those of gender/sexuality, social class and ethnicity.

Before moving on, however, I would want to introduce a note of caution. There is a danger that, in attempting to go beyond binarisms, we construct theories that act as if those binarisms do not exist. Paradoxically, in doing this, we may also be setting up a new binarism. As a lecturer at the college of higher education where I did my first degree remarked to me in 1987, 'There are two types of people: those who recognize that binary thinking is bankrupt, and those who do not'. Such new polarities are not likely to be helpful. Allan (1999: 116) argues for the importance of 'acknowledging the binarisms of special/normal or disabled/able-bodied in order to speak against them'. The task here seems to be one of naming the meanings associated with existing binarisms and of developing theories that will enable an interrogation of the material consequences of those meanings, without constructing new polarities as a result. In the context of 'racial' identity, Hall (1990: 226) argues for a 'strategic essentialism' in which binary points of identity are understood as 'not an essence but a positioning'. As Mort (writing about sexualized identities) explains, 'Within such an understanding, identities are concrete and material, but they are not innate. Hence identity politics becomes a matter of contingency, organised around a strategic rather than a naturalised essentialism' (Mort 1994: 218).

As has long been noted in the women's movement, neither the liberal pluralist 'equal but different' argument which attempts to do away with binarisms through writing them out of the picture, nor the attempt to reverse a binarism through privileging its opposite polarity, is sufficient. Weedon (1997: 28) notes that 'it is not ultimately helpful merely to reverse the rational–irrational opposition. It needs to be thoroughly revised and reconstituted'. I noted in the Introduction that the attempt to do away with difference categories at this point in time would be premature and counterproductive. In this book I attempt to engage with the social and political production and consequences of a specific set of binary differences, while also wanting to venture beyond them, to alternative, more equitable and sustainable versions of 'difference' and of change.

Notes

1 'Microcultural work' refers to the interpersonal negotiations through which the girls and young women position themselves relative to student microcultures and, in so doing, re/produce those cultures. Other groups in school – including, of course, teachers – partake in their own microcultural work.
2 Such phenomena also reflect the marketisation and commodification of education, which, in the UK, are the legacy of New Right reforms of the 1980s and 1990s.
3 It has been argued that 'increased transnational capital mobility produces new waves of short-term immizerisation and long-term environmental degradation' (Boswell and Chase-Dunn 2000: 12). The development of global capitalism, and its winners and losers over time are discussed in Dunn (1995), Kirk (1995), Modelski and Thompson (1996), Robinson (1996), Taylor (1996), Boli and Thomas (1997) and Haseler (2000).

CHAPTER TWO

'Will you put this in your book?' Researching with 'special needs students'

Introducing the school

Newbrook School for Girls is a medium-sized secondary comprehensive school in a mostly working-class inner-city locality. There are 900 students on roll, aged from 11 to 16. At 16, students take GCSE examinations, after which most leavers progress to one of three local further education colleges. Newbrook is situated in an ethnically diverse locality, as is reflected in its student population. Approximately 50 per cent of its students are from Asian (mostly Pakistani) families. This is a somewhat higher proportion than might be expected, and is usually accounted for by the fact that many of these families are observant Muslims who prefer single-sex education for their daughters. A further 20 per cent of students are of African Caribbean heritage. The remainder is made up of students from many backgrounds, principally indigenous white, African (mostly from Somalia and the countries of Western Africa), Greek and Turkish Cypriot, Eastern European (predominantly from the former Yugoslavian states) and Irish.

A 'mixed economy' of ability grouping, commonly found in UK comprehensive schools (Clark et al. 1999), exists in Newbrook. The students are grouped when they enter the school in Year 7 into tutor groups of 30. These are initially used as teaching groups for most subjects. There are six tutor groups in each year, carefully mixed for perceived 'ability' on the basis of the girls' test results in the Key Stage 2 (Year 6) statutory tests. As the students move up the school, they are grouped according to measured attainment in more and more subjects. In English, technology, arts and humanities, student grouping is resolutely mixed ability through to the end of Year 11.

Newbrook has a teaching staff of about 60, including part-time teachers: at the time of the research, I was one of these part-time teachers. About two-thirds of the teaching staff are women, and a similar proportion of the total are white and are of UK origin. There are about 30 non-teaching staff, including special needs assistants (all of whom are women), caretaking staff (all of whom are men), administrative staff (women), cleaners (women) and school meals assistants (women). The non-teaching staff come from a range of ethnic/racial backgrounds that broadly reflect that of the immediate locality. Indeed, most of them live locally, unlike many of the teachers, some of whom travel long distances (often from more middle-class districts) to Newbrook. The staff is managed according to a pyramidal structure that would be recognized in most UK schools, with a head, two deputies and three senior teachers. The three senior teachers line manage the heads of faculty, heads of year and heads of non-teaching staff respectively. The heads of faculty line manage the heads of department, who in turn manage the unpromoted classroom teachers. Thus are all members of staff held by a chain of power and accountability.

I first entered Newbrook on the day of my interview for a post as learning support teacher in December 1997. The main building is Edwardian, and I was shown into a once grand but now rather shabby and dark lobby to wait. Through the double doors I could see the school hall, honours boards around its walls, the body of the hall full of folding desks arranged in ranks. GCSE 'mock' exams were taking place. As I was shown around the school, I was struck by its orderly atmosphere. At one point, the bell sounded, and the corridors filled with laughing, chatting girls in bottle-green uniforms. A small woman, later introduced to me as Ms Cashmere the headteacher, stood at the bottom of one of the main staircases, directing the 'traffic'. I later found out that, in a version of the Panopticon, she would vary her monitoring point, so that students never knew on which staircase they might encounter her.

Other things impressed me that day. The humanities corridor was ablaze with displays relating to Black History Month, the music noticeboards contained work that challenged common-sense perceptions that all great composers and performers were and are men, and the school's equal opportunities policy – handed to me on arrival – was the most comprehensive of its type I have ever seen. In my first few weeks at the school as a learning support teacher I was made welcome by friendly and helpful colleagues. On the whole, Newbrook provided me with an enjoyable context in which to work, and few personal axes to grind.

From equal opportunities to inclusion

For me as a teacher committed to a feminist and socialist politics of egalitarian social change, Newbrook's emphasis on equal opportunities priorities was an important part of that enjoyable working context at a personal and professional level. During the three years in which I worked there, however, the configuration of those priorities changed in the context of national policy changes. The 'Gender and Achievement' section of the former Department for Education and Employment website chronicles what it calls three distinct phases of concern (DfEE 2000). The first of these it calls the 'equal opportunities phase' which was 'marked by concern mainly about girls' experiences within male-dominated structures' (DfEE 2000). This gave way to the equity and social justice phase 'where the interplay of issues of gender, class and ethnicity were highlighted'. Lastly, there came the 'achievement-oriented phase' in which whole-school approaches 'endorsed the professional responsibility of schools to base their interventions on analyses of their own performance data' (DfEE 2000). The DfEE – and its successor since 2001, the Department for Education and Skills (DfES)– make clear that they support this last, presenting the earlier phases as preparatory for this current phase.

Newbrook enjoys a good reputation locally, the consequences of which I will examine in Chapter 3. As a school which prides itself on its strong equal opportunities ethos, it publicly affirms its anti-sexist and antiracist commitments. At Newbrook, discourses associated with equal opportunities, social justice and achievement coexist, but their relationship to each other is not always as seamless as the DfES website might suggest. Although it is not within the area that constituted the Inner London Education Authority, the ILEA's 'Race, Sex and Class' initiative (ILEA 1983a–e, 1985) was important in Newbrook's development in the 1980s.[1] Discourses and strategies that characterized this initiative are still in circulation at the school. As one example, an ethos of positive discrimination lives on in Newbrook's celebration of International Women's Day, in which the experiences and contributions of women to a male-dominated world are explored and celebrated, and students are reminded of feminist struggles worldwide. Newbrook continues to claim equal opportunities as a strength, and its policy and policy guidelines in this area reflect much of what the DfES has called the 'social justice phase'. In reality, this means that Newbrook has committed itself to a version of equal opportunities that goes beyond the 'holy trinity' of race, sex and class. The school's own policy guidelines (which run to 20 pages) provide practical examples of how students can be unfairly disadvantaged, and suggestions of ways in which members of the school community can work against social injustice.

Increasingly, though, these concerns are reworked into the standards agenda which characterizes what the DfES refers to as the 'achievement-oriented phase'. Sometimes this can look like an unproblematic co-optation. For example, Newbrook's equal opportunities working party often spends its meetings 'analysing' examination results in the interests of promoting the 'achievement' of students from what might be thought to be disadvantaged groups. In such meetings it is hard to pose questions about how this might have costs for other disadvantaged groups. This is a theme to which I return in Chapters 3 and 4. At other times, the imbrication of radical equal opportunities discourses with those of new managerialism is contested. In one example of this, the listing of Year 10 students in order of their examination results for the purposes of data analysis and subsequent professional intervention has been and continues to be a matter of internal staff controversy. While residual discourses still exist, then, recent months have seen Newbrook begin to reformulate its equal opportunities concerns as concerns over (social) inclusion, again in line with New Labour priorities. The implications and effects of this reconfiguration for students who are formally designated as having 'special educational needs' are examined throughout the book.

Why ethnography?

Why, when my interests are so clearly linked to macro- as well as micropolitics, and to policy as well as practice, did I choose to do research that is ethnographic in nature and scale? Can this be a suitable way to address concerns that, while they are played out locally, are produced in and by a national, and even global, context?

> Each new class which puts itself in the place of the one ruling before it is compelled, merely in order to carry through its aim, to represent its interest as the common interest of all the members of society, that is, expressed in ideal form: it has to give its ideas the form of universality, and represent them as the only rational, valid ones.
>
> (Marx and Engels [1845–6] 1975: 65)

Marx and Engels' comments on the production of (class) domination through knowledge may seem outdated and irrelevant to the twenty-first-century world of multiplicities. But they echo down the centuries in Gramscian notions of hegemony and in the work of feminist, postcolonial and disability theorists, to name but a few. In all these cases, the production of critical knowledge is a political, as well as an epistemological, project, in which the production of knowledge(s) has close and reciprocal ties to a movement for social change.

My concern in this research was to interrogate the actions and meanings around 'success' in the context of the English schooling system. In the New Labour government's appropriation of both the moral high ground and of the language of pragmatism, it is arguably managing to present its own very specific set of meanings around what constitutes success in schooling as the only possible set of meanings. In David Blunkett's terms (cited in Chapter 3) the arguments are 'unanswerable' or, as Marx and Engels might have said, appear to be the 'only rational, valid ones' and in the interests of all groups within society. As a teacher, as a feminist and as a socialist, I have a set of questions about such a presentation of meaning. I want to know how, and in whose interests, this set of meanings about success is being constructed and made hegemonic.

An ethnographic approach appealed to me, primarily as a way of studying the imbrication of macro- and micropolitical processes with the microcultural and (inter)personal identity work through which educational policy is enacted in school. Ethnographic strategies, which involve the active participation of the researcher in meaning-making with participants over time, enable us to interrogate the working through of schooling reforms at the level of the interpersonal, and examine the interpersonal in the context of wider social and political power relations. A full history and analysis of ethnography as method and methodology is beyond the scope of this book. What is of interest here, and worth exploring, is the construction of both a politicized methodology and a methodologically informed politics. Reflecting on why she chose to use ethnographic methods, Skeggs (1994: 74) comments that she 'wanted a method of analysis which would make the links between structure and practice, between the macro and the micro; a method which would link everyday interaction to history, economics, politics and wider cultural formations'. As a learning support teacher, I already had considerable knowledge of the reservoir of things that could be said and done in the processes of constructing success and of producing successful subjects at the schools in which I have worked. An ethnographic approach, firmly situated in the wider sociopolitical context, seemed the most appropriate way for me to build on this knowledge and to use it to interrogate dominant meanings of success in school.

Introducing the research

At the beginning of the autumn term of 1999, by which time I was teaching for only one day each week, I sought permission from the headteacher to conduct ethnographic research at Newbrook, involving my presence at the school on days on which I was not contracted to teach. Having secured official permission, I talked to a group of young women students about my proposed research. The students to whom I spoke were 15-year-olds in Year 11: they all prefer to be described as 'young women' and not as 'girls'. My teaching experience and my research interests led me to focus my attention on this initial group who were considered to have 'learning difficulties' and who I perceived to be positioned in specific ways relative to dominant versions of success. They were a group of nine young women with whom I had a long-established good relationship. Two out of the nine have statements of special educational needs: one for moderate learning difficulties and one for autism. Six of the remaining seven were listed on Newbrook's SEN register (see Chapter 4) as having 'learning as a primary concern', while one was listed as having 'behaviour as a primary concern' and learning as a secondary concern. All of them were keen to be involved, and all took a letter home and returned the permission slip promptly.

Working with these nine students was enjoyable, and the methods I used were derived from our established style of working together. We were already in the habit of meeting before and after school and during lunchtimes, to work on pieces of GCSE coursework and to chat about life in and out of school. They were happy to allow me to bring the tape recorder to these sessions, and they negotiated with each other about when the tape player would be switched on and off. We agreed a set of ground rules in which anyone could erase her own comments, or switch the tape player off before speaking, but erasing another person's comments could be done only with their agreement. I did not set up any formal interviews with this group, although the questions I asked them and the directions in which I tried to steer conversations during these informal sessions were often structured by my research intentions.

I also attempted to do some classroom observations with this group of young women, on my non-teaching days. There were two obstacles to this. First, finding the students in appropriate lessons proved to be a logistical nightmare. I wanted to observe in classrooms in which I had a relaxed and friendly working relationship with the class teacher, so that I would not have to be too involved in my own microcultural work. I also wanted to observe them in lessons where they were not already being supported by another member of staff, as the presence of too many adults in the classroom was perceived by both students and teachers as intrusive. Three of the young women were very poor attenders, and would frequently be absent from lessons that I had painstakingly identified as possibilities. Second, in most cases, the young women were unwilling to allow me to observe them. If I was in the classroom, they understandably wanted me to work with them, not to watch them struggle. For three lessons, I attempted to remain detached from the action, and to write in my notebook. These occasions were unsuccessful in that the young women were completely distracted from their curricular work, spending time waving to me, and coming over and reading what I was writing whenever they could. I either had to go into a governmental role, and tell them to get on with their work without me, or I had to collude with their avoidance of classroom work. Since I wanted to do neither of these, I decided a better option was to go into the lesson without my notebook, and to support the students in my more usual way. I would go straight to the staffroom and scribble down as much as I could remember afterwards.

The other group of participants were in Year 7. These were the youngest girls in the school. I selected the group partly on the basis of convenience, from three tutor groups. Of the twelve girls asked, nine were willing and allowed by their parents to participate. These students, all of whom were listed on the special needs register, knew me by sight only at the outset of the research, though I was subsequently asked by the school to spend an additional (paid) half-day each week supporting one of them in class. I planned a complicated schedule of observations, so as to be able to be present in lessons with the Year 7 participants. They were somewhat more willing for me to take an observer's role, though it was still hard to maintain any great degree of detachment.

The interviews of the Year 7 girls were somewhat more formal. They took place between halfway through the spring term to the end of the summer term. I interviewed the girls in three class-based groups three times each. During the first interview, I asked them about their experiences as newcomers to Newbrook the previous autumn. I also asked them to invent 'successful' and 'unsuccessful' students, to describe these students and their school day in as much detail as possible, and to act 'freeze-frame' representations of their constructions. These were intended to be talking points, not ends in themselves. At the end of that first interview I gave the girls a disposable camera each, to take some pictures of their own school lives. During the second interview we looked at the pictures they had taken, and used them as prompts to talk about aspects of their experiences at school. Each girl chose her 'favourite' picture and we made a captioned display. In the third interview, the girls used a magnetic board with their own and their classmates' names attached to small magnets (Creese et al. 2000) to talk about classroom life and microcultural work. I asked them to imagine they were the teacher, and to arrange the class as they wanted. We repeated this several times, imagining, for example, what a teacher in a good mood and a teacher in a bad mood might do.

I also interviewed four members of staff, approaching three of the teachers most often mentioned by students as the ones they liked and found most understanding. In my approach to the three teachers, I told them of this. The questions I asked these teachers were mostly designed to elicit their accounts about why they were liked by students with 'SEN' and, in the process, to find out what meanings the teachers themselves attributed to teaching intellectually subordinated students. I also interviewed a learning support assistant about how she viewed her role and her position within the school.

In the student interviews, pedagogy and research overlapped, as did my pedagogic relationship and my research relationship with the student/ participants. In the case of the Year 11 informal interviews, research-led conversations were interspersed with work on overdue GCSE assignments. For the Year 7 girls, making a poster of their photographs was as much a pedagogic intervention as a research-led one. In all three year groups, interviewing the students, and attempting to make meaning with them, had pedagogic, as well as research, implications. As a teacher, positioned as an authority in relation to knowledge, this inevitably produced a specific range of things that could and could not be said in conversation with me. It simultaneously produced a form of reciprocity in the interviews, through which the students benefited from extra help and teaching, while helping me with my research.

For many of the students, the interviews provided them with a context in which to produce themselves as authorities, a position more usually withheld from them. Sometimes the interviews were heavy going, as participants struggled for words and ways to say what they meant and I struggled for words and ways to help them. Sometimes these struggles were productive in their eventual construction of the students as 'articulate'. At other times these struggles were less productive, and I had to rely more heavily on my own fieldnotes and records of less formal conversations.

Partners in research?

Since my intention was to learn about students' meaning-making alongside them, it made sense to involve them as much as possible in analysing their data. At the end of the GCSE exam period, when the Year 11 students had

officially left school, I spent two full days with some of the Year 11 participants. We listened to their interviews and talked about what they had said
and about how they now felt about what they had said. They listened with
excitement, and three young women in particular wanted to re-record parts
of their interviews as they had changed their minds. We notated some of
their key phrases and words, putting them onto cards which most of them
were able to read. I talked to the young women about some of the themes
that I thought had arisen. We added to these, and they sorted the cards into
the themes. It felt important to demystify the analysis process as far as
possible, and to give the young women an insight into what I was doing
with their accounts. These occasions also provided the opportunity for some
enjoyable reminiscences about their schooling experiences, and acted as a
closure process. I would have liked to have been able to involve the younger
students in data analysis in this way, but the demands of the timetable
precluded it.

The Year 11 students also showed interest in the magnetic board I had
used in the Year 7 interviews, and made known to me their reservations
about the questions I had asked the younger girls. With the Year 7 students'
permission, and with mutually agreed ground rules about confidentiality
and use of the tape recorder, three of the Year 11 students used the magnetic
board to reinterview three of the Year 7 students, and then discussed their
findings with me. The three interviewers, and the three interviewees, helped
me to analyse the interviews, identifying key words and sorting them into
themes.

The micropolitical implications of the research

Skeggs characterizes cultural studies ethnography as 'a theory of the research
process which combines particular methods in certain ways. It is a methodology which combines theoretical positions and political intent; it informs
how the different methods are combined and the way the researcher
approaches issues of power, responsibility and ethics' (Skeggs 1997: 23). Two
of the theoretical fields from which I draw much of my thinking – feminist
theory and disability theory – have slightly different takes on these issues of
power, responsibility and ethics.[2] Of especial concern to me were the debates
in disability theory around representation, and around who can, and cannot, speak for those who are positioned as disabled. Did I have any right
to investigate issues relating to intellectual disability when I have no claim
to a disabled identity myself? Moreover, as a teacher, I am in part involved
and invested in the ongoing production of intellectual subordination. From
a similar starting point, Bines (1995) notes that:

> Although I believe that most special needs are socially constructed
> . . . it can be difficult to maintain such social perspectives under the
> day-to-day pressure of teaching and research . . . Professional experience
> and culture has also made it difficult to agree with all of the sociological

criticisms of professional vested interests, even though I am aware that policy and provision for special educational needs are often neglected and marginalised, and that certain professional attitudes and practices need to be confronted.

(Bines 1995: 44)

Like Bines, I am located within a professional culture that positions me as complicit, makes some arguments unappealing and unpalatable and, no doubt, obscures for me some (though not all) of the practices with which I at times collude (Coffey and Delamont 2000). From such a position, is reflexivity enough? Some might argue that it is not. Barton and Clough take an undifferentiated body of non-disabled 'researchers' to task, stating that 'it is vitally important that researchers, recognising their limitations, endeavour to be more open and self-aware with regard to their own values, priorities and processes of interpretation' (Barton and Clough 1995: 143).

To return to Skeggs's triad of power, responsibility and ethics, perhaps what is of most significance here is that I was multiply positioned in relation to teachers, students and the research endeavour. As a teacher, I had contractual responsibilities, I had a clearly delineated position within the hierarchy of the school, and I was subject to professional notions of ethics. These were nuanced by the fact that I was a learning support teacher, my responsibilities configured in some rather contradictory ways around the 'well-being', as well as the academic progress, of students who are, by definition, not doing well at school (see Chapter 6). Simultaneous engagement in a research project towards a doctorate further complexified my position. Hill (1995: 104) speaks of 'the contradiction that, while belonging to one group (teachers), I was involved in pursuing the goal of another group (academics). The fact that the outlook, perception and, indeed, language of the two varied, left me in a position that was on occasions difficult'.

Issues of power, responsibilities and ethics were threaded through the research in this book. Such issues surfaced at many levels, from the ideological/conceptual, to the purely procedural. But examination of the 'purely procedural' level reveals its ideological depth, and the ideological/conceptual was usually operationalized through the procedural.

Of all the schools in which I have worked, Newbrook is the one in which I have felt happiest and most successful. It is, therefore, hard to be relentlessly critical when 'criticism' appears to connote unpleasantness and negativity, and, since the late 1970s, has overridingly been associated with 'exposing' teacher failure. To some extent, I am a product of New Labour. Part of me wants to tell a happy tale, in which things come out well for students, and in which my colleagues (especially those whom I count as friends) and myself have heroic parts to play. Undoubtedly, I have an interest, produced in part through personal and professional loyalties, in presenting what happens at the school in its best possible light. In some ways it is hard for me as a teacher to tell a critical story when, since the late 1970s, criticism has been systematically used to undermine and ridicule the efforts of teachers in schools. The unwritten rule of the staffroom is that criticism – the asking of hard and often unanswerable questions – is best done in private, between consenting adults.

> Back in the staffroom, the usual people gather to have a good laugh about the meeting . . . People congratulate Sue [the teacher who had led part of the staff meeting] on her presentation. She had been nervous, especially, she says, of me sitting writing copious notes. Nadje jokes that I'm going to be writing it in my PhD, and there is laughter. I feel myself going a bit red. One of my purposes in staying for the staff meeting was to get juicy data on the introduction of the G&T policy. I'm not sure whether this gentle teasing means that it really is OK, or whether me and my notebook are beginning to get a bad name. I wish I'd asked Sue's permission first.

(Fieldnotes 13/12/99)

Staff micropolitics were a fascinating but fraught area of exploration. If someone had an interesting conversation at lunch, my first instinct was to hunt for my notebook straight away and record as much of it as I could remember. This felt permissible in the case of the headteacher and her deputies, since their lunchtime appearances were very much in the style of public engagements. The lower down the hierarchy, the less acceptable it felt. My purpose at Newbrook was not to find people out, inspector-style, but to find out how the system operated, and informal contexts were and are central in the production of meaning. But where to draw the line? Should I take my notebook to the pub after school?

In the end, I decided that I would not take 'covert' notes where informal situations with colleagues were concerned. Since everyone involved knew that I was doing a research project in the school, it seemed adequate to wave my notebook around as a signal that I was engaged in systematic recording of what was going on, and leave it to people to make their own decisions about what to say. This did not cover every situation, as people had a habit of saying the most interesting and unforgettable things when I was putting my coat on to leave, but it was my general working principle. Staff meetings were harder. In some ways, as formal, minuted occasions, they were fair game for me. But the point of staff meetings is that they are idiosyncratic and intended for their participants only. I have long been fascinated by them as key sites of micropolitical activity. In the extract above, Sue could not stop or substantially modify her presentation when I took out my notebook. Following that meeting, I realized that I should not take my 'insiderness' for granted, and I was more careful about asking the main speakers at meetings for permission to bring my notebook. Permission was never refused, and indeed I think it would have been very hard for anyone to refuse, but I reasoned that at least people were forewarned.

The role of teacher-researcher that I was trying to take up was nuanced by the fact that the role of learning support teacher can in itself be tricky to negotiate. One problem, inherent in working as a learning support teacher as well as teacher researcher, is that of knowing how to respond when students criticize a colleague.

Suleika: And then we got stupid stinky Ms Drummond –
Amina: You shouldn't say that to Miss, they might be friends [laughs].
Miss might be friends with her, you never know, are you friends
with her Miss?
SB: Well [pause], I don't know her very well, erm, I don't see her
very often, she doesn't come in the staffroom, she stays mainly
in the faculty block, so I don't know her very well –
(Interview 9/12/99)

My position as teacher gives me an ongoing access to students and makes
me a part of their school lives. It also means I have an ongoing set of
responsibilities – to students and colleagues – and contractual obligations by
which I am bound. As a learning support teacher, there is an expectation
that I will bend the rules of teacherliness, listen to students' grievances and
sometimes mediate when things have gone very wrong between student and
teacher. It is often hard to know how far to bend those rules without breaking them: in the students' interests, as well as in the interests of the organization, my teacherliness and my loyalty to colleagues have to be preserved.
The temptation during the research period was to let my desire for interesting nuggets of data lead my decision about how far to bend a rule. With
hindsight, I can see that there were times, such as the one cited above, when
my desire to keep students talking led me into some difficult situations that
it would have been better to have avoided.

By far the most frequent 'procedural' dilemma was the one of knowing
when to intervene in the classroom, again a familiar problem for a learning
support teacher.

Theresa asks the girls to put aprons on, and come and watch her demonstrate. She's showing them how to make textured patterns on pieces of
aluminium. They're going to be doing a project involving special paints,
which will only work if the metal is textured. Josie wants to know what
happens if anyone steals the special paints. Theresa tells her they're kept
securely. Josie won't let it go. She asks what if someone broke in, found
the paints, found the key of the cupboard in which they're locked up.
I invoke the 'three strikes and you're out' routine. I know I'm supposed
to be observing, but I can't collude with Josie's invasive questioning.
(Fieldnotes 2/3/00)

There is probably no right way I could have solved this question of intervention. In some settings, and especially where Josie was concerned (see Chapter 8), not to intervene was an act of cruelty, since she could not understand
my non-intervention and perceived it as punitive. In the extract above,
my collusion with her barrage of questioning would have been very puzzling
for her. Similarly, in lessons where my targeted students were struggling
with work or relationships, there was only so far I could maintain non-
intervention. My credibility as a teacher relied on students and colleagues
believing in my ability to spot problems and in my willingness to intervene
to ameliorate them. For this credibility to remain intact, I could not, nor

did I want to, produce myself as distanced researcher with dispassionate curiosity.

Throughout the period of the research, my concern was not to seek to disembed myself from the intricacies of relationship work with students and colleagues, but to participate in it and to use all the resources it made available to me in what I hope (but cannot guarantee) was a non-exploitative and reciprocal way. Any misuse of those resources had serious implications for me as a teacher, and these were a stronger incentive towards ethical actions than any guidelines could have been. In the end it was my dual institutional location – as a critical teacher, with an ongoing responsibility towards the students and the school, and with a commitment to sustainable long-term change, and as a research student with a researcher's curiosity and a comparative freedom from institutional demands – that produced the data I was able to gather.

Notes

1 The Inner London Education Authority researched and introduced this initiative as a radical response to the inner-city uprisings of the early 1980s. Schools and teachers were encouraged and required to address inegalitarian practices through strategies such as curriculum reform and positive discrimination.
2 See, for example, Stanley and Wise (1993), Cherland (1994), Fine (1994), Holland and Ramazanoglu (1995), Kelly et al. (1995), Mirza (1995), Morris (1995), Hey (1997), Bell (1998), Edwards and Ribbens (1998), Skeggs (1998), Skelton (1998) and Mauthner and Hey (1999) for a full discussion of the ethical, strategic and political dimensions of feminist research. The issue of non-disabled researchers researching those considered to be disabled, as well as a full range of ethical issues around participatory and emancipatory research, are discussed in, for example, Clough and Barton (1995), Fulcher (1995), Peters (1995), Swain (1995), Vlachou (1995), Barton (1998), Clough (1998) and Corbett (1998b).

CHAPTER THREE

Beacon schooling and the construction of 'success'

To understand how 'effective' schooling can have unintended and inegal-itarian effects, it is necessary to look at the construction – at school and at policy level – of 'success'. This chapter examines how Newbrook is positioned, and positions itself, as a 'successful school' in relation to the standards agenda. It starts by placing Newbrook within the macropolitical context, then goes on to explore how this policy context produces a set of discourses and discursive practices in relation to which Newbrook constructs the subjects 'successful student' and 'successful teacher'. Newbrook's implementation of the 'Excellence in Cities' initiative of 1999, which requires schools to identify and provide for 'gifted and talented' (G&T) pupils, illuminates and exemplifies some of the ways in which the school produces 'success' (DfEE 1999a). This chapter uses the introduction of Newbrook's own G&T policy to interrogate how some versions of 'success' come to dominate, where they come to dominate, and what locally produced versions of success are able to coexist alongside dominant ones.

Newbrook and the standards agenda

It is the beginning of the spring term. Today's whole-school Training and Development (T&D) day is on target-setting. The consultant/fac-ilitator, immaculately power dressed in skirt with matching jacket opens with a suitably girlie, 'emotionally present' post-Christmas anecdote. She tells us that for years she has struggled to lose weight, looking (or is it my imagination) at the white women in the audience for empathic nods of recognition and fellow-feeling. She has tried many diets, none of them successful. The reason? Her targets were not SMART (specific, measurable, achievable, realistic and time-framed) enough. Had she devised sufficiently SMART targets, she would have been able to stick to her diet and achieve the body she tells us she wants. Before anyone can so much as whisper 'Fat is a Feminist Issue' she moves seamlessly on to show how her example can be applied to schooling. The girlie-ness disappears from view as she takes us through overhead after overhead of evidence as to how target-setting is that way to effective learning for *all* (emphasis on the all) pupils for which we, as teachers, have been searching. Is this an add-on to the liberal fantasy that anyone can achieve anything if they want it enough and work hard enough – now they have to have a SMART enough target? We are taken through the National Learning Targets for 2002, and how they will be filtered down (via our 'information-rich' education system) through LEAs [local education authorities] and schools to individual teachers and students. Touchy-feelie meets punitive surveillant policing in pursuit of the unsustainable.

(Fieldnotes 6/1/99)

Newbrook is known and respected locally (and knows and recognizes itself) as a 'successful' school. The single most important discourse in the production of Newbrook's success is the standards agenda. Every year, when the LEA league tables of examination results are published, Newbrook vies for top place with the other local girls' comprehensive school. This is a contest fought out on the battleground of percentages of 16-year-old leavers achieving at least five GCSE examination passes at grades A*–C. Typically, around 60 per cent of Newbrook's leavers attain this benchmark of externally recognized success. Such a figure is above the national average, and is ahead of the National Learning Target of 50 per cent of 16-year-olds achieving this standard by 2002 (DfEE 1999b). In the 'performance and assessment data analysis' document (the PANDA), Newbrook itself scores an 'A' grade when compared with 'similar schools nationally': that is, comprehensive girls' schools in which over 30 per cent of the students are eligible for free school meals.

Newbrook enjoys other external markers of success. Following a glowing Office for Standards in Education (Ofsted) inspection report in 1997, it was awarded beacon status; it subsequently applied for, and secured, funding as a beacon school. This means that key departments and aspects of work have been recognized not only as strengths of the school, but also as strengths from which other schools and teachers can learn. Newbrook has been constructed, and has taken up a position, as a 'market leader' in areas thus identified. Beacon status has brought with it validation and approbation, and also material rewards in the form of extra funding. A further official marker of Newbrook's success is the Investors in People status, which Newbrook achieved in 1998, and which was re-awarded in a review in 2000. This makes available a set of understandings around what it means to be a successful teacher, constructed through a managerialist matrix and dominated by the notion of 'performance'. In the set of official stories that Newbrook tells itself about itself, success within the parameters constructed as desirable by New Labour is a recurrent theme. Newbrook presents itself as a confident, successful school, in which new initiatives are embraced and taken forward for the good of students.

These external markers of success perform many functions, not the least of which is the production of a measure of stability in an uncertain and rapidly changing climate. Its success means that Newbrook is routinely over-subscribed, and has a waiting list of girls who have not been allocated places. Newbrook can therefore rely on secure funding, knowing that numbers in each year group will remain constant: when one student leaves, she is replaced by another from the waiting list within days. But it is not only the student population that is shaped by Newbrook's success. As a popular school, Newbrook is attractive to teachers, since standards of discipline and attainment are high, and especially so when compared to those of neighbouring mixed comprehensive schools. It has a relatively stable staff and, until September 2000, was unaffected by the spiralling UK teacher shortages. In times of uncertainty and change, then, it is Newbrook's success that has acted as a buffer, enabling security and continuity of funding and population.

But this stability is dependent on Newbrook producing itself as a school undergoing continuous improvement, in order to maintain its success in league tables and under the scrutiny of Ofsted. There is a moral discourse underpinning this apparent zeal for continuous improvement. Newbrook's tales of its own confidence and success are framed as equal opportunities imperatives. Many of the staff, including the headteacher, are passionate about girls' education as a means of working against women's disadvantage. This commitment provides the legitimizing narrative behind what can look like a wholesale embracing of the standards agenda. From such a standpoint, enabling girls (many of whom are from ethnic minority families and most of whom are working class) to achieve good exam results can be understood as one way in which to promote equality of opportunity. So Newbrook tells itself a caring, as well as confident, set of stories about itself. That caring, and that passionate belief in equality of opportunity, are recast as targets that can be set and must be met. Newbrook's stability is prized but precarious, and target-setting is one way in which the continuous improvement on which that stability depends can apparently be brought within the control of individuals, groups and the school's senior management. Paradoxically, target-setting generates its own sets of instabilities, incorporated into and enacted through student and staff micropolitics and identity work.

The facilitator of the training and development day gave us a recipe for success. In her account, certainty was ours for the taking if only we got our target-setting right. She stood before us embodying the inadequacies of her own argument as she reduced the complexities of human social action to a set of technicist behaviours to be rationally understood and controlled. Eliminating the social and political context from consideration, and disregarding the irrational and idiosyncratic may be one way to seek to reduce uncertainty. But when the production of success is made to depend on such elisions, and the real conditions of the work of embodied students and teachers are airbrushed out of the debate, the result is an increase in anxiety. The attempted removal (it is never quite accomplished) of that which cannot be reduced to bland taxonomies – the rich, complex world of social and interpersonal relations – generates a toxic mix of fear and hope, conflict and collegiality, optimism and pessimism at Newbrook. The result is a permanent sense of instability and impending doom.

Sennett (1998: 31) comments that 'What's peculiar about instability today is that it exists without any looming historical disaster; instead it is woven into the everyday practices of a vigorous capitalism. Instability is meant to be normal'. Linked to the normalization of instability is a discourse of education as risk management strategy. Levitas (1998: 121) notes that 'Security has been discursively constructed as something individuals achieve through employability, and employability as an individual obligation'. It is in this context – the normalization of instability and the individualization of risk management – that the construction of success, and the production of successful subjects at Newbrook School, has to be understood.

Successful schooling and can-do capitalism

In the run-up to the May 1997 general election, prime ministerial candidate Tony Blair famously declared his three priorities to be 'education, education and education'. Within weeks of coming to power, the New Labour government elected on this platform made it clear that 'standards not structures' were to be the key targets of educational reform. In July 1997 (two months after the election) a White Paper was published, promising 'zero tolerance of under-performance' (DfEE 1997c). School effectiveness became the grand narrative upon which New Labour's construction of the continuously improving school – achieving high standards and always aiming higher – was predicated. A version of equal opportunities was embedded into the new managerialism through which this continuously improving school was to be brought into being and maintained. As Morley and Rassool (1999: 114) note, 'Previous discourses of effectiveness have been hijacked, with an added dimension of social justice lost during the Thatcher and Major years'.

Rustin (1999) argues that a core feature of New Labour's reinvention of itself is in its mode of address. Where unreconstructed Labour spoke to and for 'we the oppressed', New Labour speaks to and for 'we the current or future beneficiaries of the new world order' (Rustin 1999). Seen thus, the New Labour project is one of enabling those who are currently excluded from the benefits of global capitalism to become successful competitors in the global marketplace. The 'socially excluded' of New Labour's rhetoric are those who need to be helped to enter and to become successful inhabitants of consumer society. This has profound implications for education. Definitions of 'success' in schooling are tightly defined and policed through a battery of coercive measures, as well as through discursive struggle. In distancing itself from 'Old Labour', much has to be left out of the New Labour agenda. In particular, the debate over what constitutes egalitarian schooling – the site of allegations of 'loony-leftism' and 'out of control political correctness' throughout the Conservative administration – has to be carefully controlled.

Where the prevailing political imperative is to insert as many 'disadvant-aged' pupils as possible into global capitalism as its successful subjects, other visions of educational equality have to be made unthinkable.

Contained within the standards agenda, then, is an unproblematic accept-ance of the inevitability and desirability of global capitalism. The purpose of schooling is equally unproblematically constructed as the need to produce 'employable' subjects with the skills to compete in the global labour market and the desire to do so.[1] In New Labour's vision of schooling, the only questions that can legitimately be asked are around how the continuously improving school can produce more and more successful players in the game of global capital. To this end, schools are inundated with more and more data about the examination results of their students, since it is these results that determine how successful a student is seen to be. Student success, measured by examination performance, becomes in turn the determinant of individual teachers' success, which becomes the determinant of school success, local education authority success and, ultimately, governmental success. But, while it is heavily surveillant, and while there is a measure of resistance to its policing functions, this target-setting regime is seductive as well as punitive. It works to make dominant versions of 'success' desirable to students and teachers in all sorts of ways.

The construction of the subject 'successful schoolchild'

Long before New Labour's election in 1997, the outgoing Conservative administration had, in its 18 years of government, established clear and reductive criteria for what was to count as student success. The Education Reform Act 1988 paved the way for the introduction of a National Curric-ulum, embedded into which was a set of expectations of 'typical' academic achievement for pupils at ages 7, 11, 14 and 16. To facilitate the govern-ment's New Right vision of a marketized education service, pupils in Years 2, 6, 9 and 11 of compulsory schooling would be tested, and their examination results collated to enable the publication of league tables of schools.[2] The National Curriculum itself enshrined the notion of linear progression via a ten-point scale according to which pupil attainment could be calibrated and compared with national norms.

The New Labour government, far from dispensing with this version of success, built on and refined it. The National Curriculum levels originally conceived of as representative of 'typical' pupil attainment are now referred to as the 'expected' standards. A version of the subject 'successful school-child' now progresses diligently and unproblematically from one SMART target to the next in the pursuit of continuously improving examination performance. But perhaps New Labour's optimal model of the subject 'suc-cessful schoolchild' is the 'gifted and talented' pupil. These G&T students, introduced to us through the 'Excellence in Cities' programme, are the ones for whom extra resources must be made available in order that they may progress further and faster through the National Curriculum to a point where they can perform successfully in 'world class tests'.

Of the many educational initiatives introduced by New Labour, 'Excellence in Cities' (EiC: DfEE 1999a) is one of the furthest reaching for Newbrook. One of its many effects has been its construction of new possibilities for 'doing successful student' at the school, as well as the staff micropolitics that the construction of these possibilities has entailed and necessitated. In the EiC document, published in April 1999, New Labour sets out its vision for the transformation of a well-worn New Right construction, the 'failing' inner-city school. Its starting point, as the document makes clear, is the poor GCSE examination results of inner-city 16-year-olds, when compared to cohorts in suburban and rural areas. In its introduction, the document explains that 'excellence must become the norm' (DfEE 1999a: 2). The construction of the subject 'schoolchild' within the pages of the EiC document is an entirely managerial one. Children are the raw materials to be processed, developed, sorted and quality-tested (assessed) for added value at regular intervals. They are creatures who have 'needs' that must be met, and 'talents' that must be unlocked. Or, to be more precise, a statutory 5–10 per cent of them have talents and gifts that are by implication inherent, and that must be provided for.

Commenting on what they call the 'effective schools movement' (ESM), Rea and Weiner (1998: 23) note that 'the "revivalist" tones of ESM appear deeply attractive to [teachers], offering salvation with a litany of redemptive recipes'. There is indeed a strongly revivalist flavour to the EiC document:

> While problems exist, there are also many success stories in the cities. There are children, schools and other educational services which perform well . . . They overcome what others would tell them are children's disadvantages in income, language or experience. We must create a climate in which this 'can do' approach can prosper. We must learn from those who succeed and spread their culture and achievement more widely.
>
> (DfEE 1999a: 5)

Such promises of hope for a brighter, more successful future can appear to leave no room for argument. They are both seductive in their appeal to social justice, and are presented as the only possible option: the imperative 'we must create' and 'we must learn' produce a sense that resistance is not only futile but inadmissible. The schoolchild is reduced in this analysis to a set of variables to be controlled for (Rea and Weiner 1998). Those variables are carefully described as 'disadvantages in income, language or experience'. Differences of class, race, gender, disability and all other structural sites of oppression are completely elided, as is the concept of oppression itself, redolent as it is with unreconstructed socialism.

EiC is explicitly part of the government's project to 'drive up' educational standards. The middle four pages, entitled 'Standards in the Cities', explain how 'we' intend to do this. There are three indicators of pupil performance to be taken into account: proportions of students gaining at least five A*–C grades at GCSE, proportions of students gaining at least one A*–C grade, and proportions of students excluded from school. The subject 'successful school-child' is thus one of a body of people who is enabled to perform certain tasks to measurable levels at required intervals, and one of a body of people who is enabled to be sufficiently compliant with their school's agenda to be institutionally included. But this successful subject does not count, and is not counted, as an individual. It is how their performance relates to the overall performance of students nationwide that is to be judged. As media panics over so-called grade inflation indicate (Bomford 2001; Henry 2001), the credibility of the A*–C benchmark depends on its continuing inaccess-ibility to a proportion of students. The successful schoolchild is not the one who gets to Point A, but the one who succeeds relative to others. This is what Kenway et al. (1997) have called the 'zero-sum' game of success. The successful schoolchild can exist only in relation to the failing schoolchild. Both are necessary subject positions in New Labour educational discourse.

At the end of the 1999 autumn term, Newbrook held a staff meeting to prepare everyone for the operationalization of the EiC reforms.

> Dorothy [the head] stands up to introduce EiC. It's her usual pep talk. The school motto – 'neglect not the gift that is in thee' – and the aim – 'quality education for all girls' – are on an OHT [overhead transparency]. EiC is to be one more way of achieving our aim, and improving our service, especially to girls at either end of the ability spectrum. Newbrook is to participate in two strands. There will be a learning mentor whose brief will include home visits. This person will be working with, for example, the three Year 11 girls who were absent for the mocks, and with disaffected 'children' lower down the school. There are nods of agreement. The other strand is the G&T – Gifted and Talented. The silence becomes a tense one. Expressions harden as people prepare to disagree. Dorothy directs us to the first aim of the school – to ensure that students reach the highest academic standards of which they are capable – and the first bullet point of the home–school agreement, which is similar. This initiative is going to be adapted 'as we at Newbrook always do' to improve education for all girls. It is to mean curriculum enhancement for all our girls *and* our very able girls . . .
>
> Sue [the newly appointed G&T coordinator] talks about the huge amount of government money. The G&T strand will be national in 15 months, and will be inspected by Ofsted. For us, it will improve standards for all students as the discussion around differentiation will percolate down and benefit everyone. It is, in her account, a question of equal opportunities – the G&T students have a right to be stretched, and after all, research shows that there is a high suicide rate among Oxbridge students who haven't learned how to fail. So G&T students have the right (by implication, like all other students) to be stretched until they fail . . .
>
> (Fieldnotes 13/12/99)

The introduction, via EiC, of learning mentors was uncontroversial. This is not surprising, given Newbrook's tradition of attention to strategies of challenging inequalities and oppression. But the G&T policy required much more hedging around. Both the construction of 'brilliant student' and the notion of providing extra resources for such students were likely to encounter resistance. Threaded though the stories that Newbrook tells itself of itself is the recuperation of those models of learning traditionally associated with girls (Walkerdine 1988; Walkerdine and Girls into Mathematics Unit 1989; Paechter 1998). The diligent, hard-working girl has been thus recuperated, and (masculine) effortless brilliance, while admired, has been painstakingly prevented from taking up a central position. The idea that some girls can be identified as G&T – as 'naturally' brilliant – is not one that could have automatic appeal in Newbrook. Additionally, Newbrook is invested in an anti-oppressive version of equal opportunities. While such understandings of equal opportunities can be co-opted within a version that valorizes successful examination performance by previously underperforming groups of pupils, the attempt to reposition G&T students as needful of extra resources was, at the point of the meeting, a discursive jump too far. Except, perhaps, for those teachers who are positioned as senior managers, and who have specific interests in promoting compliance with policy directives for whose implementation they are accountable.

> We go into faculty groups . . . We have a piece of sugar paper, and have to record our concerns on one side, and anticipated benefits to the school on the other. We start with concerns. What about the students who identify a talent, but aren't picked out to join the G&T register? Will there be an elite group? Will that elite group be monitored, for class and race bias? What about parents who want their daughters to join the register? Will our top 5–10 per cent equate with the other cluster schools (which include a special school for students with learning difficulties)? What about girls who don't want to be on the register? And what will be the position of the (orthodox) Muslim girls, whose parents tend not to be keen on extracurricular activities at school, and who certainly wouldn't let their daughters participate in mixed-sex extracurricular sessions? Pam [Head of Faculty] has had enough before long, and wants us to note down some benefits. This effectively stops the discussion. She puts down some of the points made by Sue in her presentation. We get back to concerns. What are the implications of the staff sorting out the G&T? Will we ever get away from the hierarchies in our heads? Pam doesn't write it down. She is determined to fill the benefits side . . .
>
> Back in the staffroom, the usual people gather . . . Conversation turns to the G&T. Sue gets out the pieces of sugar paper, and we gather round to have a look. Most of the concerns are about how and whether the girls and their parents will be notified, and the dangers of categorization. Nadje is uneasy with the idea of labelling and thinks that the G&T girls will not want to be picked out in this way. We laugh at the prospect of parents putting pressure on their daughters to get onto the G&T list. But it's not that far-fetched a prospect. Bozena wants to know exactly how the nine students identified by each faculty will be correlated with

the seven G&T areas. What about Jessica, who ran for Essex ladies, but whose talents were more or less confined to sprinting – Bozena doesn't rate her as talented when compared to Myrtle who could do well at any sport, though not to regional level. That is what Bozena calls talent. The English faculty have written elaborate mind maps. Every faculty has written more concerns than benefits. On the benefits side of our faculty's list, almost empty last time I saw it, Pam has written in big capital letters, 'GREAT! WE THINK WE CAN REALLY GO WITH THIS'.

(Fieldnotes 13/12/99)

The resistance of Newbrook's staff speaks to a profound distaste for 'naming and acclaiming'. Contained within that resistance is the implicit recognition, so obvious it does not need to be voiced, that the school's small group of white middle-class students are likely to be disproportionately represented on the G&T register. If there are extra resources coming in, none of the 'rank-and-file' members of staff want them used on this already advantaged group, and Sue's attempt to use versions of equal opportunities to reposition such girls as disadvantaged does not (immediately) work. Where benevolent humanitarianism can be invoked to do the work of legitimizing the normative categorization of 'SEN students', Newbrook's senior managers cannot quite manage to insert it into the G&T programme. Contrary to the construction of EiC's successful student, Newbrook's staff want to hold onto a construction of giftedness and talent that is relative and is culturally and socially situated.

Meanwhile, outside the staffroom door, lives another version of the subject 'successful student'. She is produced and produces herself through imbrications of New Labour's target-driven high-performer, Newbrook's confident pro-feminist young woman, postmodernism's multiskilled and multiply-positioned new millennium girl, and student/street culture's girl with attitude. She is typically high achieving, of high microcultural status, hetero/sexually attractive (and possibly active, though she keeps that information to herself), good at sports and arts as well as academic subjects, and popular with the teachers for her friendly and outgoing demeanour. She knows, or appears to know, where she is going in life, and is able to make use of school and student cultures to help her get there. I call her a 'starlet'.

Amina and I go to 102. Some of the starlets are there. They are quite noisy, confidently discussing Spanish exams and practising with each other, in a relaxed kind of way. I know that if I asked them to be quieter they would comply, as a favour to me, while remaining in charge of the situation. Amina and I get stuck into Spanish conversation. She wants to practise the basic questions – the date of her birthday, her age and where she lives. She has been learning these for three years. I wonder if she's getting bored with answering the same questions yet. Another starlet comes in, fresh from the exam. The others ask how it went. 'Miss' (the teacher examiner) has told her she is the best she has heard all day. There are screams of approval, and one young woman hugs the new arrival. She has an examination tale to tell. She told the examining teacher that she helped with the housework. As a follow-up, the teacher asked when she was going to clean the house. The starlet, misunderstanding, and thinking she was being asked when she was going to leave home, answered that she would do so in three years. This story is greeted with yells of excited approval and laughter. Amina doesn't understand the joke. She asks the starlet a question about the exam. The young woman comes over, and explains to Amina, in a very nice, gentle way, what she wants to know, not seeming to mind when Amina's questions make little sense.

(Fieldnotes 24/11/99)

Is the confidence that the starlets apparently exude a function of their taking up positions as 'successful' students, or is it a function of being 'the best'? This is an important question, since on it hinges on the relationality of success. In many ways, the starlets embody a femininity of which I approve. They are 'critical readers of their lifeworlds' (Kenway et al. 1994: 201), they are resistant to injustice and they treat more vulnerable students with respect, care and kindness. The starlets can afford to delight in a mistake made in an examination, since it does not threaten their status as 'the best': they have sufficient reserves of 'success' in the bank to make the occasional mistake a source of fun. They can turn that mistake into a story that confirms and reinscribes them as successful. Amina could not have told such a story, nor did it even seem to make sense to her. Success does not appear to be in jeopardy for the starlets. Nor is the stability of their friendship group, which can delight in each other's achievements, because there is plenty of success to go round. It is a stability that can permit its members to be 'kind' to those who, like Amina, are positioned as microcultural as well as academic losers, and of whom middling girls steer well clear.

Two of Newbrook's starlet leavers of 1999 returned to the school the following year, to speak publicly to the new Year 11 cohort. One of them spoke about her athletic prowess, which had led to the realization of her dream to win the local schools' sprint championship when she was in Year 9. She told the audience that she had gone on to prioritize her GCSE work, as opposed to her athletics, and had emerged with a clutch of A* and A grades. Addressing her audience as 'beautiful young women of the new millennium', she told them that they could all achieve their dreams if, like her, they set ambitious goals, believed in their ability to attain them, and worked with determination, using the support provided by Newbrook's teachers. The address of the other starlet returner was similar in content, describing a process of converting dreams into targets. Embedded in their speeches was the fundamental contradiction which lies at the heart of depoliticized versions of equal opportunities. Enabling these talented, clever young women (both of them of working-class, African Caribbean origin) to do superlatively well within a competitive culture has also enhanced the continuance of that competitive culture. As members of a group that is often disadvantaged, these young women, and others like them, have been given an opportunity to climb rungs of a ladder that they might not otherwise have been able to climb. The ladder, however, remains in place. The speeches of the starlet returners elide – slide past – the relationality of success within a competitive culture, making it invisible and unremarkable, and confirming the fantasy that everyone can insert themselves into successful subject positions within global capitalism.

If school effectiveness is a 'feel-good fiction' (Hamilton 1998), such recasting of dreams into targets that can be set and met, and the promise that success is there for everyone who works hard enough and SMART enough, are central to the plot. Newbrook's starlets have apparently learned to dream the dreams that global capital makes available to them, and are able to produce themselves as successful subjects of meritocratic fantasy, but at what cost? Boler (1999) comments that 'Meritocracy enforces the internalisation of discipline and desire for reward, thus incorporating democratically engineered individualism . . . Meritocracy places success and failure squarely on the individual, decontextualising the student from any mediating factors of social or cultural context' (Boler 1999: 47). Since equal opportunities are central to Newbrook's official, micropolitical and social life, the fiction of universally attainable success has to be maintained. The starlets – girls from social backgrounds that are traditionally thought of as disadvantaged – embody the contradictions inherent in the fiction. When they stand before the Year 11 assembly, exuding confidence and speaking their success, they are both the proof that 'anyone can do it' and the reason why everyone cannot. They are not merely 'successful' students, they are 'the best' and, by definition, that is a position available to few.

Interrogating the position taken up by Newbrook's starlets is not to argue for a return to other, perhaps more traditional, versions of success more closely tied to traditional elitist educational practices. Neither is it to pathologize a group of young women who, starting from positions of systemic disadvantage, use every resource on offer to them in order to take up the better life that they have been promised. I do, however, want to centralize two questions: what are the costs of current versions of success, and what possible versions do they displace? These questions can perhaps best be illustrated by considering the occasional non-dominant versions of success that Newbrook makes available to its students, and the conditions of that availability.

One occasion stands out. In 1996, two feminist teachers made the case for a whole-school celebration of International Women's Day. They were able creatively to deploy discourses around achievement and standards in establishing a politicized celebration that would engage with women's equality issues worldwide. Such a celebration has since become customary practice at Newbrook. On the Friday closest to International Women's Day, the school timetable is suspended, and replaced with a programme of activities, visiting speakers and external visits. The school comes alive with excitement, and there is little talk of targets. Although the day is meticulously planned, there is space for spontaneity. One year, at lunchtime, an enterprising group of young women in Year 11 facilitated a concert, with individual and group 'star turns'.

A group of Asian girls, in Year 10 I think, come onto the stage and start to dance. The hall erupts with whooping, clapping and stamping. I don't think it's that the dancing is particularly brilliant (which it's not). It seems to be more an atmosphere of excitement and appreciation of each other that's caught on. At the end of the number, the girls in the audience roar their approval. A woman I don't know – one of the day's many visitors – comes onto the stage, with a drum which she starts to play. The audience scream and clap. Then another woman leads the Year 11 girls onto the stage. There's about 20 of them, including some of the shyest, quietest young women in the school. I feel quite tearful seeing them up there. The audience continue to whoop and stamp. I wonder when people like Aneesa and Kareema have ever been the focus of 400 cheering, adoring fans. And if they ever will be again. I think everyone should be able to do this at least once in their lives. I spot Aqsa and Hafsa on the back row – I've never seen them at the centre of attention before. The audience are ethnically mixed – it's not just other Asian girls enjoying this show, but black and white and Middle Eastern as well. I'm relieved to see Asian-ness on centre stage. Asian-ness is so often missing from the success stories the school tells itself about itself.

(Fieldnotes 10/3/00)

Kenway et al. (1997: 35) remark that 'teachers invariably walk a tightrope between encouraging students to succeed in conventional terms and encouraging them to succeed differently – always with the knowledge that difference seldom wins out over dominance'. Occasions such as the one above are rare at Newbrook. During the period of fieldwork, this was one of very few incidents I witnessed in which a different version of success came close to momentarily displacing the dominant one, and in which the students with whom I work were publicly positioned as 'successful'. Newbrook's celebration of International Women's Day is explicitly linked to a political context beyond the school. The standards agenda in particular, and school effectiveness in general, demand that schools be viewed as complete microcultural entities disembedded from wider sociopolitical contexts (Lauder et al. 1998). The celebration of International Women's Day momentarily wrote that wider sociopolitical context back into the picture, and extricated social justice issues from their managerialist and instrumentalist packaging. This opened up a discursive space in which non-dominant versions of the subject 'successful student' could become thinkable, visible and desirable.

The construction of the subject 'successful teacher'

New Labour's policies on the 'modernization of the teaching profession' – especially those on performance-related pay – explicitly link pupil attainment with teacher effectiveness (DfEE 1998; Barber 2000). The construction of the subject 'successful teacher' is linked at many levels, formal and informal, to the construction of the subject 'successful student'. Such a linkage has a long history. When mass and then compulsory education was introduced in the

UK in the 1870s, teacher salaries were based on the number of pupils promoted from a teacher's class. This system was widely criticized, and abandoned in 1891. Nevertheless, many (heavily gendered) understandings of the linkage have persisted in various common-senses and popular mythologies. The 'Mr Chips' version of the dedicated public school teacher and his sister, the wise, scholarly spinster headmistress, the committed and progressive young radical who wins the hearts and minds of the local toughs in the working-class comprehensive, the warm, motherly infant teacher and the stern disciplinarian with the heart of gold all stand in the shadows of today's 'effective' teacher.

The school year at Newbrook customarily begins each September with a staff training and development day. The major item for discussion on this day is always the school's examination results. The senior teacher in charge of examinations spends the final two weeks of the summer holiday collating GCSE results, and tabulating them in a number of ways. Attention is focused on the numbers and percentage of students scoring five or more passes at grade C or above, since this is the 'expected level' and the benchmark for externally recognized success. It is also the measure used in compiling local league tables.

> Dave passes round the list of results from the top point-scorer to those who have scored no points at all. The room is full of exclamations – 'I knew she could do it!' 'Only three Cs for Zina!' 'Farhana got more then Karen!' and the like. I turn straight to the last page to see if Cassandra got any grades. She didn't get English Literature (which is no surprise) but she got an F in textiles. No one else on my row seems interested in the last page. We don't get long to look. Dave hands the next one round. It's the comparison of the faculties, with each other and with their results from the last three years. English is top again, pushing onwards towards 70 per cent A*–Cs, followed by science. Then comes the point-by-point comparison. Every student's average point score is listed, alongside the points actually awarded in each subject. These are compared not merely across faculty, but also across teaching groups, enabling comparisons of teacher 'performance' to be made. The room is now silent and tense. Every faculty will have to draft a report this afternoon explaining its improvement, or lack of it. Every head of faculty will have to account for the performance of students in specific teaching groups. More especially, they will have to account for any 'underperformance' by students taught by particular teachers.
>
> (Fieldnotes 4/9/00)

The subject 'successful teacher' at Newbrook works purposefully towards the examination success of their students. This is the bottom line, below which no teacher can produce themselves as successful. It is a competitive bottom line. The successful teacher must enable all students in their teaching group to perform at or above their average in their other subjects. More than that, the successful teacher must be continuously improving, and that continuous improvement must be demonstrable in the improving examination results of their teaching groups. The successful teacher produces students who are desirous of dominant versions of success, and, as such, are governable. In producing such students, the successful teacher also produces themself as desirous of those same versions of success, and as governable according to the rules of the same game.

The official construction of 'successful teacher' at Newbrook, like the construction of 'successful student', draws on a new managerialist version of equal opportunities. This version of equal opportunities serves to legitimize the regime of surveillance imposed on individuals and groups of teachers through examination results, by framing it as democratic accountability. Those teachers who embrace surveillance are cast as the ones who really care about their pupils, since they are willing to subject themselves to what is presented as a regime of self-examination 'for the good of the students'. League tables and numerical data are the instruments of self-examination, disliked perhaps, but tolerated. Equal opportunities is the authorizing narrative that secures the consent of teachers for the process. School effectiveness discourses link the two. Morley and Rassool (1999) note that:

> Teachers are now reassured that their interventions make a difference. They have targets, goals, visible indices of their efforts. There is a new classification and value creation machinery, based on a moral authority, backed up with quantification and a series of sign systems which represent educational excellence.
>
> (Morley and Rassool 1999: 134)

At Newbrook, discourses of school and teacher effectiveness make desirable a version of successful teacher who deploys the machinery of surveillance in the interests of traditionally disadvantaged students. The successful teacher is co-opted into the school effectiveness discourse, and takes up a (supposedly) active, agentic position within it.

New managerialism, equal opportunities and the ongoing micropolitical struggle for power, prestige and the resources they accrue, combine to do the discursive work of co-optation. It was this combination which ultimately provided the way for the unpopular introduction of the G&T policy, already noted, to go ahead.

> The work of maintaining the G&T faculty noticeboards will be done by faculty G&T reps, each of whom will be allocated half a responsibility point [a salary enhancement]. These will initially be allocated on a fixed term basis, for the three years that the EiC initiative is planned to last. There will be training and development attached to the posts, so they will present an 'excellent professional development opportunity'. Sue tells us that these responsibilities will make their holders 'very attractive' as the initiative is set to go nationwide after that time. Not only is this, in Sue's account, a professional development opportunity, it is a fantastic opportunity to raise the achievement of all our students.
>
> (Fieldnotes 13/12/99)

The successful teacher takes up professional development opportunities since, in current terms, the good teacher is the developing teacher, always ready for new initiatives that will improve their own 'performance' and thereby that of their students. Taking up professional development opportunities is also key to producing oneself as a successful teacher with a career plan and a set of personal targets in mind, thereby adding value to oneself as a 'human resource' for the purposes of investment. A very particular kind of seductive appeal inhered in the newly created posts of faculty G&T coordinators. If the successful teacher is indissolubly linked with the successful student, it is only a short step from linking the brilliant, going-places student with the brilliantly effective, going-places teacher. Within days of a resistant staff meeting, a new subject, the 'G&T student' had been constructed through some intensive micropolitics and allied teacher identity work.

It is probably true that most of Newbrook's teaching staff were co-opted into what appeared to be active compliance with the G&T policy. But what were the choices? No active forms of resistance were on offer, since central government and the local authority had decided the school would participate. Senior management cannot be seen to be sceptical without damaging their own career prospects, since progression through the managerial chain requires 'positive responses' to new initiatives. Faculty heads, directly responsible to senior management, are held to account for the positive operationalization of those new initiatives, and cannot afford to be seen to jeopardize them. Non-compliance on the part of faculty members is regarded as personal disloyalty, as well as disloyalty 'to the firm' (Reay 1998). Despite the micropolitical realities here, the new managerialist construction of 'successful teacher' cuts across school hierarchies, addressing teachers as if their interests were identical. And so a blend of coercive measures that rendered resistance futile, together with incentives that made co-optation appealing, interpellated most of Newbrook's teachers into subject positions as successful implementers of a policy with which they had initially disagreed.

The construction of the subject 'successful teacher' is the production both of historical understandings of what it means to be a teacher, and of the reinvention of the subject 'worker' as flexible specialist. New Labour has inherited an inglorious tradition of eighteen years of teacher derogation by the Conservative administration (Cooper 1989; Ball 1990; Chitty 1999). Onto the resultant image of lazy, incompetent teachers who care only for ideology and/or an easy life, New Labour has grafted a new version of the teacher. This newer version has more in common with the flexibly specialized corporate worker than with older notions of the autonomous professional. For the introduction of the G&T policy to work at Newbrook, teachers' consent must be won. When equal opportunities arguments proved unconvincing, and coercion unpalatable, the appeal was made to teachers' new understandings of themselves and their purposes. To turn down, or to appear to encourage others to turn down, a professional development opportunity in these days of flexible specialization is inadmissible. The successful teacher at Newbrook embraces new initiatives and uses them for career enhancement, in much the same way as the successful student sets goals and uses the resources around her to achieve those goals. Newbrook's successful teachers are positioned as superb technicians, asking searching questions about how best to operate new initiatives to the benefit of Newbrook's students and their own careers. What they cannot do is ask questions about why, and in whose interests, those initiatives are being introduced.

It is impossible to leave a discussion of the subject 'successful teacher' without mentioning the performance management requirements.that now statutorily link teacher 'performance' with pay. Every school is required to have its own policy for administering the system. Newbrook's Performance Management Policy, written in bright, up-beat language, enables the national policy of linking teacher pay and performance to be put into practice. The casual reader of the policy might think this was something that Newbrook's staff had collaboratively decided was a necessary absolute good. Morley and Rassool (1999: 66) argue that 'schools produce action plans, mission statements, targets, strategies and visions as a matter of symbolic compliance or legitimation'. The successful teacher is required to identify as effective through active participation in the construction of these symbols of compliance, completing a circle of moral authority which operates by deploying new managerialist discourses of empowerment, inclusion and professionalism. In this way, the coercion of teachers is made to masquerade as co-optation, and governmental surveillance and control in schooling is elided – not merely concealed, but made unremarkable. It is successful teachers who do the work of elision, and performing that elision is a prominent means by which to do 'successful teacher'.

Success and the standards agenda

Newbrook is the product of a competitive system of schooling. Fortuitous circumstances and the hard work of individuals and groups enable the school to recognize itself and to be recognized as successful within the parameters constructed by that competitive system. There is much serious engagement within the school about issues of equality. This engagement can be understood within a framework of the current expectations for schools to be self-interrogating, and continuously improving. But it also is representative of the legacies of more radical, politicized discourses of educational reform. Current discourses of success come under constant challenge but ultimately, given their systemic location, these dominant discourses, however fragile they may appear to be, are the ones that nearly always determine who can be recognized as successful, and the terms on which that recognition can take place. This pessimistic analysis contains its own ray of hope. The fact that the strategies used to enforce hegemonic versions of success are so multifarious, suggests also that the standards agenda is struggling for survival, albeit in very unequal conditions. The 400 whooping, stamping girls who participated in the International Women's Day lunchtime concert, and the teachers who watched, delighted, from the back of the hall, know that there is more to life than target-setting, and recognize that there is more to social justice than examination success. Day-to-day life at Newbrook, however, mostly obscures such perceptions and delegitimizes their articulation.

Most of the time, success at Newbrook can be recognized only in relation to the standards agenda, and all versions of success exist in relation to this dominant version. New Labour's drive to improve standards has a ring of inevitability about it. To voice disagreement with the standards agenda is, on the one hand, to proclaim oneself against an unquestionable good, much like arguing against peace, or mother love. It is also to declare oneself a dinosaur, with a politics so irrelevant and untenable as to be extinct. Levitas (1998: 113) remarks that 'the New Right naturalisation of "markets" is replaced by appeals to the inevitability of "globalisation"'. The perceived inevitability of the standards agenda stands in direct relation to the perceived inevitability of globalization. It presupposes that the overdetermining purpose of education is to produce the successful subjects of global capitalism. Making his 'case for change' in education, the former Education Secretary has stated that:

> The first argument is an economic one and *is unanswerable*. Thirty or forty years ago, developed countries could tolerate substantial under-performance in their education systems mostly because there was a plentiful supply of unskilled or semi-skilled jobs in the economy. This is no longer the case. The combined forces of globalisation and technological innovation mean, as a recent World Bank report put it so succinctly, that 'education will determine who has the keys to the treasures the world can furnish'.
>
> (Blunkett 2000b, emphasis added)

The standards agenda operates as if standards are absolute, and the legitimizing narrative operates as if those absolute standards can be made accessible to everyone. The ultimate aim of the successful, continuously improving school is to produce entire cohorts of students who attain the national average standard or better. Such an aim is cruel, as well as being manifestly nonsensical, since an average standard, by its nature, requires half the population to fall below it. Towards this end, however, Newbrook's successful teachers routinely stand in front of classes exhorting students to work hard towards their exams. The fiction, that everyone can be successful if only they work hard enough and their teachers are effective enough, is reinscribed lesson-by-lesson. The costs of continuous improvement remain largely unspoken. When ripples of concern do surface, as they did at Newbrook in the debate over the G&T policy, a complex and impermeable blend of coercion and co-optation operationalized through micropolitics and identity work forces them back beneath the glossy waters of the standards agenda pool.

Notes

1 The concept of 'employability' has been central in the Labour Party's reinvention of itself as 'New Labour' (DfEE 1997a, 1998; Blunkett 2000a, 2001). Arguments originally deployed in the 'education for employability' agenda re-emerged as 'life-long learning' discourses, in which individual obligations to progressively reskill are

presented as entitlements to an undisputed good. See for example Levitas (1998) and Rustin (2000).

2 The Education Reform Act was a major piece of legislation, heralding a wave of New Right educational reforms based on the principles of neo-liberalism and neo-conservatism. For a fuller discussion of these reforms (in the UK and elsewhere) and their implications for equity issues, see, for example, Goacher et al. (1988), Jones and Mahony (1989), Norwich (1990), Johnson (1991), Arnot and Barton (1992), Barton (1993), Epstein (1993), Lunt and Evans (1994), Tomlinson (1994), Apple (1995), Gewirtz et al. (1995), Griffiths and Troyna (1995), Kenway (1995), Apple (1996), Dehli (1996), Hey (1996), Kenway and Epstein (1996) and Lowe (1997).

CHAPTER FOUR

'SEN', inclusion and the elision of 'failure'

This chapter looks more closely at what happens to notions of 'failure' in the successful comprehensive school that Newbrook perceives itself to be. How does the school explain the failure of particular students to reach the benchmark requirements of the standards agenda? Like Chapter 3, this chapter examines how prevailing macro-discourses are operationalized through micropolitics and identity work. In particular, it looks at the way notions of 'inclusive education' are co-opted via school effectiveness models into a version of the standards agenda, and the implications of this. Newbrook produces its 'special needs students' in relation to these newer discourses, and in relation to older historical models. The school's learning support department plays a central role in this production, and this chapter looks at the micropolitics of learning support provision. The case study of a final-year student writing her valedictory statement shows the production of a 'special needs student' in action, and suggests that what is going on is not the production of 'failure' but something potentially far more harmful: its elision. The discursive practices in play at Newbrook slide past notions of 'failure' in ways that obscure and obfuscate, but do not eliminate, their continuing inegalitarian social and material effects.

What's wrong with inclusion?

Thomas and Loxley (2001) note that 'inclusion' is becoming something of a cliché. Where it might once have meant policies and pedagogies that explicitly set out to make anti-oppressive schooling available to all students, and which engage with the politics of identity and difference in creative and challenging ways, it has been evacuated of much of this meaning. This is largely to do with developments on the macropolitical stage. There has recently been a political sleight-of-hand in which 'the oppressed' have become 'the excluded'. The increasingly hegemonic solution to this version of exclusion seems to be the insertion of supposedly excluded people into global capitalism (Rustin 1999, 2000). Once 'the excluded' have been 'empowered' to become the successful producers and consumers of global capital, it is implied that there will no longer be a problem.[1]

Similarly, 'inclusive education' has (though not uniformly) been co-opted Lloyd 2000). There is a growing tendency for policy debate on inclusive schools to be located within the (highly reductive) school effectiveness paradigm (Lunt and Norwich 1999). As such, it gives rise to, at best, bland debate about 'valuing diversity' in which the politics of difference are cast as irrelevant and are prematurely discarded, and into which dominant disabling courses can be absorbed (Slee 1997). It has no way of engaging with the petitive nature of the standards agenda, or of interrogating the politics which the standards agenda is located. At worst, it upholds the fiction minant versions of success can be universally possible. Moreover, .e term 'inclusion' was always supposed to preclude the construc-. of a new binary subject position (Allan 1996, 1999), the recent slippage between inclusion and social inclusion has enabled politicians, educators and others to produce the 'excluded child' as the subject and object of concern and provision (Smith 1999).

This chapter examines the production of the 'special needs student' at Newbrook in the context of current debates around inclusion. Barton and Slee (1999: 7) point out that, 'It is the broader political, economic and cultural context that needs to be engaged with in any serious attempts adequately to understand and explain failure within the educational system'. But the micropolitical production of 'special needs' at Newbrook, and the policy context in which this production is situated, explicitly rule out any such engagement. In consequence, a framework for understanding and engaging with student failure has not been developed, and failure itself becomes elided through complicated narratives of remediation and 'banal and vacuous' versions of 'inclusion' (Wilson 2000).

Levitas (1998: 7) notes that 'Exclusion appears as an essentially peripheral problem, existing at the boundary of society, rather than a feature of a society which characteristically delivers massive inequalities across the board and chronic deprivation for a large minority'. It is in the context of a schooling system that delivers similarly massive inequalities that I want to interrogate the micro-production – or, as I will argue, the elision – of failure at Newbrook school, in its macropolitical context. Newbrook's 'special needs students' are not enabled to produce themselves as successful according to dominant discourses (see Chapter 7). This is a function not of their own failure, or of the failure of specific teachers, but of a system that, in setting some up to win, also requires some to be positioned as losers.

> After break, we go into separate faculty groups to work on our targets. This is supposed to give us 'ownership' of them. I think I am supposed to feel empowered by this, but I don't. We have been provided with

copies of the school's overall targets for the next three years. The SATs targets have no apparent relevance for the learning support department.[2] Our Year 9 students will not be amongst those reaching the 'expected standards for their age' which is what counts in the statistics. Our Key Stage 3 students don't then exist in official terms: their built-in failure has rendered them invisible. So we don't have to bother with SATs targets. Maybe we can go home early. When it comes to Key Stage 4, we have only one set of targets to concern ourselves with. The percentage of students getting at least one A*–G grade. The other targets – the five A*–Cs and the five A*–Gs are equally inapplicable. We have finished by lunchtime. In the afternoon, we try to fill the time with desultory discussion on IEPs (individual education plans) and target-setting for individual students.

(Fieldnotes 6/1/99)

Students who have been identified as having SEN are at the sharp end of the standards agenda. Many (though not all) discourses of school inclusion require that these students are educated in mainstream schools and, at best, that mainstream schools adapt to value the diversity such students supposedly embody. Newbrook, with its emphasis on education for *all* girls, takes seriously its responsibility to provide as well as it can for these students. But this involves accommodating multiple contradictions. On the target-setting training and development day, we in the learning support department were exempted from setting departmental targets for improvement, since our students are not amongst those who are expected to succeed in dominant terms. That exemption, though, was not allowed to challenge the legitimacy of the target-setting process, which remained intact. I would not want to argue that the 'SEN students' were excluded from the process, since this side-steps the question of what they were to be included in, and suggests that what already exists – in this case, target-setting – is unquestionably right, and the only remaining problem is how to make it accessible.

The micropolitical production of the 'special needs student'

Procedures for identifying students with perceived 'learning difficulties' at Newbrook are clear. At the time of the research, they operated within the framework set out by the Special Needs Code of Practice (DfEE 1994; Riddell et al. 2000), itself derived from the Education Act 1993, though this has now been superseded by the Special Educational Needs and Disability Act 2001 (SENDA). When Year 7 students enter the school, all those whose Key Stage 2 test results were below the 'expected standard' of level 4 take the local education authority's reading and spelling tests. Those who achieve a reading age of less than 9 years are allocated additional funding from the LEA, in order that the school can make additional resources available to meet their 'special educational needs'. These students' names are entered onto Newbrook's SEN register. Their combined scores in the tests are used to calibrate their distance from the norm, and accordingly to determine at what stage of the Code of Practice their name is entered, and the amount and nature of the support to which they will be entitled. The special educational needs coordinator (SENCO) allocates in-class support to students, and individualized reading tuition, on the basis of their stage on the SEN register. Each year, students on the SEN register are retested, and they can be moved to different stages of the register, or off the register altogether, based on progress made. Some students enter Newbrook at stage 5 of the Code of Practice, and therefore have a statement of special educational needs. For these students, levels of support are agreed by the LEA, and these are monitored through the annual review process.

Students whose names appear on the SEN register, and who are thereby formally identified as having special needs, have an individual education plan (IEP). On the IEP is a set of targets for the student, together with a strategy through which the school will enable the student to achieve each target. In most cases, these targets are formulaic: it is standard practice to require a student to raise her reading age by 6 months over the course of the academic year, or to learn a particular multiplication table. It is the SENCO who is responsible for administrating the targets. Given the number of IEPs that the SENCO is expected to write and oversee during the course of the year, their formulaic nature is in many ways understandable and inevitable, though it also works to hold a technicist approach in place. Through the IEP targets, students' failure to make progress according to national norms can be reconfigured as personal achievement. While 6 months' progress in reading age over an entire academic year might more usually be considered as 'underachievement', the IEP will present it as success. Whether this success has currency in anything other than a deficit discourse is questionable. It is a question to which I will be returning in Chapters 7 and 8.

Following the assessment of the incoming Year 7 students, letters are sent home to alert parents and carers when a girl is put on the SEN register.

> Pam comes over to give Tony a message. Sereena's mother has phoned to say that she 'doesn't want her daughter to have special needs'. We laugh. Other anecdotes surface. Quratulain's parents have objected that she was put on the register because she made three mistakes on the reading test. Daisy's mother has told Tony that on no account must Daisy 'be special needs'.
>
> (Fieldnotes 15/10/00)

Within the official stories that Newbrook tells itself of itself, there is no place for the suggestion that a stigma, born out of inherited meanings and structures, still inheres within the designation of 'special educational needs'. The conundrum of whether and how to position various kinds and extents of special educational needs as socially constructed means that Newbrook, with its attention to social justice and its imperative to achieve success in normative terms, has to negotiate multiple contradictions. One of the overriding imperatives in this process of negotiation is for the school to position itself as acting in the best interests of its 'special needs students'. Back in the early

1980s, Tomlinson (1982: 5) noted that 'Special education is permeated by an ideology of benevolent humanitarianism which provides a moral framework within which professionals and practitioners work'. Ten years later, Norwich (1993) wrote that:

> Much of the appeal of viewing special educational needs as socially constructed or created is that it encourages a belief that difficulties associated with special educational needs can be overcome. It does this by placing the responsibility on social attitudes or institutions, like schools, with the assumption that schools and teachers, unlike individuals, are extensively adaptable.
>
> (Norwich 1993: 53)

At Newbrook, this discourse of benevolent humanitarianism operates via the managerialist version of equal opportunities to construct a contradictory view of SEN and of 'special needs students'. 'Divergent discourses' of learning difficulty appear to coexist (Skidmore 1999a, 1999b). On the one hand, the school's SEN register exists to provide for individual students the help they apparently need to succeed on the same normative terms as other students. One measure of the school's success in SEN provision is how many students it manages to remove from the list on the grounds that they no longer require extra provision. Tales of such removals of students' learning difficulties can be added to Newbrook's collection of stories about its effectiveness, and imply a social constructionist view of learning difficulties. On the other hand, the register exists to provide legitimation for a student's apparent failure to make the 'expected progress for her age' by defining her as a 'special needs student' and therefore intrinsically unable to achieve this standard of performance. The very designation, often heard in the staffroom, of 'special needs student', speaks not only of the cumbersome way in which these students are now officially categorized, but also of the residual understanding that 'special needs' are intrinsic to the student. There is a clear attraction in this. The current surveillant 'blame and shame' culture in schooling means that someone (be it student, parent, teacher or administrator) has to be blamed for below-average examination performance. Designation as a 'special needs student' is one way to avoid institutional blame.

One of the functions of the special needs register, not admissible in public discourses at Newbrook, is to calibrate students in terms of their distance from the norm. To this end, the reading test, as a delineator of 'objective' measurement, can be invoked seemingly unproblematically, to justify the provision of additional resources. As such, it is impossible to argue against, and the idea that a parent can argue with the resulting designation, or that there can be any reason to argue with that resulting designation, is so ludicrous within staffroom discourse that it elicits laughter. Weedon (1997: 94) comments that 'it is the need to regulate disparate forms of subjectivity in the interests of existing power relations that motivates the language of common sense'. In staffroom common sense, the existence of the subject 'special needs student' is so obvious as to render these parents' objections ridiculous. The converse is also true: in responding to these parents' objections as if they were ridiculous, we reinscribe and thereby regulate the existence of the 'special needs student' and her location on the special needs register. Through what in effect is a restatement of institutional common sense, we make other functions of the register – the positioning of some students as 'needy', and their inscription within a set of discursive practices that have worked to materially and socially disadvantage those so designated – marginal to the discourse of benevolent humanitarianism that still pervades. Partly, though, the language of common sense is invoked as a way of dealing with the perplexing dilemma in which Newbrook finds itself in relation to those of its students who will underperform according to national norms. The subject 'special needs student' *has* to exist in order for Newbrook to account for those students, while simultaneously she *cannot* exist since her existence proves the impossibility of the fiction of universally accessible success.

The refraction of benevolent humanitarianism through a managerialist lens has further functions and effects. It constructs the process of identification and assessment of SEN as an entirely rational and technical enterprise, in which the irrational, the emotional and the interpersonal are factors to be objectively noted, monitored and controlled. While the Code of Practice has perhaps ensured that certain minimum standards of provision are met, it has also produced an understanding of SEN as a phenomenon that can be objectified and quantified given effective sets of techniques and apparatus. The apparent rationality of the stages model both suggests that it can be applied identically in every local context, and obscures the terms and the nature of its own social and political construction. One of the problems with any apparatus used to measure learning difficulties is that it is inescapably the product of the machinery of constructing relations of dominance and subordination.[3] Such relations are not constructed without struggle, but the form of the Code of Practice, and the interventions it legitimizes, conceal these struggles by the use of 'neutral' terminology within a techno-rationalist discourse.

Inclusive education and the standards agenda: some policy contradictions

New Labour's policies on provision for pupils and students with SEN are outlined in and informed by the Green Paper *Excellence for All Children* (DfEE 1997b). This document reflects an uncertainty, similar to the one that perplexes staff at Newbrook, about how to frame 'special educational needs' and how to represent those pupils who are considered to have such needs. Its introduction gives a twin definition. Pupils are considered to have SEN if they have 'learning difficulties' or disabilities that mean they cannot use resources commonly provided in mainstream classrooms *and* they require special educational provision over and above that required by pupils who do not have such needs. In other words, students have special educational needs not because of *either* intrinsic deficiencies *or* institutionally located ones, but because of a combination of *both*. This take on causality is fine, as far as it goes, in that it allows that both factors are necessarily associated with the production of 'special needs students'. What it does not do is interrogate the meanings held in place by the identification and assessment of pupils and students considered to have SEN, or the social and material consequences for individuals who are categorized in this way.

In his foreword to the Green Paper, the former Education Secretary David Blunkett sets out his rationale for promoting inclusion, which is in this context defined as the education of children considered to have SEN in mainstream schools. He explains that 'The great majority of children with SEN will, as adults, contribute economically; all will contribute as members of society' (DfEE 1997b: 4). In many ways this represents a step forward from benevolent humanitarianism, in that it starts by positioning people not as needy, but as contributors. Children with SEN are to be included not primarily because they have something to gain, but because they have something to offer. Blunkett finishes his foreword by stating that 'Where all children are included as equal partners in the school community, the benefits are felt by all' (DfEE 1997b: 4). As a statement of principle, this again is positive. It challenges the normative function of schools and problematizes the assumption that it is solely the pupils with special needs who stand to gain from their admission to mainstream provision. It is in keeping with much of the writing on inclusive education, which draws attention to the fact that it is in the interests of all pupils for mainstream schools to function in ways that celebrate diversity and a diverse range of talents and abilities (Bailey and Furby 1987; Hulley et al. 1987; Thomas et al. 1998; Ainscow 1999; Dyson 1999; Bines 2000).

To promote the inclusion of pupils and students with SEN in mainstream schools, Blunkett writes that his government 'shall remove barriers which get in the way of meeting the needs of all children' (DfEE 1997b: 5). Again, this is in keeping with much of the writing on inclusion which increasingly addresses barriers to participation. In the case of pupils and students who experience physical and sensory difficulties, the phrase is wholly appropriate. But while the rationale for applying a similar term in relation to students experiencing learning difficulties in understandable, its use in this context is more problematic. The social and political meanings still attached to 'learning difficulties' are overwhelmingly negative, and the notion of removing barriers cannot adequately explain the complexity of the task facing educators and the students themselves. The removal of barriers implies that schools, as complete microsystems, are able to manage their communities so as to change these socially and politically situated meanings. While I would not want to argue that schools or teachers are powerless in the process of the construction of meaning, it is a mistake to think that the meanings they construct can float free and independent of the discursive matrix within which they are embedded. The meanings that schools are able to make available, and the practices they can legitimize, necessarily exist in relation to those of the society and communities beyond the school gates. To suggest otherwise is to set schools and teachers up for failure.

Later in the Green Paper, the theme of removing barriers is expanded. 'Inclusion is a process, not a fixed state. By inclusion, we mean not only that pupils with SEN should wherever possible receive their education in a mainstream school, but also that they should join fully with their peers in the curriculum and life of the school' (DfEE 1997b: 44). I would want to agree in principle with much of this. But, again, the issue of what 'pupils with SEN' are to be included in has been side-stepped. What does it mean to 'join fully with their peers in the curriculum and life of the school' when 'their peers' are engaged in the formal work of pursuing the competitive standards agenda and in the microcultural work that dominant versions of success make possible? For students who are not going to succeed in dominant terms, the standards agenda is instrumental in *constructing* barriers to their participation. Here lies one of the most fundamental contradictions at the heart of New Labour's educational policy. The kind of full inclusion process apparently promoted in *Excellence for All Children* implies a set of values about intrinsic human worth which has effectively been overruled by the competitiveness of the standards agenda.

For the source of this contradiction we have to look again at the underlying imperative, obscured in the Green Paper, behind what New Labour means by inclusion. Levitas (1998) traces how New Labour has moved away from a redistributionist discourse to draw on combinations of moral underclass and social integrationist discourses. She argues that:

> Social inclusion now has nothing to do with distributional equality, but means lifting the poor over the boundary of a minimum standard – or to be more accurate, inducing those who are sufficiently sound in wind and limb to jump over it – while leaving untouched the overall pattern of inequality, especially the rich.
>
> (Levitas 1998: 156)

Educational policy, like other areas of New Labour policy-making, is similarly designed to legitimize the overall pattern of inequality necessary for the reproduction of global capitalism. When Blunkett cites the World Bank's observation that the keys to the world's treasures belong to the educated (see Chapter 3), he not only de-problematizes unequal distribution, but also inscribes it as right and proper, and an unarguable good. Where the standards agenda and the drive towards 'inclusive education' work together is in their colonization of the moral high ground. Both present themselves as if they were egalitarian in intent and effect. But a closer look at parts of the Green Paper already cited shows that this morality is, in fact, a utilitarian argument. When Blunkett describes children with special educational needs as 'contributors to society' he is making this utilitarian argument as if it were a moral imperative. This toxic mix of utilitarianism and morality cast as common sense and presented in 'can-do' language obscures, at a practical and theoretical level, the relations of dominance and subordination it continues to reproduce. Looking at the discursive practices that produce and are produced by the 'inclusion' of 'special needs students' is one way in which these relations can be made visible and interrogated.

At Newbrook, the standards agenda inscribes such students into relations of intellectual subordination through inserting them into deficit discourses. Students on the special needs register are positioned in one of three ways, and their 'neediness' defined accordingly. Those who are situated closest to the intangible border at which 'learning difficulties' merge with 'normality' are positioned as needing help in order to get as close as possible to, or even attain, normative levels of success. Most are positioned as needing help in order to achieve their personal best, since normative levels of success are clearly inaccessible to them. And a further small group is identified as 'really disabled', and needful of help not to make academic progress, but to be socially included in the life of the school. While all three positions can be legitimized, the deficit discourses also serve to position intellectually subordinated students outside of the dominant versions of success that the school works so hard to make desirable to the rest of its students. This is a theme to which I will return in later chapters.

The micropolitics of learning support

The standards agenda requires Newbrook to make above-average examination success available and desirable to a continuously increasing proportion of its students. The inclusion agenda appears to require Newbrook to provide schooling for students of all abilities and inclinations, irrespective of whether they are going to be able to perform at average level or above. These apparently contradictory imperatives are transmitted to students in many ways. One key site of this transmission is the learning support department, via which the school's micropolitical response to policy and discursive contradiction is enacted.

The learning support department is part of the pastoral faculty at Newbrook. It consists of the head of department (Tony), two part-time teachers covering a full-time post (Barbara and myself) and three learning support assistants (Saima, Caroline and Simone). The head of the pastoral faculty (Pam) also does some support teaching within the department. In parallel with the learning support department is the ethnic minorities and traveller education grant (EMTAG) team, of approximately the same size. The EMTAG teachers and support assistants are based in the school, but paid directly by the local education authority, and so have a slightly different relationship with Newbrook's line management system. In April 2000, a learning mentor (Ariadne) was appointed to a two-year post funded by 'Excellence in Cities'. Ariadne is line managed directly by Pam and, like the EMTAG team, she works in parallel with the learning support department. Her post has been created specifically to promote the inclusion of 'disaffected' students who are at risk of 'social exclusion'.

In general terms, the policy of the learning support department is to offer support to students in subjects with a high literacy or numeracy content. This means that support is usually allocated when students are in an English, maths, science or humanities lesson. The exception to this is for students who have statements of educational need specifying other support require-ments. A support teacher or learning support assistant will usually support two or more students in any one class. There is a long-running dispute about this apparently rational allocation policy. Teachers in some faculties, and in particular the Creative and Performing Arts (CPA) faculty, believe that they are disadvantaged, and their curriculum areas marginalized, because of it. Newbrook is officially committed to offering all of its students a 'broad and balanced curriculum'. The head of the CPA faculty (Alex) argues that she is not able to offer such a curriculum to some students because of lack of support. Underlying this argument is the sense that subjects such as music and drama, which form part of the CPA grouping, are being positioned as less important than the more 'serious' subjects. As a former teacher of music, and as a friend of Alex's, I tend to be perceived as her ally in this argument and often find myself taking her part in staffroom debate. That debate can get very heated. Ball (1987) comments that:

> The talk is of winning and losing, and the person and the personal are part of the conflict and the 'stake'. This is no cool rational process; it is a conflict between persons, groups and ideologies. It is a matter of confrontation, influence or the lack of it, and emotions. It is micropolitics.
>
> (Ball 1987: 46)

Tony's view is that we are supporting the student, not the faculty, and that a student's gains in literacy are transferable across the curriculum. Alex (and I) argue that students are as entitled to have access to music and art as to literacy-based subjects. The ideological and the personal are entwined and between them construct the debate. Although it appears to be about contrasting notions of what constitutes 'right' provision for students on the special needs register, this argument is as much about the power and prestige of 'recreational' subjects as it is about student entitlements. There is a seldom-voiced personal dimension to Alex's apparently rational argument, which is about how she is positioned as a music teacher and head of CPA if her subject and her faculty are positioned as relatively unim-portant. Alex's strongly held views about the purpose of learning support provision, and the moral and ideological base for that provision may therefore be, in part, produced through her own struggles for power and prestige.

If this is true of Alex, it is certainly true for those of us in the learning support department. Arguments that 'professionals and practitioners have vested interests in the expansion and development of special education' (Tomlinson 1982: 5) which run through sociological writing in special and inclusive education have what I believe to be a partial ring of truth at Newbrook. As a professional and a practitioner, the notion of professional vested interests is a thought with which I find it hard to engage, and one that I always want to complexify. Undoubtedly, though, we have an interest in listing students on the special needs register. By doing so, we justify our own jobs at the school: funding from the LEA for special needs provision is delegated according to the number of students on the register. If students do not get registered, our jobs do not get funded. We also have an interest in lobbying for the school to become more inclusive. When Newbrook admits students whose learning difficulties are perceived to be beyond the expertise of most of the subject teachers, those of us in the learning support department who have the required experience are positioned as experts, and our advice is eagerly sought. The ideological commitment to moving towards inclusion, which is held by many of us in the learning support department, is thus produced in the context of the personal/professional implications that more flexible admissions policies would have for us.

While the micropolitics of special needs support are played out on the personal/ideological stage of allocation and admissions debates, they are also played out, day-by-day, in classrooms (Kugelmass 2001). Newbrook's policies on the provision of classroom support may appear highly rational, and challenges to them constructed through the ideological debate of what is perceived to be best for the students. But the provision of such support, and its take-up by students, can be far from straightforward. The operationalization of Newbrook's in-class support policies is fraught with interpersonal complexities for both students and adult workers. Chapter 6 will look at student responses to classroom support, and the kinds of identity resources that the act of offering classroom support makes available to students. It is important also to note that adult identity work produces, and is produced by, the in-class support context.

> I sit down next to Aneesa. Actually, I'm supposed to be supporting Bridget, but she would have a fit and tell me where to go if I sat with her. I think Larry has forgotten that I'm supposed to be with Bridget. Anyway, Bridget sits next to Laura, who's perfectly capable of giving any help needed. Larry attempts to allocate parts for *Macbeth*. Several students refuse to read, so he will take the parts not filled. Aneesa is given the third witch: Larry always gives her a part to read when I am there. He wants there to be a 'stage' in the middle of the classroom. First and second witches take up their places. I ask if we can do our part from where Aneesa is sitting – I would be completely mortified if I had to go and stand on the 'stage' in front of the class, although Aneesa probably wouldn't mind. We take advantage of Larry's struggle for the class's attention to practise the first line Aneesa will say. When it gets around to her turn, she has forgotten it, and we stumble through, with me telling her every other word. I'm hot with embarrassment and feel like I should be doing a better job. Larry says that he's not going to let anyone spoil the lesson by talking at the wrong time, and that he will exclude from English the next person who talks. At one point he threatens Bridget with the duty room. She has just returned from her temporary exclusion, and is on a contract, so this is visibly effective. She argues that she wasn't the only one making a noise, but doesn't push her luck just in case. I would feel terrible if she were to be excluded from a lesson in which I was supposed to be supporting her. I hope no one finds out.
>
> (Fieldnotes 5/1/00)

Just as failure is elided for students, so it is differently elided for those of us who work with them. As a learning support teacher, I come to share in the embarrassment and shame of Aneesa's inability to decipher the text to an expected level. Even though no one points this inadequacy out, I am acutely aware of it. I also come to share in the guilty and furtive nature of Bridget's transgressions: I, too, fear the consequences should my deliberately counter-authority abandonment of her be found out. Like the students, we as teachers have sometimes contradictory motivations (Bines 1989). These may be partly constructed through rational arguments about how we understand our classroom purposes, but they can also be, at times, profoundly irrational. It is in the classroom that the immaculately pieced-together jigsaw of Newbrook's SEN policies gets shaken and scrambled by the jostling inconsistencies of interpersonal negotiation and identity work.

Eliding failure in the new millennium

It is important to remember that the current New Labour government has not invented the discursive field of 'special education'. The government's policies on inclusion reflect inherited meanings, structures and practices in the provision of schooling for intellectually subordinated students as well as systemic inequalities in wider society and globally. I do not intend in this chapter to undertake a lengthy exposition of how students use this discursive field in their identity work, since this will be fully considered later in the book. Before moving on, however, I want to present one example of how policy imperatives and inherited meanings combined with school micropolitics to inscribe a Year 11 student in some fairly traditional relations of subordination across multiple axes of difference through the elision of 'failure'.

Aqsa is in Year 11, her final year at Newbrook. Early on in the academic year, the students are required to produce a personal statement for their record of achievement (ROA). This document, essentially a file containing a record of the student's examination results and some 'personal best' pieces of work (in practice often randomly chosen) together with any certificates the student may have gained, informs the references that the form tutor will write for colleges and employers. The personal statement is a student's own view of the transferable 'key skills' she has gained, together with her career aspirations. Local colleges always ask to see a copy of the personal statement. Writing the statement presented multiple challenges to Aqsa, and she brought it to me for help in writing something that would satisfy her form tutor and keep her out of trouble.

> Hafsa and Aqsa collect me from the staffroom after the bell goes. Aqsa has her ROA personal statement, which has to be handed in tomorrow, and she's in a bit of a panic. So far, she has written two sentences; 'I am not brit [bright] girl. I am v v lazy'. Somehow, within an hour, we have to construct a narrative of her life that will illustrate all the transferable skills she has acquired. We start with her educational background,

reducing the upheavals and complexities of her history to a bald statement of how long she spent at school in Pakistan, France and England
respectively. She has been in school for a total of seven years. The rest of
the time – spent in hiding, and in refugee camps – we don't write about.
We list the subjects she is currently studying. I ask what her favourites
are. She doesn't like any. This won't do, and I press her to nominate two
or three that she finds less horrible than the rest. We note these down as
her favourites. Hafsa helps us construct a paragraph about Aqsa's interests. Aqsa doesn't want to admit to liking Indian films, as she thinks I
will read this as 'lazy'. She feels the same about her enjoyment of Indian
music. Between us, Hafsa and I talk her into writing these down. We
write that she is good at cooking, since this is one of her home responsibilities, although she detests it. Interests at school are harder. We're
stuck for a while, until Hafsa remembers the community party in Year 9.
Aqsa, whose English then was less fluent than it is now, had hung
around on the sidelines. They talk about the experience, which neither
of them had enjoyed. It turns out that Aqsa had hung someone's coat
up at one point, and had also managed to hand round a jug of orange
juice. We write about how she had been responsible for 'receiving guests'
and 'serving drinks'. A paragraph at the end on Aqsa's future ambitions
turns out to be the hardest. She wants to go to college, but thinks she is
too stupid, and doesn't like to think about what she might do there in
case she does not get good enough results to go at all. So we write about
how she is 'not yet sure' what she wants to study, and end with her
wanting a job in which she can 'use the skills I have already learned, and
develop new skills'. I'm disturbed by how much of the language of
corporate managerialism I've absorbed, and how easy it is to use it. And
by what it leaves out.

(Fieldnotes 1/11/99)

The coherent, unified narrative of the skills and competencies Aqsa had
supposedly accrued during her school life was in most ways a travesty. Not
only did we elide Aqsa's failure to make the academic grade in the terms of
the standards agenda. We elided the complexities of her refugee background
in our Eurocentric account of her schooling, and we de-problematized her
inscription into traditional feminine domesticity. We rewrote her, western-
style, as an individual with a portfolio of skills, aptitudes and abilities, all
supposedly transferable into resources that she could use to her personal
advantage in future study and employment.

It is unlikely that Aqsa will emerge from compulsory schooling with more
than two GCSEs at grade G. She is, whatever euphemisms we might care to
use, a failing student of a system that needs to produce failing students in
order to produce successful ones. In this example, however, our joint task
was to narrate her as if she were successful. We narrated her as if she were
academically enthusiastic: the three school subjects she hates least became
her 'favourite subjects'. We narrated her as if she were a corporate 'team
player', milking her participation in compulsory school activities for all it

was worth, teasing out what she had done, and recasting it as demonstrable competencies. And we re-presented her bleak hopelessness about what the future holds for her as an amorphous ambition to develop new and existing skills. In so doing, we commodified what learning had taken place, so that Aqsa could demonstrate she had accrued some 'masteries' worth trading on the marketplace.

But the kinds of goods we argued she had accrued were those that could enable her to insert herself into the global labour market on its feminized bottom rung: making use of her skills in cooking and providing domestic services. I am not arguing that this institutionally legitimized production of Aqsa's personal narrative is the only institutionally legitimized narrative she has produced in the course of her construction of herself as 'special needs student'. But the ROA personal statement occupies a privileged space in that it is the document a student takes forward to college or employment as her statement of entry to the adult world of work.

Aqsa left the library that afternoon beaming with a satisfaction which I think owed more to finishing a task that had been worrying her than it did to pleasure with the completed narrative. The ROA personal statement has to be written in bright, up-beat, positive language. There is no space within the genre for the articulation of failure or of the fear of failure. Sennett (1998: 118) writes that 'Failure is the great modern taboo . . . As with anything we are afraid to speak about forthrightly, both internal obsession and shame only thereby become greater. Left untreated is the raw inner sentence, "I am not good enough"'. The inherited meanings, structures and practices of the English schooling system in general, and 'special' schooling in particular, privilege academic achievement and attach negative meanings and consequences to perceived intellectual inadequacy. The New Labour education reforms, building on the marketization of education under the previous Conservative administration, have incorporated some of these meanings and consequences. Under the umbrella of 'inclusion', and using a version of social justice based on social integrationist and moral underclass discourses (Levitas 1998), these meanings and practices have been recast.

In today's system, where failure in education exists, it can only overtly be ascribed to teachers and schools. Since Newbrook is a 'successful school' and cannot be interpellated into narratives of institutional failure, Aqsa's failure to achieve good exam results cannot be articulated as failure at all. And yet she is about to leave school with poor examination results. New Labour's version of social justice draws on a complex blend of social integrationist and moral underclass discourses. People like Aqsa, who 'fail' in spite of the opportunities they have been offered are thereby implicitly traduced as responsible not only for their own failure but also for the consequences to society of that failure. At Newbrook, Aqsa can be positioned as a 'special needs student', and her failure can thus be accounted for, and recast through her IEP targets, as personal success. But beyond the school gates, Aqsa has no claim to a disabled identity. She is a materially impoverished immigrant young woman who, if she manages to take up a place in the labour market, is likely to find herself doing the most poorly paid and least prestigious jobs.[4] Such contexts need to be written back into accounts of 'inclusive education'.

This chapter has presented an overview of the ways in which government policy for SEN appears to contradict the standards agenda in its drive towards inclusive schooling, even as it acts to shore up the inconsistencies of the standards agenda through its location within discourses of effectiveness. Newbrook's discourses of failure are similarly complicated. Drawing on an historical set of meanings in which intellectual attainment below a certain (changing) level has been cast as irretrievably shameful, as well as on a current set of discursive practices profoundly shaped by the standards agenda, failure has become unmentionable at Newbrook. Discourses of success, and discourses of SEN and inclusion slide past some students' failure to meet culturally and politically produced norms. This elision obscures the political situatedness of the standards agenda, and contributes to its daily reinscription as common sense.

Notes

1 Levitas (1998) notes the shift in New Labour rhetoric from 'the poor' to 'a new workless class' in speeches reported during 1997. She cites, for example, Tony Blair's speech, reported in the *Guardian* 27 September 1997, saying that this 'new workless class' must be 'brought back into society and into useful work' (Levitas 1998: 138).
2 When statutory testing of achievement in maths, English and science was first introduced in the early 1990s, the tests were called 'standard attainment tasks' and abbreviated to SATs. The term has officially been replaced by the wording 'national tests', but schools, students and the media tend still to refer to SATs.
3 Walkerdine (1988) examines the evolution of normative pyschoeducational discourses and associated means of measuring 'intelligence', arguing that these have been central to the production of hierarchical relations of class, capital, gender and race.
4 The Labour Force survey of 1999, cited in NACETT (2000), shows unqualified women earning one-sixth of the average earnings of degree-holding men.

CHAPTER FIVE

The micropolitics of student identity work in Year 7

Chapter 4 argued that an unspoken 'failure' is central to Newbrook's production of special needs students. The next chapter looks at the identity work of a group of Year 7 (11-year-old) participants, in order to illuminate how this works. The chapter begins by looking at how the girls use – or, more correctly, avoid using – the term 'special educational needs'. I then use the girls' accounts to identify three distinct subject positions available to them: 'sweet little girls', 'big bad girls' and 'lazy girls'. Although these three positions can be identified, this is not to say that they are water-tight, or that the act of negotiating entry into one of them is a simple once-and-for-all act. Such negotiations are constantly in process, they are enacted through many overlapping discursive practices, and they rely on complex manoeuvres and power contests. And so the chapter ends with a fieldnote account of a maths lesson, through which some of the intricacies of these processes can be analysed.

The production of 'special needs students'

> *Meera*: When you come to this school, you have to work hard, and my Mum said, when I got a place at this school, like that's good, yeah, 'cause at this school you can achieve, and so I thought when I come to this school I'd get gooder in reading, but I didn't get gooder in reading. When I come to this school, I'm not gooder in reading more than I was in Year 6, and when I was in Year 6 there was these people what used to call me 'dumb' and I thought when I come to this school I would get good in

reading, but I never . . . And I still ain't, I'm still not good in reading, even when I come to this school, not even any bit gooder, and I'm still, you know, um, if you ain't good in reading you're dumb.

(Interview 4/4/00)

The Year 7 participants bring with them (in most cases) a history of academic failure in their primary schools, confirmed in the SATs (statutory) tests taken at the end of Year 6. In their primary schools, they were all identified as 'special needs children'. None of them, however, applied this formal designation to herself or referred to herself as a 'special needs student'. Neither did I, at any time, use this designation in front of students, or hear any other member of staff do so, in spite of the fact that they are routinely described in this way amongst members of staff in the professional privacy of staffroom and office. Why, then, did the girls use the apparently much more pejorative 'stupid' and 'dumb' to describe themselves, when they could have used the apparently neutral language of special needs? And why did the staff (including myself) consistently refrain from using the designation in front of the students?

Shazia: Why do you want to know what we think, Miss? I mean, 'cause we don't know nothing, we're just all the stupid girls, we don't know nothing to say, there's lots of girls in my class, they know what to think, you should talk to them.

SB: I'm interested – I really am – I think you've got lots of, um, interesting things to say, I do.

Fozia: Why did you, why did we get choosed?

SB: Well, um, you know when Mr Elliott wrote to your parents saying you were on the special needs register, that you would get extra help, I decided I wanted to talk to some girls who were on the school special needs register, and see what they thought about the school.

Fozia: What's special needs register? I ain't never heard of it.

Shazia: It's for all the stupid girls, so you can take a register like in registration, only not, so you know who is all the stupid girls, so they can all go like on one side, when you take a register of all the dumb girls.

(Interview 12/3/00)

One reading of Shazia's interpretation of the special needs register would suggest that she is resistant to the construction of herself as part of a deviant group, its deviance subject to heightened adult surveillance. Allan (1999: 21) argues that, 'surveillance of pupils with special needs enables professionals to show their concern for their welfare and acquire knowledge about their condition and the progress they are making. It also constructs them as objects of power and knowledge'. The special needs register, as maintained by Newbrook and other schools, depends for its legitimacy on the acceptance of a complex web of discourses around human and educational needs and entitlements. First, that people have a 'need' for education. Second, that people under a certain age are entitled (by law) to have that need met. Third, that some people are more educationally 'needy' than others, and that need can be objectively, or at least reliably, determined. And fourth, that it is an act of professional benevolence and caring to meet the needs of the more needy.

The 'special needs student' is produced as the object of governmentality and also of care. The dependence connoted through constructions of SEN as intrinsic to the student is dependence on a professional (or group of professionals) who can operate the technical machinery of identification and assessment from a position of caring for the needy. The 'special needs student' is positioned as doubly needy. Her educational needs must be managed more carefully than those of other students through the rational (and therefore traditionally masculine) apparatus of monitoring and target-setting if those needs are to be met and she is to make progress. But the framework for meeting those needs is the traditionally feminine realm of care and compassion for the vulnerable.

The Year 7 girls are thus offered a subject position that is highly problematic from the outset. It is a position that carries with it the stigma of outsider-ness, since it refers to a discourse of intrinsic need that stands in contradiction to 'normal' culturally produced educational need, and since it refers to a failure to make the linear progress associated with schooling. It is a position that also refers to failure to make academic progress according to norms set out in the standards agenda, and as such, cannot be articulated, especially in a successful school such as Newbrook. And it is a position that inscribes the girls within a bureaucratized regime of governmentality legitimized through benevolent humanitarianism (Tomlinson 1982; Slee 1995) and a version of equal opportunities. While they can and do refuse to recognize the label 'special needs student', and while all members of the school community can and mostly do refuse to address them as such within their hearing, these girls nevertheless have to position themselves in relation to the discursive practices that produce them, in specific sites, as 'special needs students'.

The Year 7 participants are all invested, to some extent, in producing themselves as compliant, hard-working students. None of them overtly rejects what she perceives to be the academic or disciplinary aims of the school. Already, however, they are beginning to be recognizable as members of one of three distinct categories: 'sweet little girls', 'big bad girls' or 'lazy girls'. Fozia, Shazia and Ambrine tend to produce themselves as the 'sweet little girls' of the group. All are of Asian origin and are observant Muslims. Kerry and Josie tend to produce themselves as 'big bad girls', though, as I argue in more detail in Chapter 8, this production is fraught with difficulties for Josie. Kerry is from an indigenous and secular UK family, while Josie is African Caribbean. Meera and Sunna tend to produce themselves as 'lazy girls'. They are from Asian Muslim families. Josephine, whose family are Jehovah's Witnesses from sub-Saharan Africa, tends to occupy a midway position between 'sweet little girl' and 'lazy girl'.

'Sweet little girls'

In his work with young children, Connolly (1998) notes the tendency for boys and girls of South Asian origin to be infantilized, and referred to by teachers and others as 'little'. The three girls, all of Asian origin, who take up this position are all physically small for their age, and they manage to code themselves as childlike. They wear shoes with low or no heels, they do not use make-up, and they specialize in a shy version of a smile, while looking down at the floor to suggest submission and eagerness to please. Like many of the Muslim students they wear *shalwar kameez*, and Fozia also covers her head. But whereas many of the Newbrook's Muslim girls manage to play with the dress code so as to suggest hetero/sexual attractiveness, these girls present themselves as completely desexualized, and, in both interviews and informal conversations, made clear the distance between themselves and the hetero/sexualized Other girls.

The 'sweet little girl' position is in many ways an obvious one for 'special needs girls' to take up. The official version of 'special needs student' constructs them as people who are young, vulnerable and 'needy' of help. In addition, many of these girls find the hurly-burly of the microcultural work that goes on amongst their peers difficult to understand and often frightening:

Fozia: They shouldn't let you out of lessons. There's some girls, they're like in Year 10 and 11 they go out, they say they have to go out to the toilet, and then they go out and meet their friends and they do their hair, and talk about who's got what boyfriend. They didn't want to go to the toilet, but they're in there, and when you have to go, yeah, like if you really want to go to the toilet, and you got out of lessons, and they're all in there, and when they're doing their hair, you go in there, and it's sort of embarrassing, cause it's like they're Year 10 and 11, and you're all like 'Oh no, I don't wanna be in here'.

Shazia: And you think they're all looking at you, like, 'What are you doing in here?' yeah, and, um, when I went out of maths that time, and I was really like I really needed to go, and I didn't even dare go in, and I was waiting round the corner, um, in the students' bit, you know, and I'm thinking like I don't know what to do –

Fozia: And you wish a teacher would come and um, and tell them they have to go to their lessons. It would be better if they didn't let you out, cause some girls, they just do their hair, and, you know, um, talk about their boyfriends, and like where they're going after school, um, and it makes you scared to be in there.

(Interview 12/3/00)

High-speed, high-volume and heterosexually coded ways of doing girl, associated variously with 'girl power' and with transgression, appear to make these girls afraid. In their accounts, theirs is an altogether gentler, more childlike and apparently more passive version of femininity (Walkerdine 1989, 1997). But this apparent passivity can hide the fact that the girls have to work actively at producing themselves as 'sweet little girls'.

> *Ambrine*: In humanities, Sir he sometimes says, 'Get in groups' and we have to choose, but you can't have more than five 'cause he thinks we'll all be argue, and if you've got like six friends, you're looking at the floor 'cause you want to be with the people what helps you, and me and Asma this time, in humanities, when we was doing about the castles, when Sir said to go in groups, we was both trying to look all sad, and looking at the floor, 'cause it's Gulshan who's in charge, who's always in charge, and she would, um, would only let the person stay who was all sad and who needed help, and if you didn't have needed help, you would have to go in another group, but it was alright because Sir he came over and we was both looking at the floor, me and Asma, we was both looking all sad, and Sir he said we could both stay, me and Asma, if we all did what Gulshan said.

> (Interview 4/4/00)

Skeggs (1997: 116) notes that the young women who participated in her study 'usually "did" femininity when they thought it was necessary'. It is likely that something similar is happening here. The position of 'sweet little girl' is not without a certain power. These four girls (and others whom I witnessed deploying similar strategies in classrooms) have developed a means of eliciting and retaining adult and peer help, which in many instances is crucial if they are to be able to participate in routine classroom activity. But in doing so they are also inscribing themselves in hyperfeminine discourses of vulnerability and dependence.

'Big bad girls'

Kerry and Josie, the 'big bad girls', are both very tall for their age, and both are apparently strong and athletic. They both wear shoes with high heels, and both flout the school's rules on make-up as openly as they dare, wearing nail polish and transparent or pale lipstick. Both have a reputation for making a lot of noise in class: they are frequently told off for talking or playing about, and moved away from their friends for failing to get on with their work. The position of 'big bad girl' is apparently an oppositional one, resisting the school's academic ethos and its imperatives to work hard and allow others to work hard at all times. It is, additionally, a hetero/sexualized position, involving students in producing themselves as hetero/sexually active and attractive.

While there is a reluctance on the part of both teachers and students to allow girls in Year 7 to take up positions as 'big bad girls', Josie and Kerry nonetheless act in ways that often have disruptive effects on their classes.

Kerry comes from an indigenous white working-class background, and Josie from a materially impoverished African Caribbean family. Given that most of the school's teaching staff are white, institutionally positioned as middle class, and academically successful, there are few, if any, identifications that Kerry and Josie can make with their teachers. They are the Others of the dominant official discourses through which Newbrook produces its youngest students: they are Other to the construction of incrementally developing, target-reaching student which Newbrook strives to make available and desirable to most girls. They are also Other to the construction of endearing, vulnerable little girl: the position Newbrook makes available to a large number of its 'special needs students'.

Kerry and Josie's positioning as 'big bad girls' is highly unstable, however. It is especially precarious for Josie, who is unable to do the microcultural work that would be necessary to produce herself as hetero/sexually active and attractive. Her position as 'big bad girl' has been achieved more through mis-recognition of her intentions than by her active insertion of herself into the discourse. Kerry, too, is unwilling to abandon altogether the possibility of becoming a successful student. She is aware that there may be costs, as well as benefits, in taking up an oppositional position in relation to the school's official agenda. But hers is not a rational analysis of the costs and benefits. In role-play during a fieldwork interview, she presented the 'big bad girl' as both the dangerous and undesirable Other, and as a natural option for a 'girl like me'. Talking to me about her role-play character, she commented:

Kerry: My girl was called Anne, and she was wearing a black mini-skirt, a black mini-skirt all the way up to here [indicates and grimaces, apparently indicating distaste], and black tights, and shoes with heels like this [indicates]. And lipstick, loads of lipstick, she puts it on after line-up. She's bad [grimaces again]. She was in English, and she wasn't listening to what the teacher said, she was all the time writing, but it wasn't English, it was to her friend, it was about their boyfriends that evening and after school. And her friend she wanted to listen to what the teacher was saying, but she couldn't because Anne kept on writing to her a note and saying like, 'Take it, take it', and her friend would have been scared if she hadn't've taked it.

SB: What did she do at lunchtime?

Kerry: In lunchtime, um, she went outside of the gates, and she made her friend go with her, even though her friend didn't want to go, and she said, 'Do we have to' and Anne said, 'Yes you have to come with me to where our boyfriends is'. And Anne's friend she was all scared because she wanted to go to her lessons and she didn't know where their boyfriends worked – did I say that, did I tell you their boyfriends they worked in – um – they – um, their boyfriends was out at work in, um, somewhere down the High Street. And Anne and her friend, they goes out of the gate when the teacher wasn't looking. Well, the teacher was looking, it was Ms Rivers, but Anne didn't care but her friend she didn't want to get in trouble, she said, 'We can't go, Ms Rivers will see us' but Anne said, 'Yeah, we've got to, the boys are expecting us'. Cause Anne had phoned them on her mobile phone, even though you're not supposed to, and she'd said, 'We'll come and see you this afternoon, down the High Street, at where you work'. And so they walked up to the gates and just walked out, and Anne's friend she was like, 'Oh no, Ms Rivers has seen us, and she'll tell the other teachers, and it's science, my favourite subject this afternoon and I wanna go to it' but Anne she didn't care, like she didn't care who saw her, and missing science, and going to their boyfriends. Even though it's a girls' school and her Mum thought she wouldn't have a boyfriend. And her friend she didn't want to miss science, and, um, maths, it was maths last lesson, but Anne she didn't care . . .

SB: Why did you, I mean, why do you think Anne doesn't care?

Kerry: Um, well I think she does care a bit, only she, what she really cares about is her boyfriend, and, um, don't know if I can say this [giggles], she, um, she wants to, [pause] *it*, you know, Miss [giggles]. It's not like she doesn't care *at all* about school, but, um, it's her first time and she wants to do *it* with her boyfriend. Ms Rivers isn't going to hear this is she?

SB: No, no, I'm not playing the tape to anyone at school, don't worry. So what I'm wondering, is, if Anne cares a bit about school, well, can you say a bit more about the things she cares about?

Kerry: She does care a bit, but only a bit, and, well, when she was in Year 7, she was just a girl like me, she was just a girl like me, you couldn't tell she was failing, except she was a bit scruffy like me, but then when she got in Year 8 she got fed up of all the teachers going, 'Blah, blah, you aren't getting no better at science, you have to work more harder, you have to do good for your exams, blah, blah' like that. And it just, I dunno, it got on her nerves, cause she'd been working hard, she did work hard, well not very hard, but a bit hard, and she just said, 'Well, I ain't gonna do good in exams, cause I've been all the time trying, and so I'll just get a boyfriend'. And she just did, and that's all, and that's how she got like she didn't care. But in Year 7, when she was in Year 7 she was just a normal girl like me.

(Interview, 21/3/00)

The SEN discourse is one place in which the notion of child-in-danger meets with the notion of child-as-danger (Boyden 1990; Hunt and Frankenburg 1990; Walkerdine 1997). The child-as-danger (as well as the child-in-danger) is a thoroughly classed, gendered and racialized subject: Boyden (1990) shows that one important strategy in the global export (and imposition) of the western bourgeois version of childhood is the presentation of street children (violent boys and sexually promiscuous girls) as a threat to their communities. Walkerdine (1997) argues that:

> The little working-class girl, produced by and consuming popular culture, becomes a central object of social and moral concern. She is one of the figures (along with the violent boy) who most threatens the safe pastures of natural childhood, a childhood free from adult intervention and abuse, a childhood so carefully constructed as a central fiction of the modern order, the childhood which will ensure the possibility of a liberal democracy.
>
> (Walkerdine 1997: 4)

Current definitions of SEN embrace both understandings. The child-in-danger is primarily the child with learning difficulties, who can be constructed as vulnerable. The child-as-danger is the student with 'emotional and behavioural difficulties': the student whose effect on classrooms can be disruptive, and who risks becoming 'socially excluded'. Complex elisions and distinctions are made between the two groups at different times in Newbrook. But it seems fair to say that staff and students alike go to considerable lengths to avoid recognizing Year 7 students as 'child-as-danger'. Pressures on schools not to exclude students, teachers' desires not to fail any student, and the students' desires for a measure of success in the schooling endeavour combine to make it very problematic for a Year 7 student to take up a 'big bad girl' position. Where the younger girls are concerned, formal identification as child-in-danger tends to override formal identification and informal (mis)recognition as child-as-danger. For a Year 7 'special needs student' who has been identified as having what the school terms 'learning as a primary cause for concern', any oppositional activity will tend to be formally interpreted as proof of further neediness, and will often trigger further offers of support.

Kerry's ambivalent and problematic investment in doing 'big bad girl', containing as it does something of the quality of a moth flying around a candle flame, also appears to contain the knowledge that she will never be fully recognized as a 'big bad girl', and that the act of working to produce herself as such will involve some intensive changes for 'a normal girl like me'. In her description of the role-play she and Josephine had constructed, it could be argued that she identifies both with 'Anne' who once was like her, and with Anne's friend who is more obviously invested in achieving academic success, and is even able to find lessons pleasurable. Anne appears to contain the unknown and unknowable desires which only a complete disinvestment from academic endeavour makes accessible. Anne's friend, on the other hand, contains the longing for the safety provided by investment in the rationally knowable and (so the story goes) controllable world of working for and achieving academic targets.

The two are irreconcilable: to remain friends with Anne, the unnamed girl must abandon – literally walk out on – her desire for academic success. And she must take a step into what is the complete unknown for both girls, the enigmatically and euphemistically coded 'it' of hetero/sexual intercourse in a venue whose precise location remains unspecified. 'Somewhere down the High Street' implies a world that is both more public and more adult than the world of school. The setting is prosaic and everyday, but the ambiguity that surrounds the exact location renders it exotic and mysterious. In Kerry's account, Anne takes with her to the High Street not only her own desires for the exotic and adult world of hetero/sexual activity, but also her friend's desires for academic success. The episode Kerry imagines has something of the quality of a modern-day Cinderella story, a story in which a cocktail of compliance with and rebellion against unreasonable authority brings rescue, romance and fortune. 'Anne' and her 'friend' make the exotic and adult world of heterosexual activity geographically and socially accessible through locating it in working-class female territory, imagining the public site of domestic labour as a setting for romantic encounters (Hey 1997). But her concluding comments, in which 'Anne' gives up on academic achievement and gets a boyfriend instead, suggest that Kerry does not easily position herself within such a world, viewing it as both second-best to the world of academic achievement, and as mysterious and frightening. Her investment in producing herself as 'big bad girl' is thus configured through an intricate blend of (often contradictory) fears and desires, in relation to a number of equally contradictory discourses of childhood, academic success and femininity, worked through the material conditions of white working-class girlhood.

'Lazy girls'

Sunna and Meera tend to position themselves, and describe themselves, as 'lazy girls'. Unlike the 'big bad girls', they do not act in ways that can be interpreted as oppositional to the school's formal agenda and authority, and their effect on classrooms is not disruptive. They are observant Muslims, and dress in *shalwar kameez*, but unlike the 'sweet little girls', they augment their uniforms with discreet make-up, and they wear shoes with heels. When speaking to adults, they usually make eye contact, so their general demeanour does not code submission. Josephine, however, does code herself as more submissive, customarily looking at the floor, and appearing to welcome adult support. I would tend to include her in this group for three reasons. First, she describes herself as 'lazy'. Second, she deploys a 'rescue' discourse when talking about her academic struggles. Third, teachers perceive her as 'lazy', although this is often euphemized as a problem of 'low self-esteem'.

Students who take up positions as 'lazy girls' do something very complex with the connotation of helplessness and vulnerability that attends the SEN discourse. On the one hand, they appear to refuse it, and portray their struggles as arising from their recalcitrance, or an untenable situation, rather than from lack of ability. Meera uses the unsatisfactory secondary school set-up, and her habit of procrastination, to account for the poor academic performance that is worrying her;

Meera: It's more, it's like there's more to worry about 'cos you like get all this homework in one day, and you just worry about more things . . . I'm a loafer – I procrastinate.

SB: [laughs] What do you mean when you say you procrastinate?

Meera: I was supposed to so something yesterday, and I end up – and I'm supposed to be doing something and I end up doing something else. It's like, say you're, it's a really sunny day, and you can't be bothered to sit in your house and do your homework, so you like go on a bike ride or something, and you're like, 'Oh no, I forgot to do my homework' it's like nine o'clock in the night.

(Interview 20/3/00)

But while Meera and the other 'lazy girls' appear to resist the helplessness of the SEN discourse, they are inscribing themselves into a different version of passivity and helplessness. Alongside references to themselves as lazy, and therefore exercising conscious agency in relation to their academic struggles, the girls suggest that 'rescue' is the only solution and the only way to attain the academic success they all appear to want. All three of them express their disappointment that taking up a place in Newbrook School has not, in itself, been enough to effect the rescue. Newbrook promotes itself as a successful school, deploying in that promotion the fiction that academic success can be attained by everyone. These girls appear to have believed (or at least wanted to believe) in the promise:

Josephine: I was all excited on the first day, on the first day when I come, and I was putting on my uniform, and I was all excited. And you had to go in the hall when they read out your form group, and I was in 7T, and Ms Cashmere, I didn't listen, not the whole time. And Ms Cashmere she was talking about Newbrook, and how you all do good when you come here, and how you all get good in your work and she was saying you all get good in your work, and in your reading and your Maths. And my Mum says it's a good school here, but I've been here two terms, and it's just like in primary school, like in Year 6 but it's just like Year 6. The only thing what's better is there isn't any boys, 'cause in Year 6 they used to throw things, but anyway it's just like Year 6.

(Interview 27/3/00)

The 'lazy girls'' accounts draw also on a version of the entitlements discourse that is daily becoming more prevalent in the educational landscape of the UK: the notion that it is schools and teachers who must be held responsible, and held to account, for 'pupil performance' (Barber 2000). The 'lazy girls'' deployment of this discourse in this way constructs their own 'poor academic performance' as something shameful that must be blamed on someone. Their accounts are replete with people and systems who appear as culprits: teachers, boring lessons, unviable quantities of homework and other students who distract them. Sometimes these culprits are aspects of themselves, such as Meera's loafing, but there is a sense in which these aspects of themselves have somehow become disconnected and they are not responsible for them. What is clear is that their understanding of academic struggle is not framed within the apparently neutral discourse of SEN.

For Meera, Sunna and Josephine, their struggles are, in the words of government imperatives, 'poor academic performance'. Poor performance connotes failure and deficiency, in which blame necessarily inheres, and which must be displaced onto someone else or a distant and disembodied part of themselves. And so the 'lazy girls'' refusal of the SEN discourse and its attendant suggestions of helplessness and passivity appears to be inscribing them in another version of helplessness and passivity. In this version they wait to be rescued, with what appears to be a decreasing belief that rescue is possible. The accounts of the 'lazy girls' imply a deeply contradictory impasse, in which they simultaneously believe, and refuse to believe, in the possibility of rescue. While they describe themselves as needy of such rescue, they also produce themselves as beyond rescue. This may in part be an intricate way of working out what it is possible and realistic to want (Bourdieu 1984; Reay and Lucey 2000), as the girls go about negotiating the contradictions in which they are embedded: caught between the promise that they, too, can get good exam results if they work hard enough, and the reality that those exam results are out of their reach.

Identity at work in a maths lesson

The three subject positions of 'sweet little girl', 'big bad girl' and 'lazy girl' tell only part of the story, and I would not want to suggest that they give anything approaching a complete picture of any girl's identity work. Students seldom enact a 'pure' version of any of these (or other) subject positions, and are always positioned simultaneously within a number of discourses. The discourses through which dominant versions of success are constructed have to be re-enacted and renegotiated in every lesson. Each lesson presents a microcosm of student identity work, as students engage in the project of doing student in tandem with their official curriculum work. This is not to suggest that each lesson is a blank slate. Common rules are drawn on, existing relations of power (including those between teacher and student as well as amongst students and groups of students) are confirmed or challenged, and common histories on the macro- and micro-stages frame the current performances of identity, of academic attainment, and of identity constructed through academic attainment.

In the following maths lesson, my role was explicitly that of observer. I knew a few of the girls by sight, but had spoken to none prior to the lesson in question, with the exception of my targeted students. What follows are extracts from my fieldnotes, with the chronological order of events preserved. The fieldnotes, and my analysis of them, do not try to give an accurate overall picture of the entire lesson. They present, instead, a series of snapshots that give an impression of how the identity work of two students,

Fozia and Ambrine, is negotiated in the context of the lesson, and in relation with other students and the teacher.

> When I get to Jean's room, some of the girls are already settling. There are a lot of girls I don't know. I sit with a white middle-class group, from where I can see Fozia and Ambrine – I don't sit on Fozia and Ambrine's table, as it's nearest to Jean, and I don't want to be so near the front when she's talking to the class. She goes over the homework, for which they have another two days. Then she reviews the work they've been doing on volume. She holds up a cuboid and asks 'What shape is this?' Hands shoot up, and Simone gives the answer. Simone is something of a mystery to me still. A good African Caribbean girl, adult- rather than peer-focused, about in the middle of the perceived ability range. Jean asks the difference between a cube and a cuboid. Rachel is the only girl with her hand up. Even the gifted and talented Leah doesn't offer the answer. Jean talks them through it, rather than ask Rachel. She then asks how to find the volume of a cuboid. Again, Rachel is the only person to raise her hand. This time, Jean asks her. Having given the right answer, Jean then asks other girls to do the calculations. She asks Bridget to calculate 4×6. Bridget doesn't know, and other girls on her table, including Rachel, whisper the answer to her. They look collectively pleased when she gets it right . . .

Many teachers at Newbrook begin their lessons with whole-class question-and-answer sessions. It is a common means of 'warming the class up'. As a way of beginning the lesson, it also serves to remind everyone of their position in semi-formal and informal hierarchies: it is an opportunity to rehearse the roles people take, and to restate the boundaries of who can do what and say what. Although I had not previously been in this class, I already knew the names of the 'gifted and talented' girls (Rachel and Leah) since they had been so noticeable in other classes I had visited.

Jean's agenda is clear, and there is no doubt that what she wants the students to do is to listen, and to put their hands up to answer questions. Two versions of compliance are therefore on offer. The lowest order of compliance is to listen without interrupting. The higher order of compliance is to offer answers on the public stage. Students who want to position themselves as 'good girls' can do either or both of these things, but the type of 'good girl' is different. The good girl who offers answers is both 'helping' in what is being presented as the joint enterprise of constructing knowledge, and is 'not helping' in that she prevents other students from speaking up. While the 'good girl' who listens quietly is both 'helping' in as much as she allows the teacher to proceed unhindered, but is 'not helping' in the collective knowledge-production project. Moreover, she is positioned as someone who 'needs help' in the form of encouragement, and, if the teacher were to have time, in the form of differentiated questioning, in order to enable her to play an active role in the class. The eagerness to answer Jean's first question would tend to suggest that the first version of 'good girl' is more attractive to the students, but that this role becomes less and less available as the questions become more challenging. The 'good girl' who gives answers produces herself as clever in offering those answers, as well as helpful and compliant. But there appears to be a tacit understanding that the cleverness produced through answering questions is relative, and if the question is an easy one, there is not much cleverness to be demonstrated.

> Jean gives out the two worksheets that they'll be working on this lesson . . . The first worksheet can be done using multilink, if the girls want, and Jean puts some cubes on each desk. The second sheet, with bigger units, has to be calculated using long multiplication. Which seems like a good way of differentiating. Leah has nearly finished the first sheet by the time Jean has finished explaining what they have to do . . . Fozia and Ambrine and the other two on their table are making the multilink models whose volume they must then work out. The girl sitting opposite them is called Afshan . . . The four girls seem to be quite happy making their models, so I go over to Simone, who has her hand up. She wants to work out the answers without making the models, but is stuck on one of the more difficult ones. It's not my strength, either, so we try to work it out together. But in the end, we need to get the right answer, so I get Jean's answer sheet. We haven't got it right, but manage to work out where our mistake lies. It's a lot slower doing it this way, and Simone has been overtaken by the others on her table who are now on the second sheet. I experience this as pressure to get on with it . . .

It is not only the SEN students who can produce themselves as 'sweet little girls'. Arguably, this is partly what Simone is trying to do, but there are many factors that make such a production problematic for her. First, she is physically big. So although she dresses 'young' (with white socks and shoes without heels) and has a perfect version of a shy smile, it is hard for her to be recognized as 'little'. Second, she is of African Caribbean origin. It is extremely hard for students with this background to be recognized as 'sweet little girls': their 'racial' background appears to connote the opposite of dependence, gentleness and vulnerability (Mirza 1992; Hatcher 1995; Wright et al. 2000). Third, she has no obvious learning difficulty, and, what is more, she appears to be invested in not producing herself as a 'special needs student'. She wants to be clever, and helpful, and give the right answers, while still wanting adult help and attention. Perhaps the sticking point for Simone is the impossibility, in a girls' school, of a not-clever student being positioned as 'helpful'. So three key routes to doing a recognizable version of 'sweet little girl' – small stature, Asian-ness and not-cleverness – are closed to her. Simone is neither clever enough, nor sporty enough, nor popular enough, nor confident enough, to produce herself as a successful African Caribbean student. As she cannot 'do starlet', she is left with a version of 'good girl' that is barely recognizable within Newbrook's range of microcultural possibilities.

> Back on Fozia's table – the 'special needs table' – the girls are still making models. The last questions on the first sheet involve making rather large

towers, which is time- and resource-consuming. They keep having to supplement their multilink supplies. By now, almost everyone else in the class is busy with long multiplication, except for this group who are building towers. I go over to Iram, who is sitting on her own, and has refused to go and sit with anyone else. She is stuck with the long multi-plication. I go through it with her, using the method with which I'm most familiar and find easiest. I can't do it the way Jean usually teaches it, but she's flexible over method. Iram is a sweet girl. I enjoy sitting next to her doing long multiplication . . .

Iram faces no such difficulties. She is a tiny Asian girl, who looks much younger than she actually is. She is very easily recognized as a 'sweet little girl', whether or not she appears to work at it actively. She does not have to produce herself as 'needy' in order to work on her positioning in this discourse – the position is available to her, seemingly irrespective of whether or not she wants it. Her middle-of-the-road cleverness (she is able to do long multiplication with help) appears to be overridden by her size, physical appearance and demeanour.

Fozia and Ambrine have now finished the first sheet, and have gone on to the second. There is no choice but to do the long multiplication now. Some of the other girls have finished both sheets. Jean has given Rachel a chart, with the pentominoes investigation on it. Fozia and Ambrine are struggling. Afshan is making the last question on the first sheet last as long as possible . . .

Fozia and Ambrine, as 'sweet little girls', have dutifully worked their way through the first sheet and onto the second. Afshan, however, appeared to realize that completion of the first sheet would mean she would have to do the more difficult second one. As a 'lazy girl', she finds the obvious way out of this dilemma, extending the time she must spend doing the work she can understand, as a strategy of avoiding the work she can't. This would appear to be a completely reasonable strategic approach. It is also a prime example of how she becomes reinscribed in discourses of 'laziness', and of how Fozia and Ambrine become inscribed in discourses of 'neediness'. Where Fozia and Ambrine plough on into work that they cannot do without adult interven-tion and help, Afshan tries to find ways of avoiding the work that would involve her in seeking and retaining that adult help, seeming to prefer, instead, to appear 'off-task'. In Year 7, the discourse of 'success' often over-laps with the discourse of 'hard-working'. Fozia and Ambrine, by virtue of being hard-working as well as 'sweet little girls' have access to a version of success through hard work: this version is situated within the deficit dis-course of success which I will be exploring in Chapter 7. Afshan, as a 'lazy girl', not completing the easy first worksheet, cannot access even this second-rate version of 'success'.

Meanwhile, Leah's table have finished both sheets. They are calling Jean over, repeatedly chanting the word 'Miss' to the tune of Jingle Bells. This is more like Jean's lessons as I have known them. Jabida, next to

Fozia, is trying to build a model of $30 \times 6 \times 15$ rather than work it out using long multiplication. Over on the high-achievers' table Gail has made a giraffe out of multilink, and Janette has made a mobile phone, which she is walking around, talking to. The positions are now reversed. Instead of the 'special needs table' making multilink models while everyone else engaged with the serious stuff of long multiplication, now it is they who are struggling with hard sums while everyone else plays with multilink. But it has a different meaning. My girls were making models because the sums were too hard for them. Now the other girls are making models because the sums were too easy. Jean asks Janette, 'What's the volume of your giraffe?' Leah replies, 'Who cares?' Jean and I burst out laughing. She has such a good point. And because she's making the challenge on our rational, middle-class terms, we can identify with it and accept it . . .

The high-achieving girls have managed, in this extract, to position themselves alongside the teacher, using their middle-classness and their successful positioning in discourses of rationality to bridge the institutional power differential that exists between themselves and the teacher. Their use of humour as a discursive practice appears to be key to this renegotiation of power. The girls' status as high achievers is not in jeopardy, so they can afford to indulge in what might be derided as 'babyish' activities, knowing that these will be read as humorous. Their undisputed success as rational, incrementally progressing students means they do not have to worry about being mis-recognized as 'immature'. They can go on to challenge the nature of the work with which they are engaged without positioning themselves as oppositional, and, in the process, can make the lesson fun. Fozia and Ambrine, meanwhile, have not been offered the opportunity to do this. The tasks are too hard for them to use as 'play' activities. Their choice is stark: either get on diligently, or refuse to do the work. As 'sweet little girls', the second option is unavailable to them, so they carry on with work that is difficult, and through which they are reinscribed as needy of help.

Afshan has jumped from the first sheet to free model-making, leaving out the stage of the long multiplication sheet. She announces that she's making a 'famous person in this school'. Fozia looks disapproving and tells me, 'She's naughty'.

(Fieldnotes 6/3/00)

It is possible to look on at students taking up positions as 'sweet little girls' and imagine them completely passive. But, as Ambrine quoted earlier in this chapter makes clear, it is a position that requires careful maintenance: simply being an Asian girl identified as having SEN is not enough. Fozia's disapproving comment about Afshan's 'naughtiness' is not just a disinterested piece of information for my benefit, but also constitutes a piece of identity work. Fozia distances herself from such naughtiness and, in so doing, polices the boundary between 'sweet little girl' and 'lazy girl', making it clear where she is located. In this maths lesson, as in the rest of their school lives, Fozia and the other girls are constantly involved in the identity work made possible by a range of local and societal discourses, including that of SEN.

This chapter has explored how Newbrook's youngest students negotiate their entry into positions as 'special needs students'. I began by looking at the students' refusal of the SEN categorization, and at how this maps onto the ways in which they take up positions as 'special needs students'. I introduced the three identifications that appear to be most on offer to them – 'sweet little girl', 'big bad girl' and 'lazy girl' – and considered how these positions are gendered/sexualized, and further nuanced by differences of 'race'/ethnicity, religion, class and physical appearance. In a discussion of Jean's maths lesson, I showed how these positions are renegotiated and always in process. The next chapter takes up the theme of the three identity positions, in the context of Year 11 students in their final year of compulsory schooling.

CHAPTER SIX

The micropolitics of student identity work in Year 11

Like the Year 7 girls, the 15-year-old Year 11 participants can also be recognized as 'sweet little girls', 'big bad girls' and 'lazy girls'. This chapter looks at the responses of these three groups of young women to the learning support they are offered, and at how this response maps onto their production of themselves as specific versions of the subject 'special needs student'. After examining this in some detail, I go on to look at some of the practices located around the borders of Newbrook's SEN discourses. I consider the positioning of two young women who, while they have not been formally identified as having SEN, produce themselves in a particular context as needy of help. The chapter ends by considering some of the theoretical problems that are thrown into relief by the attempt to explain what goes on in the 'SEN borderlands'.

The disappearance of 'special needs students'

By the time they reach Year 11, the young women who appear on Newbrook's special needs register mostly describe themselves in terms of their institutional location, as students who 'get learning support'. Corbett (1996: 2) notes that ' "special needs" is becoming a most unacceptable term. Most prefer the words "learning support". However, these words apply specifically to the provision, not to the people'. By Year 11, the 'special needs student' has largely disappeared: even the staff do not use the designation. Learning support staff talk of 'our girls', and other members of staff talk about 'learning support girls'. In some situations, when the whole cohort's projected exam results are up for discussion, these students are collectively described as 'the tail'. In many ways, the struggle over who is a 'special needs student' has taken place long ago. By Year 11, everyone knows who has, and who has not, been officially identified as having SEN. It is a matter of common knowledge that has passed into common sense. This combines with the sense of shame associated with 'not-cleverness' to make the designation 'special needs student' a completely unsayable one: it *need not* be spoken because it is so obvious, and it *cannot* be spoken without implying failure.

The young women in Year 11 continue to describe themselves as 'stupid' and as 'thickos', although they mostly take care not to be heard doing this by members of staff. In more public and formal settings, they are more likely to position themselves around the designation of 'getting learning support', and in relation to their response to whatever support is offered. The 'sweet little girls' are generally positive towards learning support and towards its providers, often going out of their way to ask staff for help during lunchtimes and after school. They are popularly referred to by the learning support department as 'support junkies'. The 'big bad girls' tend to be strongly resistant to leaning support, and publicly repulse it, except where it is offered by high-status teachers or in times of exceptional urgency. The 'lazy girls' have an ambivalent response to learning support. They alternately repulse and seek help, often making appointments but failing to keep them, to the annoyance of learning support and other staff.

'Support junkies'

The 'sweet little girls' amongst the Year 11 participants are Aqsa, Sana, Hafsa, Aneesa and, more problematically, Cassandra (see Chapter 8). The first four are young women from observant Muslim families, and three of them are part of the same extended family. Aneesa has a statement for learning difficulties, and the others are listed on Newbrook's SEN register as having learning as a priority concern. Aqsa had arrived in the UK three years previously, and entered Newbrook in Year 9, at which point her command of the English language was very limited. The others have all been in Newbrook since Year 7, and went to the same local primary school. All four routinely stay behind at the end of the school day for help with their homework, and to chat to me or to any other member of staff who is willing to help them. During one conversation after school, I tried to find out how Aqsa understood herself as a recipient of learning support.

> *Aqsa*: And we hope to – and we have to – and we have to do our courseworks when is too difficult, learning support helps you with your courseworks so you not get in trouble, innit, and is learning support to help you, when you go there, when you want help with your courseworks, is to help –
>
> *SB*: Why do you need help with your coursework? I mean, what, what makes you decide to get help with your coursework?

Aqsa: Is you get help when you not know how to do your courseworks, like in science, Sir he get angry when you not do your courseworks, and one time, you remember Miss, innit, when I had all subjects, subjects, subjects, all lots of subjects, and I keep come to learning supports, and we didn't do science because we was all other subjects, and Sir he say to me, 'where is your courseworks?' and I go all red, and he tell me off, but is not my fault, because I doing learning support with all lots of subjects, is when you decide to get learning supports, is when you have all subjects, subjects –

SB: You might think this is a funny question, well it *is* a bit of a funny question, but you said you go to learning support for help with coursework, but is there any other reason you go, I mean, apart from getting your coursework finished? Does that make sense?

Aqsa: Is I go learning support sometimes because is Sana and Hafsa is there, and we is all talking, with you innit, Miss, and we is all talking, talking, and at home, is boring, I have to do all courseworks on my own, I have to look after my little brother, I have to do cookings, and is no one there, but in learning support is Sana and Hafsa and Aneesa, and we can have good time with Sana and Hafsa, and we can be talking and at home is more boring innit, is only my brother.

SB: Right – so it's a way of passing the time before you go home, that's right?

Aqsa: And is also I go learning supports in lunchtime, in breaks and in lunchtime, because is fun, you not have to go outside, you not have to be – have to be, like where me and Sana and Hafsa is we stand, innit Miss, we stand, you know, outside the new building, and is more fun in learning support, you can be with Ms Benjamin and you can be talking and is no one come in, innit. And when we is standing outside new building, is lots of girls, and they is make very noise, is make lots of noise and they sometimes is be very rude, and is more private in learning support, and is you not have to worry about – there is very rude girls sometimes, you know, in Year 11 innit, there is very rude girls in my year and is not in learning support, is more private.

(Interview 24/11/99)

The 'sweet little girls' tend to position teachers as allies. In some cases those allies are constructed as strict, and the young women are afraid of them, but even frightening teachers are regarded as having the best interests of the students at heart, their strictness brought about by the desire to enable the young women to achieve high academic standards. In many cases, the 'sweet little girls' construct their teacher allies as caring, supportive and, above all, 'nice'. 'Niceness' appears often in their accounts, as the quality most appreciated in teachers. Aqsa positions 'nice' teachers as her allies against the demands of strict teachers, against the loneliness and compulsory domesticity of home, and as providers of refuge from the reviled 'very rude girls'.

Theirs is a pro-teacher, pro-school culture, through which their designation, now unvoiced, as 'special needs students' can be configured as an advantage through which they can access the teacher time and help that they have come to enjoy and find rewarding.

While it is important to recognize the positive outcomes for the students of taking up positions as 'sweet little girls', it remains important to question some of the less positive outcomes, namely their reinscription into traditionally feminine discourses of helplessness and vulnerability. It appears significant that a high proportion of the 'sweet little girls', including the four participants here, are from (often orthodox) Muslim Asian backgrounds. The link between some traditional versions of femininity, Asian-ness and 'sweet little girl-ness' is one that needs to be explored. It could be the case that Asian Muslim 'special needs' students are too readily recognized as 'sweet little girls', and that adequate room for manoeuvre does not exist for them to explore alternatives. In the case of these four young women, and possibly of others within the school, it is also important to look at the nuances of class in this picture. Aqsa, Sana, Hafsa and Aneesa are all from families who were powerful and wealthy under Benazir Bhutto's government. Although all four of them currently live in materially impoverished circumstances, they come from families that are invested, to some extent, in the norms of middle-class professionalism. In her study of Asian Muslim girls in two single-sex secondary schools, Haw (1998) found that:

> As Pakistani immigrants in Britain, these girls face multiple barriers from within the community and from the host context. The socioeducational structure and system in Britain present certain barriers to the educational achievements of Muslim girls in Britain, but these are also embedded into deeper issues of female role and status within Islam and the current practices within the community which further influence the schooling of these girls.
>
> (Haw 1998: 150)

The resulting complexities were too intricate, in Haw's study, for the non-Muslim school to pick its way through. As outsiders, the staff at 'City State' were not able to appreciate fully the complex positionings of Muslim girls. Nor were they going to be trusted by the girls or by their families to provide a space in which the students could explore pluralism without having to repudiate their religion and their community. Haw (1998: 172) concludes that, 'in City State, the Muslim students needed a more complex set of discursive responses than it could offer'. This could apply equally to Newbrook. Perhaps the school is just not able to provide a space in which Muslim girls can have room to manoeuvre around the complexities of what it means to be a young Muslim woman in an economically disadvantaged community in a plural city (Bhatti 1999). Also bearing in mind that at the same time, some of those students are dealing with very complex class positions. Perhaps the discursive field at Newbrook is not broad enough to make 'not sweet' positions easily available to Muslim students, and especially to those for whom academic learning is a struggle.[1] And perhaps the only permissible and recognizable response for some of the young women is to take up positions of dependence and vulnerability, in which they increasingly look for and demand help, and are consequently positioned as ever more 'needy'.

'Support repulsers'

The 'big bad girls' in Year 11 are known for their antipathy towards the provision of learning support. As such, few of them would consent to be interviewed: the potential losses, for a 'special needs student', in being seen to spend time with a learning support teacher, are too significant. Chantelle, a young woman from a working-class African Caribbean background, was the only 'big bad girl' in Year 11 who allowed me to interview her. By the time they reach Year 11, some of the young women whose special 'learning needs' were identified in their childhood have well-developed strategies for repulsing learning support. These are often manifested in overt hostility. Occasionally a young woman will manage to produce herself as so oppositional that her official designation will be changed from 'learning as a primary cause for concern' to 'behaviour as a primary cause for concern'. This, however, is very much the exception. For most of the young women who struggle to repudiate their 'neediness' in this way, their very transgressions are interpreted by the staff as further evidence of 'neediness', and attributed to lack of confidence and poor self-esteem.

What the young women *have* managed to do, in many cases, is repulse offers of learning support in ways that are unpleasant and often intimidating for whoever is offering that support. This is especially the case with learning support assistants, themselves at the bottom of the staff hierarchy: the 'big bad girls' would risk serious loss of face if they were seen to accept help from one of these low-status women. The acceptance of help from the head of faculty (a 'strict' teacher of whom nearly all of the students are scared) has a different meaning, and one that does not threaten a student's production of herself as 'big bad girl' in nearly so obvious a way.

> Sarah [the class teacher] is punctuating her talk to the class with exhortations for silence. Tana, Ijenyah and Chantelle are wearing their coats. This is a fairly standard challenge to authority: it means, 'I'm not going to be a good girl'. If the teacher tries to challenge the challenge, the girls bring out a well-rehearsed stock of complaints about the cold, lack of hanging space, and so on. Sarah is not risking a public confrontation today, but everyone in the room knows that the coat-wearing gauntlet has been thrown down, and it is unlikely to be a trouble-free lesson . . .
>
> The three girls on my table (their usual place in the corner) make heavy weather of their graph . . . Meanwhile I'm aware of, and vaguely wanting to listen to, the bad girls' conversation. Tana, Ijenyah, Vicki and Chantelle are talking loudly about boyfriends. They have their books open in front of them. Sarah has managed to persuade all of them to take their coats off, but they are making it clear they intend doing the lesson their way.

When Sarah tries to reconnect them with the task, they protest loudly
that they are doing their work, and it is true, to a point. Of the four,
only Chantelle has a blank sheet of paper in front of her. Sarah takes
advantage of this, and moves Chantelle to the table just behind us, on
her own. Chantelle continues to talk to the others, only more loudly, as
she is no longer at their table. I have a bit of a dilemma. I know that
Chantelle can't do the work, but I don't want to embarrass her in front
of her friends by offering help. I decide there's not a lot I can do about
her for the moment. If I were to try to intervene, she would probably
tell me where to go in no uncertain terms, as she is deeply involved in
the microcultural work going on. I don't think science, or me, could
compete at the moment. So I stick with Aqsa, Sana and Hafsa, and their
attempts to get the graph done . . .

Sarah stops everyone about 5 minutes before the bell. She wants to tell
them the overall game plan for science, after the mocks are finished.
Again, the bad girls interrupt, talking loudly and making a show of
putting their coats on. Sarah begins to lose patience, and says she will
keep in anyone who talks, or who tries to pack their things away, before
the bell. Aqsa, Sana and Hafsa talk quietly throughout, and pack their
things away unseen. It is not actually the packing-away that Sarah is
objecting to. It is the performative nature of the packing-away, and
whether the performance is intended as a challenge to authority . . .

(Fieldnotes 10/11/99)

Chantelle is undertaking some very hard identity work in this extract. I
think I was right in my on-the-spot prediction of a probable hostile response,
were I to have offered my services. But her intense involvement in the
microcultural work of the lesson was not simply in producing herself as 'one
of the bad girls' as I thought at the time. She faces multiple challenges in
producing herself as one of the young women in charge of the lesson: how
can someone be simultaneously 'needy' and 'in charge'?

This is a problem for Chantelle, especially in the middle part of the lesson,
where the young women's strategy for controlling the lesson is not accessible
to her. The amount of work they do is sufficient to enable them to demonstrate a particular contingent compliance to the teacher when necessary:
a compliance that would make her look ridiculous if she tried to take them
to task. But Chantelle is not able to do the work, flagging her 'neediness' to
all those around her. Chantelle's response is to intensify her 'badness' by
talking loudly (which also signalled to me that I had better keep away), so as
not to intensify her 'neediness'. The two are in direct conflict at this point.
For Chantelle to take up a position as 'big bad girl' she has additionally
to produce herself as tough and anti-education. This is not a position she
especially wants to be interpellated into, as she explained to me afterwards:

Chantelle: Aw, come on miss, you know I never did no work in that
lesson [kisses teeth]. So Tana and them lot, they was taking
it easy, you know, a bit of work, a bit of chat, a bit of work, a
bit of chat, that's how it goes. Me? [laughs] Not me. I do the

bit of chat, but then I can't do the work, so I do a bit more chat, play with pencil – la, la, la, la, la – a bit more chat, then comes Miss, 'What's going on here girls?' And who is it with the blank sheet? Well, it ain't Tana and them, that's for sure. So who does Miss move? Well, she ain't got no reason to move Tana, or she'll get backchat – and I mean real – heavy – backchat – we're not talking fun and games you know. So who is it has to go? Yes, it's me. And then what'm I supposed to do? Can't do no work, that's for sure, so it's a bit more chat, nice and loud, you know sort out the old social life a bit – well, you've got to haven't you? – and a bit more chat, and a bit more chat, and then – no more lesson – bingo!

SB: I'm interested in that. I mean, how you kind of took the blame?

Chantelle: Aw, just think about it, Miss, just think about it one little minute. If you had these two people in front of you, right, if you had these two people, Ms Connor and Tana in front of you, right, who would you be scared of? And I mean the *most* scared of?

SB: Well, I think it's different for me. 'Cause, I don't have to be scared of Tana, because if she's rude to me, or really goes over the top, if it came to it, I could just send her to the duty teacher. And if it was really bad, she could even get excluded. OK? So it's different.

Chantelle: Yeah, Miss, *exactly*. See, you said it yourself, exactly. 'Cause I can't go off running to no duty room. See, you can go running to the duty teacher, or Ms Cashmere, 'Help, save me, save me, Tana's coming to get me' and poof! No more Tana! In a puff of smoke. Yeah, just like that, in a puff of smoke. You go running to the duty room.

SB: [laughs]

Chantelle: But me, there ain't no puff of smoke for me. I've gotta *live* with it, yeah, I've gotta *live* with her, and I'm telling you Miss, I ain't ready to die yet. No, no way. I've gotta *live* in this place, and you think I can do that without I take a bit of care of Tana? If you think that, Miss, you're wrong, you've got it *badly* wrong, let me tell you. So Ms Connor tells me off in science? I can live with it. What's Ms Connor to me? But *Tana*? You think I can piss her off and live? You've got it *badly* wrong, you think that.

(Interview 10/11/99)

Chantelle positions herself within a culture that is in many ways anti-school and anti-teacher, but not anti the educational enterprise itself (Wright et al. 2000). Her anti-school and anti-teacher friends are crucial to what she sees as her survival at Newbrook. Teachers are mostly constructed as 'boring' within the 'big bad girls'' microcultures, and the challenge is one of alleviating that boredom through acts that are trangressive enough to be exciting, but not so transgressive that they threaten the young women's desires for academic success. If Chantelle were compliantly to take up a position as 'needy' she would almost certainly lose the respect and friendship of her peer group, and she appears also to fear reprisals from them. Where Chantelle differs from her friends is in the fact that they are able to produce themselves as 'big bad girls' without having to be seen to reject completely the dominant ethos of hard work.

> *Chantelle*: Yeah, so time goes on, and it ain't Year 7 no more. And then it's Year 9 SATs and all of a sudden it's, 'Get on with your work, girls, in the Hall, in rows, no talking, no looking around you, no breathing' and Ijenyah and that, they don't want to be shown up. See, they don't want to get no Threes. So you know, Miss, Aqsa and Cassandra and that, they get Threes or worse, and all of a sudden Ijenyah and that they think they're gonna be Threes if they don't get on with it. So they starts working. Not all the time, not in every lesson, but a bit. And who is it ends up a Three? You're looking at her, and Ijenyah, she makes like it's cool, but I'm telling you, there ain't nothing cool about being a Three. Not in Year 9, no way. Then it's GCSE, and they're still doing it. Workchat, chatwork, workchat, chatwork, that's how it goes. Me, I do the chat. Not the work. No way. And you know what Miss? You know what, tape recorder? What'm I gonna get in the mocks? You've guessed it. Zero. *Zero*. Forget threes. We're talking zero. I've been here five years, and we're talking zero.
>
> (Interview 10/11/99)

Chantelle is well aware that producing herself as 'big bad girl' involves costs in terms of her curricular progress. The 'big bad girls' of the SEN register have to struggle to maintain their microcultural status: this is problematic when their designation as 'special needs students' positions them as vulnerable and needy. Unlike the *real* big, bad girls of the school, they have to struggle to be recognized as oppositional, since the subject 'big, bad special needs student' is something of a contradiction in terms. There is a sense in which, by Year 11, the *real* 'big bad girls' demonstrate their grown-up-ness through a degree of investment in academic success – or at least in credentialization. Chantelle has to choose between the lesser of two evils: either she demonstrates her 'uncoolness' and powerlessness through taking up a position as 'needy', thus accessing a measure of help that may (or may not) help her to improve her exam grades. Or else she has to demonstrate the 'uncoolness' and powerlessness associated with poor grades, at the same time producing a version of herself as tough and anti-education.

The 'big bad girls' of the SEN register are overwhelmingly of either African Caribbean or white working-class origin. They tend to position teachers not as actual enemies, but as Others who must be kept at bay. Where more middle-class or higher-attaining girls (such as the high achievers in Jean's

Year 7 maths lesson) can at times position themselves alongside teachers, the 'big bad girls' of the SEN register have few resources with which to bridge the institutionalized power chasm. Their characterization of teachers as 'boring' contains an active Othering of teachers as out-of-date, out-of-touch and either asexual or sexually undesirable. Their anti-teacher-ness and anti-school-ness is lived largely in and through their production of themselves as hetero/ sexually active and attractive. In Year 7, the 'big bad girls' were faced with the challenge of demonstrating their 'maturity' through the production of themselves as hetero/sexually attractive and active against a formal school culture that positions its youngest students as rationally developing, target-achieving children. By Year 11, this is not the case. Common-sense understandings of young women as gendered and sexualized subjects permeate both formal and informal cultures at Newbrook. If anything, it is the 'sweet little girls' who have become Other to these readings of what it is (and must be) to be a young woman. The formal and informal cultures in circulation at Newbrook enable the production of differing modalities of sexualized young woman. There is the 'starlet' version, through which academically successful students can produce themselves as confident, assertive, attractive and audacious young women. There is the 'dangerous' version, through which students who are not positioned as 'needy' can produce themselves as streetwise and rebellious. Then there is the version, most available to the 'big bad girls' of the SEN register, in which students, through apparent investment in the 'dangerous' version, are positioned instead as 'girls-at-risk': the focus of current moral panics around teenage pregnancy and the target of Social Exclusion Unit intervention (Bullen et al. 2000).

'Support butterflies'

By Year 11, the 'lazy girls' appear to be maintaining their ambivalent position in relation to learning support. Amina and Suleika, young women from Somali Muslim backgrounds, are classic support butterflies. They appear to want, welcome and actively seek out help one moment, only to repudiate it the next. During the course of their time in Year 11, they made numerous appointments for help with particular pieces of coursework outside of school hours, only to break the appointments with no explanation. This exasperated many members of staff (myself included), many of whom had no hesitation in declaring Amina and Suleika 'lazy' and 'unmotivated'. Passivity looms large in the accounts these young women give of their school experiences.

>   *Suleika*: And we're just sitting there, and so we don't do, we're just
>   sitting there –
>   *Amina*: And another thing, yeah [laughs], no, I mean it, we didn't know
>   what to revise for our exam, and there's not much, there's seams,
>   and there's industrial processes, and there's fabrics, yeah, like
>   those tests. And I said to Miss, 'Miss, what do I have to revise?'
>   and she just says, she goes like, 'Everything'. *'Everything!'* I mean,

that doesn't help me, how does that help me, there's so much, you can't just do *everything*, you wouldn't do any other subjects [pause], you'd just be like textiles, textiles, all day long and all night –

Suleika: You'd just be sitting there, and I'd be crying, 'cause, like, you don't know where to start, and then I can't get my brain going, 'cause I'm just sitting there and I don't know what to do first – erm – and all the time, I'm thinking, when I'm starting on one thing, I'm thinking 'Supposing it doesn't come up', yeah, and I'm worrying in case it isn't the right thing, and I'm thinking should I be doing something else –

Amina: And you get – you know – you get like you just wanna forget it all, and you've got other things to do, it's not like your life stops just for exams, just for coursework, your life doesn't stop just 'cause of textiles, and you get like you wanna do something else, 'cause, like when I'm trying to revise, my brain it wants to do something else –

Suleika: Yeah, even you can be just sitting there, and it's like your brain doesn't wanna be there, even you can be just sitting there –

(Interview 9/12/99)

The accounts of the 'lazy girls' are saturated not just with ambivalence towards the schooling enterprise, but with apparent disconnection from it. The rescue motif is present, as it is in the accounts of the Year 7 girls. Here, there is more anger when whoever has been set up as rescuer does not play their part. Amina is clear that it is the textiles teacher who is to blame for not responding adequately to Amina's request for information. There is a sense in which Amina has cast the teacher as the all-powerful holder of the knowledge to which she needs access in order to effect the rescue. When the teacher apparently withholds that knowledge, Amina can feel justifiably aggrieved. Her objection can be understood within a schooling system that overwhelmingly casts the teacher as the giver (and therefore potentially the withholder) of knowledge. It can also be understood, more specifically, in relation to the standards agenda, which requires teachers to act in ways that emphasize the necessity for students to acquire and master predetermined measurable units of knowledge, and thereby intensify their positioning as knowledge source.

The discourse of teacher-as-giver-of-knowledge and the concomitant student-as-seeker-of-knowledge, combined with both the apparatus of 'special needs' and the reality of years of experiencing struggles with academic work appears to be locking Amina into a cycle of dependence which ultimately results in her disconnection from academic learning. Suleika's disconnection is equally apparent. Her recalcitrant brain has apparently made an escape from her essential self, which has been left 'just sitting there'. But it is not only Suleika's brain which must be disavowed. The 'lazy girls' typically perceive themselves as hetero/sexually inadequate, and they evince the longing to escape from their 'unattractive' bodies.

Amina: And we was all standing by the gates, that time, remember, when that girl in Year 10 got her boyfriend and his mates –

Suleika: Yeah, she got her boyfriend, that girl did, um –

Amina: and his mates, and we went out there, 'cause everyone was shouting –

Suleika: oh, I remember that time. Everyone was shouting, and you could hear them, everyone was shouting

Amina: and everyone was shouting, like 'There's boys at the gates' [laughs], I mean it. I don't know her name, that girl.

Suleika: And we went 'cause everyone was shouting, they was all shouting –

Amina: We both went too –

Suleika: and we went to see, 'cause that girl in Year 10, she's *so* pretty, not like just pretty, but *so* pretty, and I wanted to see, um, but I wanted to be really pretty, not like this. And me and Amina we started to go the gates, but then we didn't go, we just stayed by the wall, we was just standing there –

Amina: Have you ever seen her Miss? She's really pretty. She's got loads of boyfriends –

Suleika: She's like not just pretty, she's *so* pretty, and we both went, but I was thinking like I wanted to be pretty like her, not just pretty but really pretty. And if I was like her, and not like me, I'd be really pretty, oh, I don't know, um. And if I was like her, if I didn't have to keep being like this, [pinches her arm] then I'd have loads of boyfriends when I go to the gates –

Amina: and if we had loads of boyfriends they'd come, like, um, they'd come to the gates, and everyone would be shouting, 'Did you see Amina's boyfriends?' [laughs]

Suleika: Yeah, they'd all be shouting, 'Did you see Amina and Suleika's boyfriends'

(Interview 1/12/99)

Suleika's narratives describe a passivity in which both her brain and her body have fled leaving an empty shell behind, 'just sitting there' or 'just standing' by the wall. On the one hand, she describes her desire for the evidence of success. She apparently *wants* to do the 'right' revision for her exams, and she *wants* to be one of the hetero/sexually successful students who are 'pretty' enough to attract boys at the gate. What she is left with is the evidence of failure. She is left 'just sitting' in the exam room because she has done the 'wrong' revision and her brain has escaped. And she is left 'just standing' by the wall, because her body is not 'pretty' enough even to take her to the gates, much less to meet a boyfriend there. Her descriptions evoke for me the image of the countless lessons in which I have sat, worrying about 'my students' who so often appear to be 'just sitting there', faced with work they cannot do: the hard evidence of their inadequacy.

As 'special needs students', Suleika and Amina seldom get into trouble for their perceived laziness. In much the same way as the 'big bad girls'' production of opposition will be read as further proof of neediness, the 'lazy girls'' production of laziness tends to be read as another manifestation of their special needs. In Newbrook School, with its pride in its own success, there is considerable investment in discourses that allow for individual remediation. So the 'lazy girls' amongst the 'special needs students' will often be read within a discourse of low self-esteem (Kenway and Willis 1990; Renshaw 1990), and teachers will work hard to remedy this perceived lack of self-belief.

> *Sarah*: I'd just give them a sheet of A4 'cause they couldn't, they *really* couldn't do the test at all. I'd give them a sheet of A4 with some very simple questions on, and I'd say, 'Right, *try* and do the test, but when the test is up, when you've finished everything on the test, do this sheet that I've added on the back'. Er, they would have been, they would have looked at the test, and if they hadn't had that sheet, they would have looked at the test, and you know, 'Waaaaah, oh I'm useless,' but they, they looked at the test, did as much as they could, got about two or three marks between, um, each, and then they went on to the simpler sheet and they got a lot more out of doing that, because I suppose I'd made it even simpler for them, and asked them, asking them sort of questions that maybe I've already asked them in class, so there was stuff there that they could answer. And then when they got six out of ten for that sheet there, it made them feel, it gave them a little bit more self-esteem inside, if they got three out of thirty for their original test, but then they got six out of ten for their next test, and that gave them a bit more sort of self-esteem in themselves, which was a good idea.
>
> (Interview 6/4/00)

Of all the teachers in Newbrook, Sarah is one of the most positive about teaching 'special needs students'. Her analysis draws on a Warnock-like view that 'special needs' arise in the relationship between a student's inherent difficulties with learning, and the curriculum that they are offered. She is positive about taking steps to change her pedagogic practices in the interests of enabling 'special needs students' to 'access the curriculum' (Fletcher-Campbell 1994; Thomas et al. 1998; Dyson 1999). While I do not want to derogate her efforts, or present her as anything other than a caring, reflective and committed practitioner, I think it is important to note that any attempt to remedy the perceived low self-esteem of students such as Suleika and Amina is unlikely to be successful. Suleika and Amina take up positions as 'lazy girls' in response to being positioned as 'needy'. Reading this response as a measure of lack of self-esteem further inscribes them into cycles of 'neediness'. Moreover, the self-esteem discourse implies that their problem is one of *feeling* powerless in relation to school, and that, if only their feelings could be changed, they would become empowered. In reality, though, their problem is that they *have been positioned* as powerless (Davies 1994).

A curriculum that is constructed through what Slee (1998) calls 'curricular fundamentalism' is premised on producing a hierarchy of students according to their ability to demonstrate their mastery of that curriculum. Newbrook's emphasis on success, together with its strong equal opportunities ethos, constructs a fiction that mastery of this curriculum is available to everyone, so long as they work hard enough and long enough. While this fiction contains the knowledge that such demonstrable mastery must be hierarchically ordered and differentially available, it also contains the imperative that this knowledge must be masked and euphemized (Apple 1995, 1996). It is the 'special needs students' who most challenge the continuance of the fiction: none more so than the 'support butterflies'.

'Support junkies' and 'support repulsers' both appear to operate as if the promise of success for all were true. The 'support junkies' take up the offer of help that is officially supposed to move them towards demonstrable mastery of the curriculum. The 'support repulsers' repudiate that help, and in doing so, construct themselves as tough and anti-education, their failure the result of their attitude and, in many cases, home background. But the 'support butterflies' appear fundamentally to disbelieve the fiction, even while they may contradictorily appear to be the most invested in promises of rescue. It is this ambivalence – between desperately wanting to be rescued from their educational 'neediness' and tenaciously holding onto the impossibility of rescue – that constructs them as passive occupiers of the middle ground, not wanting to repulse learning support, but not being able to make good use of that support. And, as such, it interpellates them into a very subordinated, 'victim' version of femininity.

Whose educational needs are special?

To suggest that the notion of 'special educational needs' is entirely fixed and located within particular students would be not quite accurate. It is true that the young women in Year 11 are well aware of who is on, and who is not on, the special needs register: who 'needs' support is a matter of public knowledge. 'Sweet little girls' and 'lazy girls' have mostly established relationships with 'their' support teachers, and 'big bad girls' have established relationships of resistance to adult help and intervention. It is unlikely that any student will be formally identified as having SEN, and added to the special needs register, during Year 11. But even so, some fluidity still exists.

> After school it's History Club. Amina and Suleika get there before me. Anna meets me on the way over, and explains that she and some of the girls who have finished the coursework are going over to watch 'bitesize'. Lisa directs me to a girl I don't know, whom she's asked to sit with Amina and Suleika as she might need extra help. The young woman, whose name I don't remember, looks very worried. In fact, with drooping mouth and drooping shoulders, she's coding misery with every fibre of her being. I think Lisa thinks I'll give her some TLC [tender loving care] as well as basic history, while she gets on with the girls who aren't so 'needy'. I know all the girls on the SEN register in Year 11, and this

young woman isn't one of them. Perhaps being unhappy is enough to position her as in need of special help.

(Fieldnotes 16/2/00)

Among the staff, a common sense appears to prevail that learning support teachers operate within a discourse of self-esteem. We are seen to be in the business of enhancing students' capacities to learn by working some kind of pastoral magic that will enable failing students to feel good about themselves as learners. We are also positioned, by staff and students, as benevolent 'aunties'. We have access to the authority that is inherent in our institutional position. At the same time, there is an understanding that we are 'on the students' side' as much as possible. We are expected to take the part of students who are in trouble. Even though the head of the learning support department is a man, we are expected to operate the traditionally feminine skills of empathic listening and comforting the needy (Martin 1985; Urwin 1985; Bines 1986; Davies 1989). We care. Despite attempts to masculinize the enterprise of SEN provision through IEPs, monitoring and other techno-rationalist managerial strategies, our academic role is usually, I think, perceived as secondary to our caring one. This is not to say that other teachers do not also have a 'caring' role, or that they are necessarily 'uncaring' towards their students. But I think it is true to say that an assumption operates that most teachers will put 'discipline' first – in its curricular and governmental senses (Slee 1995). By contrast, there is an assumption that learning support teachers will put 'discipline' second.

Like all social and microcultural constructions, these starting positions are enacted in a multitude of ways by different members of staff. They are nuanced according to a range of individual and structural phenomena, such as personal disposition and inclination, and position in the formal hierarchy, as well as by class, race and gender/sexuality. Nonetheless, the infantilization that inheres in the special needs discourse serves to inter-pellate learning support teachers into positions within that discourse as care-givers, in which our primary roles are perceived to be about taking care of the most needy, and not about disciplining the majority.

While it is true that the surest way for a student to get support is through the official route, some students can, if they want and conditions are right, position themselves as 'needy' and access support in a more informal way. A student who wants adult help has more chance of procuring it if she positions herself as needy in relation to a caring discourse than if she positions herself as needy in relation to an academic one. The common-sense, informal understanding of support teachers as caring aunties can swing into operation much more easily than the bureaucracy involved with formal identification of quantifiable learning 'needs'. In addition, it is in many cases much less problematic and far-reaching for a student to position herself as needing to be cared for, than it is for her to produce herself as stupid.

Iqbal (the 'unknown' young woman in the above extract) appeared to want more help than Lisa, busy with the huge group of 'middling' students, was going to be able to offer. And one way to get it was by producing herself as unhappy, in need of care and a boost to her self-esteem. This is not to imply that she was not genuinely miserable: I think she was. But she was also taking up a position in discourse as needy of care, which brought her into the learning support fold. Perhaps the caring discourse of SEN was operating to interpellate her into the momentary take-up of a 'special needs student' position, always with the knowledge that misery is or can be a temporary phenomenon, and that she could withdraw this version of herself by cheering up.

Iqbal's identity work is of relevance here since it shows that, in practice, the implication that the 'special needs student' is an absolute binary position is false, even though the SEN discourse most usually operates as if it were true. In this case, Iqbal is not placed at an extreme position of the SEN continuum, although she could be positioned as 'underachieving'. In that sense, it could be argued that she has 'special needs' because with the 'right' kind of intervention (and the SEN discourse is predicated on the efficacy of professional intervention) she could achieve more than she is currently doing. And it could also be argued that she is intellectually subordinated since, for whatever reason, the existing curriculum and conditions in which it is delivered are not sufficiently accessible to her to enable her optimal learning. But her needs are not 'as special' as those of some of the other students since she is capable, when she really has to, of doing the set work more-or-less independently. And she is not 'as intellectually subordinated' as some since, if she makes enough effort, the curriculum and the demands it makes can be brought within her reach. This analysis leaves us with many problems, not least with voluntarism. For example, in Amina's case, the GCSE curriculum and the conditions of its delivery are always going to be beyond her. She is not able, no matter how hard she tries, to make independent sense of what goes on in history lessons. This constructs a very passive, and always 'needy' position for her in relation to mainstream schooling. Again, much of the problem seems to be associated with the demands of the curriculum. Even though Iqbal demonstrates here that SEN is a continuum, not a polarity, the curriculum, as both tool and product of the standards agenda, acts to push students towards one or other end of that continuum. It acts to move students to a place that operates as a binary divide, and from where specific students can be intellectually subordinated.

For Iqbal, it is 'lack of confidence' and anxiety that are perceived to be the root causes of her distress. With the 'right' professional intervention (care and reassurance) her underachievement could, in theory, be put right. Much of the SEN rhetoric (if not the reality of its deployment) is based on the understanding that special needs can be 'met' by skilled and caring professionals, following which those needs will not be 'special' any more.

Iqbal is in a complete tangle over Question Two. Not surprising. It's a compare-and-contrast, between a black historian's description of the purposes of black education in the 1970s, and a section of the Bantu Education Act. The two don't lend themselves to a comparison, and the passage from the Act is very hard to deconstruct. I more-or-less let it go with my students, and got onto something more manageable, but, knowing nothing about this young woman, I wonder if I should help her have more of a go at it. I ask her what mark she's hoping for overall. Her eyes fill with tears. She wants a C, but has been predicted a D. We should really have a go at the question, then, as she won't get a C unless she makes a reasonable attempt at it.

(Fieldnotes 16/2/00)

It could be said that the particular demands of this subject and this piece of coursework have constructed Iqbal as intellectually subordinated. She has, for very understandable reasons within the current micropolitical and educational climate, come to want a C grade for her work, and her realistic fear is that she will get only a D: a grade that does not really count as success. This has pushed her to the margins, where she has taken up a subordinated position. Again, her needs are not 'as special' as Amina's. They are not perceived to (and in my view, do not) require official mechanisms to be put in place. Her misery is enough to position her, momentarily, as a 'special needs student', but she is not invited into an officially inscribed, signed-and-sealed identity as such. When it comes to intellectual subordination, she certainly *feels* miserable (and possibly disempowered) in relation to the institutional grading scheme in place. But it could also be argued that her misery is also a form of resistance to subordination, since it is that very misery which has enabled her to access the help that just might result in a better grade.

But still there are problems with this analysis. It implies that Iqbal's 'special needs' and her 'intellectual subordination' are almost nothing *but* social and political constructs. Iqbal, and others like her, are not readily positioned at the extreme end of the continuum, and so they have room for manoeuvre in relation to the positions they take up. They can inhabit the distinctions that mark out SEN and intellectual subordination with some degree of creativity, if not exactly choice, whereas for Amina and most of the young women with whom I work, 'special needs' and 'intellectual subordination' are not so much social constructs as material realities. Their perceived and ascribed 'neediness' defines who they can be and aspire to be at school. And a degree of 'real' intellectual impairment underpins the social and local construction of these young women as 'needy'. They have to inhabit these categories, not only because they have been categorized, but also because they really are less able to acquire mastery of the curriculum than those students to whom normative levels of academic attainment are accessible.

One of the problems here is the implication that the degree of social construction present in the formal and/or informal designation of 'special needs' varies according to how impaired a student's intellect can be said to be, and according to how far her intellectual abilities are perceived to fall short of the norm. A post-structuralist reading of this implication might suggest that SEN operates as a discursive field in which the degree of agency available to any individual student engaged in the project of producing herself and re/producing the discourses contained in the field, correlates strongly with her (perceived and material) academic ability. To make use of such a reading requires us to hold on to two discourses often posited in opposition to each other: that intellectual ability below the normative range is both socially produced *and* has a material base.

It is not my intention here to attempt to tease out, or to try to separate, the 'real' from the 'discursive'. Instead, I am interested in how they produce each other, and I would suggest they cannot be reduced to their component parts. As soon as we begin to think about, and to measure, perceived intellectual ability, we use conceptual tools and instruments derived from politically located discourses, and in order to examine the discursive practices around intellectual ability, we have to study their material effects. This chapter has examined such practices and effects through discussing the identity work of a group of students who are, in part, engaged in negotiating their way out of the school and into the institutions of young adulthood. In the first part of the chapter, the young women's accounts demonstrated how their inability to access dominant versions of success is worked through the material and discursive practices of learning support. Their accounts showed how differential responses to the provision of such support is a crucial part of these students' identity work, embedded as these responses are in student microcultures. In the second part of the chapter, a discursive analysis of the 'borders' (Johnson 1997) of the SEN discourse demonstrated how multiple understandings of special educational neediness can be kept in play. But these understandings are not endlessly fluid, as the next chapter shows.

Note

1 The events of 11 September 2001 and their aftermath, which took place after this research was finished, will undoubtedly affect the positioning of Muslim students at school in the UK.

CHAPTER SEVEN

Making the grade: exams and the 'consolation discourse' of success

Where Chapter 6 argued for a multiplicity of meanings around SEN, this chapter looks at the limits of that multiplicity. I use the school examination process, and the discursive practices it produces and through which it is produced, to analyse how and where this contingent fluidity around notions of achievement and academic progress becomes solidified. I start in the examination hall itself, looking at how the examination process produces students and teachers. I then look more widely at the identity work that the examination makes possible in the context of student microcultures and school micropolitics. Central to this is the discourse, constructed through schooling policy and Newbrook's response to policy, of a 'consolation' version of academic success: a version that may at first glance look humane but in fact operates to reify the subject 'special needs student' and to close down the discursive spaces available to her.

The examination

There is a sense in which exams are ever-present at Newbrook. Teachers routinely invoke them as a motivational strategy when they exhort students to work hard. Students are often represented in terms of their exam marks, real or projected: the Americanism of 'she's an A* student' is increasingly used. Teachers too are measured and represented in terms of how their students perform, or are expected to perform, on the big day. The examination is the site at which student and teacher 'performance' is monitored, quantified and made tangible in the form of a grade. The omnipresence of the examination means that it generates identity work on a multiplicity of fronts, material and symbolic. The moment of public examination functions as one very important site of such work.

> I walk down the aisle, conscious of every sound I make. The floorboards at the back creak, and I'm horribly aware of it. I feel obliged to do some patrolling. The rows of desks are just about far enough apart for someone to walk between, with care. I don't like patrolling along them. As well as all the ideological objections, I keep thinking I'm going to bump into someone. Dave's in charge. A 50-year-old white man in charge of rows and rows of mostly ethnic-minority young women, and of the older women who are supervising under his direction. Bentham's Panopticon flashes through my mind. I don't like being a jailer. It's the English Lit exam. A girl I don't know asks if I will spell 'sarcastic' for her. I tell her I can't, I'm not allowed, but then I talk her through it anyway. We smile in comradely fashion at each other, momentarily united against adversity, and I go on down the row. Danielle has drawn a work of art in her anthology – she's obviously given up on English. Time drags. I try not to look at what 'my' girls are doing. I just hate seeing them sitting in isolation at their desks, not able to do the paper, and not able to ask for help. I'm supposed to stay in the hall next lesson, and when the bell for break goes, Dave asks me to go into the dining hall, to keep watch in case anyone should have the temerity to try to use it during break . . . When I get back to the hall, Lorraine has taken over in charge . . . Most of the girls have finished. We cannot let them leave. Vikki asks to go the toilet. We have all been given express instructions not to let her. She will stay in the hall, under surveillance, whether she likes it or not. As the hands of the clock creep towards finishing time, the rustle of papers becomes a roar. At some point, I think the majority of the girls must have realized that too, and it seems as if they are resisting in the only way they can. Spirit-of-the-Blitz-like, they rustle in collective chorus. They know they can do this with Lorraine in charge. It would be different with most of the other superintending teachers.
>
> (Fieldnotes 6/12/99)

It is hard to know how to start to deconstruct a piece of examination theatre. It is both a bizarre and a commonsensical schooling event, and a very familiar part of the schooling process with which I grew up. It can appear to defy questioning. *Of course* public exams must be rigorously supervised to prevent cheating, and *of course* this has to be done by responsible adults. But rows and rows of young women sitting working in silence, when the hundred-or-so of them who are crammed into the hall could so easily be ungovernable, must surely look strange to the outsider. And, as such, it is worth asking a few questions about how such a situation is maintained, and about how the consent of these young women has been won.

The physical arrangement of the hall might be a good place to start. It had been set up as rows of desks, in precisely ordered ranks. The desks had been placed far enough apart to satisfy exam regulations and the need for aisles wide enough for supervisors to patrol. They were also close enough together to meet the administrative need to squeeze 180 young women into two rooms so as to minimize disruption to the rest of the school. On the platform, facing the students' desks, was a desk wide enough to accommodate three teachers. Behind the students' desks and to the side of them were a scattering of chairs, intended for teachers' occasional use as we undertook our patrols of the hall. Every student had to be visible at all times from a variety of angles. Two blackboards at the front of the hall showed the school's name and number, and the starting and finishing times of the exam. A clock stood above each blackboard. All of this can be justified as being eminently reasonable and a good, sound, common-sense response to the demands of the examination board. But the practical reasons for setting the hall up in this way should not obscure the other meanings that can be read off from such a division of space. Foucault (1975) argues that:

> Disciplinary space tends to be divided into as many sections as there are bodies or elements to be distributed. One must eliminate the effects of imprecise distributions, the uncontrolled disappearance of individuals, their diffuse circulation, their unusable and dangerous coagulation.
>
> (Foucault 1975: 143)

The fact that sitting each student at a desk from which she can be seen from a variety of angles is a practical necessity does not mean it is not also a technology of power: it simultaneously functions as both. The magic of surveillance is such that its power operates (or must be seen to operate) to regulate students in the known absence of any members of staff of whom they are especially afraid. This is a 'practice' (not a 'real') exam, so none of the direst penalties for cheating would be invoked, and yet, even when Lorraine is left in charge, none of the students act in ways that have been expressly prohibited. But at the same time the regulatory power of surveillance is not total. The collective rustling of papers at the end of the exam was an implicit challenge: you can regulate our bodies, but you cannot stop us finding creative ways to resist with our minds. It would have been inconceivable for Lorraine to have made a public announcement, during the exam, about excessive rustling. The paradox of the surveillant power of the examination room is that it has to be seen to be total. If Lorraine had issued a directive about rustling, she would, in effect, have been pointing out that discipline was not absolute. To disrupt the fiction of total surveillance in this way would have been unthinkable. So the examination room cannot be understood as the perfect Panopticon,[1] but it needs to operate as if it were. The 'state of conscious and permanent visibility that assures the automatic functioning of power' (Foucault 1975: 201) has not *quite* been achieved here (although it very nearly has): it would need to be supplemented by the actual embodied presence of an individual who will evoke fear.

One of the challenges that the fiction of total surveillance cannot allow is the challenge of someone physically removing themselves without permission. Of all the young women sitting in the hall that day, Vikki alone was willing to make what, on the face of it, was an entirely reasonable request, to go to the toilet. In many ways it is outrageous that one person should be able to refuse another the right to go to the toilet. For children and young people at school, going to the toilet is of particular significance. In schools (as in many workplaces), the toilet is the most surveillance-free space, and student toilets are the place for escaping adult supervision. But in the context of an exam, all reasons for leaving the room are illegitimate and regulated against. Vikki's request, to leave the school's most surveillant space and go to its least surveillant, was never going to be allowed. Simply making the request was enough for her to produce herself as a 'bad girl'.

The inadmissibility of Vikki's request points to further readings about power and control in the examination room. Vikki is, by official and unofficial consent, one of the most oppositional young women in what is regarded as an especially oppositional year group. And yet, without the required permission, she does not so much as stand up, much less leave the room as she had requested. In many contexts, Vikki is constructed, and produces herself, as someone who wants attention. Surely, in the silent examination room, she could have had all the attention she wanted. She only had to stand up and speak, and more than a hundred people's attention would have been hers. This is often the way she operates in ordinary classroom situations. But the examination room does not produce any possibilities for this kind of individual resistance. Foucault (1975) argues that compulsory visibility, which he likens to the Panopticon, produces docile bodies which then enact a non-corporeal version of 'discipline'.

> He who is subject to a field of visibility and who knows it, assumes responsibility for the constraints of power: he makes them play spontaneously upon himself: he inscribes in himself the power relation in which he simultaneously plays both roles; he becomes the principle of his own subjection. By this very fact, the external power may throw off its physical weight; it tends to the non-corporal.
>
> (Foucault 1975: 202)

In the examination room, Vikki presents an extreme example of how power and control, and perpetual visibility, combine to make transgressive acts unthinkable. The fact that she will not leave the room without permission is remarkable only when considered in the context of her generally oppositional response to schooling in general, and towards authority in particular. So it is important not to exaggerate the power of the examination room to regulate in every instance. Although the examination, and the prospect of the examination, produces students as docile bodies containing consenting minds, the extent to which this production carries over outside of the examination room varies considerably. It is important, too, to bear in mind that the power produced in perpetual visibility is deeply felt, as well as embodied. Exams typically produce fear in students, and the prospect of shame and embarrassment. In this context, it is highly unlikely that a student will want to further individualize and visibilize herself by acting in a non-docile way. Added to this are the very real material consequences of the examination process. At the end of Year 11, the young women will leave school with a clutch (or not) of credentials that will bear very direct relation to the options that will be open to them, and to the standard of living that they can expect. These, too, form part of the apparatus of power that compel the attendance and compliance of the young women, and make impossible a request to leave the room.

The physical presence of teachers is equally compelled. I thoroughly dislike supervising the exams. Apart from anything else, it is very boring. But it would be unthinkable for me to refuse to 'invigilate', or to subvert the exam by not supervising (or not being seen to supervise) properly. This can be explained in large part by my contractual obligations. I am contractually obliged to be in the hall as and when directed, and I am equally obliged to invigilate in the directed manner. I would not be allowed to sit in the hall and read a book. Even as I write this, however, I am aware that I have never asked, on grounds of conscience, to be released from this unpalatable aspect of duty. It has never occurred to me to ask. Foucault again:

> Although surveillance rests on individuals, its functioning is that of a network of relations from top to bottom, but also to a certain extent from bottom to top and laterally; this network 'holds' the whole together and traverses it in its entirety with effects of power that derive from one another: supervisors, perpetually supervised.
>
> (Foucault 1975: 176)

In the examination room, I am careful to do enough patrolling so that I will be seen to be doing my job: seen by whichever teacher is superintending, and, to a lesser extent, by the students themselves. I tell myself I have no alternative. So what consequences can I imagine were I to ask to be released from invigilation? Senior management would, I am sure, enter into a discussion with me, and not just dismiss the request out of hand. But questions would be raised about my loyalty. I would be positioned as 'not a team player' for letting down my colleagues, and forcing them into a disproportionate share of supervision. I would equally feel bad about this aspect. Probably, questions would also be raised about the 'luxury' of the position from which I can afford to challenge perfectly reasonable demands. In all probability, I would not like these or any other of the consequences, all of which would be in the nature of penalty for disrupting the network Foucault describes.

But this is not the whole story. The management of exams at Newbrook is in many ways a metaphor for the management of the school. In modern management terms, the power and the undisruptability of the network relies on a combination of power not being seen to be seen (although we all recognize that we recognize it) and of this unspoken phenomenon (which we may not talk about because it cannot be known that we know about it) unquestionably operating in the interest of the greater good. It is not quite that power – dominance – is operating so cleverly that we are unaware of it, more that we have too much to lose by naming it. It is as if the unremarkableness of power means it cannot be challenged, or organized against. How can you organize against something that does not exist, and anyway, if it does exist, exists only to make everyone happy and the organization function effectively? And if we even think about thinking about power as dominance, we risk positioning ourselves as dominating and dominated: something which would be officially unthinkable within the prevailing discursive field at Newbrook. This means that in a sense what exists in the hall cannot be named as power, and certainly cannot be conceived in terms of dominance and subordination. The unwilling supervising the unwilling becomes a function of common sense and good administration.

GCSEs have a privileged place in the construction of what counts as success in Newbrook, since they are the exams that determine the options open to any student when she leaves school. But they are not the only public exams the students take. At the end of Year 9, they take SATs in English, maths and science. And in 2000, for the first time, Newbrook's Year 7 cohort took the Cognitive Attainment Tests (CATs), as a form of 'baseline assessment' for the school to use in its measurement of 'value-added'. These tests are non-statutory, and take the form of a battery of assessments of verbal, numerical and spatial skills. They are marked by computer, and the results arrive back in school as a list of student attainment, ranked in order from the highest attainers at the top of the list to the lowest at the bottom. Also supplied is a profile of each student's supposed strengths and weaknesses, and a projection of that student's expected GCSE results in each National Curriculum subject. Puzzlingly, the threshold of attainment at which the test starts scoring, is the mysterious 'attainment age 10'. This suggests that most of the SEN students would not score on it at all, since their mastery of the curriculum is below that of an 'average' 10-year-old. The flawed nature of the tests and the even more flawed nature of the arguments underpinning them was apparent to many of my colleagues.

> Helen asks me if I think the test will tell us anything worth knowing. She thinks what they are measuring is very narrow . . . She tells me that 'we stopped doing the optional SATs in technology for the same reason: they didn't tell us anything we didn't already know, or couldn't find out, and they didn't make sense from a teaching point of view'.
>
> (Fieldnotes 22/3/00)

This, however, was not the dominant story that was told about the CATs tests. The official managerial picture was that the tests had gone well – much better, in fact, than had dared been hoped for. The reason for this was the 'excellent behaviour' of the girls. Even the most disruptive Year 7 students had produced themselves as eminently governable (Foucault 1988) during the tests. This was felt to have the positive consequence of making officially desired exam behaviour (such as lining up in silence, and not looking around while in the hall) normal and unquestionable from the students' first year in the school.

> 7Q line up in register order and walk across to the hall in silence. My primary teaching days flood back, as I make them wait at strategic points to make sure they're all in line, then carry on walking. Their primary days are presumably near enough for them to remember and respond to this

kind of treatment. Pam sees them into the hall, marking them off on her
register as they go in. She's much more smiley than she was yesterday.
When 7Q come in we talk publicly about them being the best form. I'm
not sure whether they still like this or not . . . Today's tests are the 'Quantitative Battery'. The instructions are unbelievably complicated. I'm looking at the CATs book, but I can't really follow. Simone is with Josie. I
hover around the girls who are doing this for the first time, in case they
need help following. At last Pam reaches the end of the instructions. The
girl I was helping has no idea of what to do. We work it out together. I
go on patrol. Not that you really need to, it's not like GCSE where you
have to walk up and down, but I think some of the girls find it harder to
put their hands up than they do to catch my eye as I walk past them.
Several girls ask for help when I go past. Natelle wants to know why
there's a number before a bracket with no sign as to what to do. I
whisper to her that it means she's to multiply it – 'I shouldn't tell you
this, but it means times'. Simone tells me that Josie has bitten her nails
down so far that they're bleeding, and she has been to get her a plaster.

The test lasts for only 10 minutes. Then Pam asks them to put their
pencils down, and begins on the next set of instructions. These are even
worse. They go on for a good 15 minutes. It's all scripted. There are
practice tests to be taken though. Josie doesn't know where to put the
answers for the practice tests. I don't know how Pam is keeping a straight
face through this lot. The head of maths, who's also invigilating, whis-
pers to me that most of this work hasn't been covered in maths yet.
There's a whole long spiel in the script about 'parentheses' and whether
to multiply or add first. It's like a big classroom, with 90 students listening in silence to Pam, irrespective of whether or not they understand.
Natasha puts her hand up on the second practice test. She doesn't know
why the answer is what Pam has said it is. I explain briefly and unsatis-
factorily. I don't want her to get behind in the last set of instructions.
When Pam finally gives the word to begin, a forest of hands goes up.
Amna prefaces her question with 'I was listening, but I didn't understand', as if she thinks I will tell her off for not having paid sufficient
attention. This test is too hard for most of the girls sitting in the hall.
That's if the instructions didn't put them off altogether. Josie tells me
she is 'guessing them all'. There are 12 minutes allowed – 12 minutes for
most of the girls to sit and know they are inadequate . . . Pam ends by
telling the girls they have been 'fantastic – so responsible – even more
grown-up than Year 9'.

(Fieldnotes 22/3/00)

For the Year 7 girls, the examination is constructed in ways that draw upon
their experiences as primary school subjects. The familiar assemblage of
primary school-style directives – walking silently in line, and receiving public and collective praise for being 'good' – are reformulated as a secondary
school-style imperative towards self-control and displays of responsibility. As
the youngest and newest students in the school, these girls are in many ways

the easiest to control and coerce. Their compliance in the exam room is fed back to them not in terms of how obedient they have been, but in terms of how responsible and 'mature' they were in producing themselves as docile bodies. The message is a complex and contradictory one. The reality in which they did as they were told became a fiction in which they did as they wanted, but crucially in that fiction they wanted that which authority wanted. It is a complex form of enforcing consent and compliance, yet it is a familiar and much-used strategy in Newbrook and other schools.

When the dominant story of the success of the CATs tests was told, it was the girls' apparent consent that loomed large in the telling. The deduction that was made from this was that, having been won, the girls' consent for the examination process could henceforth in their school careers be taken for granted. It would not have to be struggled for in the Year 9 SATs or in the Year 11 'mock' GCSEs.

The hall had been set out as it always is for exams, with rows of desks in serried ranks. In the GCSE exams, and in the SATs, a blackboard is used to delineate starting and finishing times. In the CATs, time is much more sharply divided, and much more within the control of authority, seen to be embodied within the form of the superintending teacher. She may appear to control the passage of time, but as all of us in the hall are aware, the regulations about the divisions of time have been set down by the examining authority, and she is merely carrying out their directives, on behalf of the headteacher, who wants this test carried out in the prescribed way. There is no escape from the passage of time as an organizing narrative in the CATs tests. Foucault (1975) remarks that:

> Discipline . . . poses the principle of a theoretically ever-growing use of time: exhaustion rather than use; it is a question of extracting, from time, ever more available moments and, from each moment, ever more useful forces . . . the more time is broken down, the more its subdivisions multiply, the better one disarticulates it by deploying its internal elements under a gaze that supervises them, the more one can accelerate an operation, or at least regulate it according to an optimum speed.
>
> (Foucault 1975: 154)

The sharply delineated passage of time within the CATs tests served a number of purposes. It ensured that the responsibility for the correct administration of the test remained with the superintending teacher. It focused us all on her, at given intervals, for instructions on how to proceed. It established the CATs tests as somewhat different from the daily run of school life, in which time is usually divided into rather larger chunks marked off by the bell: for those taking CATs tests, the bell could be ignored as an irrelevance. This served to dislocate those in the hall from the normal passage of time as constructed by the school day. The delineated nature of time in the CATs tests provided some alleviation, at least, from what was a boring (and, for some, unpleasant) set of tasks: although each set of boxes-to-be-ticked was tedious, and distressing for those students who were unable to work out what to do, no set lasted very long. There was the constant promise of a new set of questions, and perhaps a set that might be more interesting or more feasible. This may not seem very relevant here, but it is undoubtedly true that the alleviation of boredom and unpleasantness is a force to be reckoned with in winning students' consent to any activity. All of these taken together meant that the control of time in the CATs test helped to construct a finely controlled reality. This reality was one in which students were obliged to produce themselves as governable. Their governability could be read (and could be read back to them) as consent.

While the dominant story of CATs was one of governability, the achievement story could only ever come a poor second. At the moment of examination, the girls' academic 'performance' was (for the superintending teacher at least) a secondary concern in relation to their performance of compliance and consent. And so asking for help, something that would normally be encouraged and read back to a student as praiseworthy involvement in the learning process, could be read as non-compliance. There was some confusion for the girls about whether or not they could in fact ask for help. In some ways, this had an equalizing effect. Many of the girls, not just those who had been identified as having SEN, were positioned as 'needy' by a set of barely comprehensible instructions, and by the ambiguity that surrounded asking for help. Nearly all were constructed as deficient in relation to a set of questions relating to work they had not covered. Moreover, the demands of the test tended to position them as comrades united against adversity, even when they had consented to the conditions adversity imposed.

But this should not obscure one of the main purposes of the tests. The production of what Foucault calls 'docile bodies', and what I prefer to think of as consenting subjects inhabiting consenting bodies, may have been (or may have functioned as) the paramount concern at the moment of examination. But the rationale behind the tests, and the organizing narrative that legitimized their administration, was the perceived need to measure the girls' academic 'performance' and map it, according to an ages-and-stages developmental model. The map produced charted each student's projected path through to GCSE, and, perhaps more significantly, produced a hierarchized list, from the top achiever to the bottom.

Consent was enlisted not just to embodied docility, but to a means of measuring 'cleverness' that will be used to produce girls as differently able students for the next four years of their school lives and beyond. Through giving (or being positioned as if they had given) their consent to this examination process, the girls implicitly consent to their insertion into discourses of rational and incremental development towards (differential) mastery of the curriculum. Walkerdine and Lucey (1989) present such processes as part of the regulative fantasy of liberal democracy.

The democratic fantasy holds that power gained through reason rather than coercion is good, reasonable power. In psycho-educational discourse this is the power gained from discovery and proper conceptualisation. It is the mastery of reasoning . . . This transformation of power into mastery understands it as a possession and therefore implicitly denies it as regulative at all. Right at the heart of it is another fantasy, of omnipotent mastery over a universe which acts according to the laws of reason.

(Walkerdine and Lucey 1989: 108)

The CATs examination room produced girls as consenting subjects in consenting bodies in relation to a given discursive field. That discursive field is one in which the organizing narratives of reason and mastery predominate, and in which learning is understood as a technicist enterprise. The CATs tests are part of a process in which students' consent is secured for a system that Hamilton (1998: 13) has called 'eugenic because it privileges the desirable and seeks to eliminate the negative'. The students who have been identified as having SEN will occupy the lowest positions on the chart the CATs tests will produce. At best, the tests will produce these girls as needy of help and intervention, in order that their 'special needs' may be fixed. At worst, the tests will produce them as the failures that SATs tests have already shown them to be, destined for failing grades at GCSE and a lifetime of poorly paid jobs or no jobs at all.

Feel the fear and do it anyway

The promised deferred gratification of exam grades that count as success are not the only way in which students' consent to the examination process is secured. Fear plays a crucial role in securing that consent. Before they even arrive at Newbrook, most girls know that the success or otherwise of their schooling will be measured and officially signed, sealed and delivered through the public examination process.

Meera: Um, my um brother and sister right, um, this was in Year 6, before I done my SATs, my brother and sister goes, 'those SATs don't matter as much as in Year 9 SATs and your GCSEs' and they said loads of stories, only I can't remember any of them.

Ambrine: I can remember one, if you don't do your GCSEs, if you don't do well in your GCSEs you have to start back in Year 7 again, I was like, 'Oh no', like you'd be so old, and I thought I'd have to start back in Year 7 again, and I was like [sigh] and my sister's like 'You should start revising now' and I was like suicidal, 'cos you've got all this homework to worry about, and now you've got to start worrying about your GCSEs in Year 7.

Meera: And that's when you start losing your hair.

Ambrine: My sister's losing her hair.

Meera: Yeah, that's from stress in the mocks, it was like gunks of it all coming out, not loads but, it was like she was losing her hair.

SB: That's awful.

Ambrine: *My* sister's *worried* worried.

(Interview 22/3/00)

Most of the Year 7 students can tell horror stories about the stress and worry generated by public exams. Entry to secondary school seems to make the distant prospect of GCSEs much more real. Twice a year there is a period of several weeks in which the school hall is arranged for examinations, when students are forbidden to walk past it, and when notices around the corridors remind everyone that they must be quiet because 'GCSE exams are in progress'. For the Year 7 students, it appears to be the process that generates anxiety, not the potential outcomes. They compare the prospect of GCSEs with the SATs they have already taken. And, like teachers discussing an Ofsted inspection, they agree that the build-up to the surveillant moment is much worse than the moment of examination itself.

> *Ambrine*: It's like. They was gonna be so hard, it's like they was something to do with secondary school, like. It wasn't that hard, it was sort of hard. It's like in Year 6 you go over more, but then when actual SATs comes they're just easy.
>
> *Meera*: In Year 4 – this is something to do with SATs – in Year 4, I mean in Year 3, I thought that when you do your SATs it was, it was like whether you pass or you don't pass, and if you don't pass you have to retake Year 6.
>
> *Ambrine*: I was really scared of my SATs, you know.
>
> *Meera*: And, um, in Year 5, my Year 5 teacher, whatever we do, she's like '*In* your SATs you can't do that, *in* your SATs you have to do that, *in* your SATs you have to remember that,' and that went on from Year 5 to Year 6, and that was really annoying.
>
> (Interview 22/3/00)

The production of fear in relation to the examination process should not be underestimated. On the face of it, Newbrook's public examinations appear to function as a means of co-optation, in which students' consent is secured through a process of recasting their enforced compliance as voluntarily given. In this way, the fiction that students consent to the examination process and its outcomes can function as truth (Foucault 1980; Walkerdine 1990). But the centrality of fear in the process of ensuring compliance might suggest another reading: that exams are functioning as a means of coercion as much as of co-optation. This may be part of the reason why 'special needs students', who appear to have so little to gain in a system that will officially position them as deficient, apparently collude with, and consent to it.

What counts as success?

The examination system at Newbrook produces young women who, by and large, consent to a process that sorts them out according to dominant notions of success. Emblematic of that success is a 'C' grade in the GCSE exams. The fiction contained within school improvement literature is that everyone can, with hard work and good teaching, aspire to membership of the five A*–C elite. Newbrook aims to enable 60 per cent of its Year 11 cohort to obtain five A*–C grades. This leaves 40 per cent who are, implicitly, the failures of the system. And among those will be the 'special needs students', some of whom will obtain, at best, a few F and G grades.

Two distinct discourses are deployed by staff in relation to the construction of this group as potential examination failures. The first of these is the dominant discourse, in which these students' examination 'performance' is judged to be substandard. Strenuous efforts are made to help students raise their grades, since, within this discourse, the higher the grade the better. Teachers deploying this discourse make constant reference to the importance of exam results for future success. It tends to be a discourse that distances itself from the past, and within it, students can aspire to dominant versions of success despite whatever they may have done before. However, a second discourse can be invoked in relation to many 'special needs students', as a kind of consolation prize. This discourse is a cousin of the self-esteem discourse: it produces students as inherently unable to aspire to reach the prestigious grades that count as success for the majority, and values their individual progress, even though such non-normative progress cannot be recognized within dominant notions of 'success'. Teachers deploying this discourse typically refer to a student's progress by comparing her present achievements with those of her past. It tends to be a discourse that does not take the future into account. Perhaps this is because, in the discursive field constructed by exam performance, bright futures cannot be imaginable for those students whose performance does not reach 'expected levels'.

It is worth citing again the observation of Kenway et al. (1997: 35) that, 'Teachers invariably walk a tightrope between encouraging students to succeed in conventional terms and encouraging them to succeed differently – always with the knowledge that difference seldom wins out over dominance'. In practice, the two discourses – of dominant versions of success and of individual progress – have to coexist side-by-side. It is an uneasy match, and one that opens a contradictory space.

> Two young women I don't know arrive in the room with their maths things. We all know they are here because they did so badly in the mocks that they can't now be entered for the Intermediate paper. Some of the young women commiserate loudly, mostly with irony, somewhere between teasing these new arrivals for their poor performance and sympathy for their plight. Don tries to retrieve the situation, saying there is nothing wrong with being in the Graduated Assessment [lowest] group. They are the girls who need to 'take things more slowly', not girls who are destined for failure. Asma asks why, then, they will be taking the Foundation paper, which has a ceiling of a 'D'. Don tells them it is merely a first step, and they can retake maths to a higher level in college. He then goes on to congratulate Almaas who has done well enough to move up (if she wants) to the Foundation Assessment group – a move that could mean, if she does well enough, that she will able to take the Intermediate paper, and possibly get a 'C'. The young women scream their congratulations at her. Almaas looks undecided. She risks losing her position as the 'clever one' in a group in which she does not have to

work particularly hard to keep up, and in which her friends contrive to have fun through subverting the teacher's agenda whenever possible. She stands to gain a position as a struggling student in a class working at a level that will challenge her to keep up, and in which hard work will have to be the order of the day. She is not the only one who is confused. I am wondering about Don's message to the class. If there is no disgrace, and no attached connotation of deficit in being part of this 'slower learning' group, why congratulate Almaas for deserving to escape from it?

(Fieldnotes 28/1/00)

Most of the time, in the Graduated Assessment maths group, the consolation discourse around exam performance is allowed to predominate. Students in this group will, by definition, not be able to aspire to the 'C' grade benchmark. So, most of the time, the dominant discourse of exam performance must be ignored, and the consolation discourse of individual progress must be deployed in order to provide these young women with a reason for continuing to work. But the arrival of two demoted students, and the possible promotion of Almaas, bring the dominant discourse into the room.

In its wake come some contradictory understandings of what the young women and the teacher are doing in that room. Are they preparing for an imagined future in which the dominant version of examination success is within their reach, albeit a little later than they might like? Are they working with reference to a past against which their individual incremental progress can be measured and celebrated, even though the outside world will never value it? What does membership of this group mean when escape from it is presented as a cause for celebration? Almaas's ambivalence about whether to move up (which was later resolved in the decision to stay where she was) contained within it the profound confusion associated with this particular contradiction.

Almaas: I don't know really, I don't know if I want to move up.
SB: What is it you're unsure of?
Almaas: All my friends are in this group. And Mr Tudor helps you when you don't know something. In the Foundation group, you can't muck about because if you miss something Ms Williams won't tell you later. I don't think I'd be able to do the work, and then I wouldn't get any grade for my GCSE. At least in this group, Sir says I'm good and I can get a 'D'. Which is better than no grade at all, which I might get in Intermediate.
SB: You don't think you could do well in Ms Williams's group?
Almaas: The good thing about going up is I could get a 'C' maybe. But I don't think I could, because in Ms Williams's group, you've got to be one of the best ones to go in for Intermediate. Some of them do Foundation, you don't automatically do Intermediate when you're in that group. I wouldn't be one of the ones who did Intermediate, not when I've been in Mr Tudor's all this time. So I'd have all the extra work for no reason. There's no

point. I can stay in this group and have a good time with my friends and still get the same grade, so there's no point in moving up.

SB: Sounds like you've decided to stay in this group? Is that right?

Almaas: I don't know. In some ways it would be good to be in Ms Williams's. At least people think you might be going to get a 'C'. You might be going to do Intermediate. But I don't think I'm good enough for Intermediate, no matter what class I'm in.

(Reconstructed from notes 28/1/00)

Caught in the contradiction, Almaas cannot let go of the possibility of an Intermediate exam entry, and of a 'C' grade, even though she (realistically I think) appears to see it as highly unlikely. In making her overall decision about whether to stay in her present group or move up to the next, she has to take the microcultural consequences into account. Present experience as well as future success have to be weighed against each other, but since they are measured in different currencies, this is far from easy. On the one hand is a group in which she can have some fun alongside her friends, but in which the 'C' grade is necessarily out of reach. In the Graduated Assessment group, her performance can be judged successful, even if only according to the consolation discourse. On the other hand is a group in which she thinks she will not have fun, but in which the possibility, however remote, of a 'C' grade can remain intact, and in which the outside world will perceive her as potentially performing according to 'expected standards'. However, in the Foundation Assessment group, Almaas's performance can be judged as successful only if she succeeds in dominant terms, as the consolation discourse is not available to this group of aspiring 'C' students. Finally, Almaas decided that the possibility of success in dominant terms was too remote, and that she was not prepared to risk her success within the consolation discourse in favour of almost certain failure within the dominant one.

The possibility of transfer into a higher maths group is not one that need concern most of the 'special needs students'. Most of them will not be offered that option: they are destined to remain in the Graduated Assessment group until the day they leave school. In their accounts, the Year 11 'special needs students' are often well able to distinguish the two discourses around exam success. Although many of the young women have come to realise that examination success within the terms of the dominant discourse is unavailable to them, they mostly continue to aspire, or continue wanting to aspire, to dominant versions of success. They recognize these versions as the ones that really count.

Hafsa: C – it's – it's a grade where you can pass, really. It's a grade where you can get certain jobs if you get a C, you can get certain jobs. But with a D you've got – you can't – you can get *certain* jobs, depending on your other grades, you know, how you do well in science and English and maths – these three subjects are really, really important and any, like, I don't think D is a great, is a great

show of achievement, like you can only get that in Foundation.
You can't get higher than that and I don't think that's right,
I think you should get a C – erm – because if you don't do that in
science – if I don't get a C, because I can get that, I've been
entered in foundation. If I get a C, right, that's great, I'd be really,
really surprised if I can get a C and, you know . . .

SB: So, what does C count for that D doesn't?

Hafsa: Erm – well D [pause] I don't know really, I think C's
a higher grade and a D? Well, I personally think it's a low
grade – erm – there's a lot of difference in between them – a lot
of difference. Well like – erm – it's difficult – erm, well personally
I wouldn't feel really, really great if I got a D. I think C makes
you proud, it makes you proud of like you're getting something,
and C, well, like I think it's my ambition, my ambition is to get
a C. I dunno – 'cause it's like basically when you're at secondary
school and you've learnt the basics and you're going to college,
and you, you, you, when you get to college, there's no point
retaking it, is there? Because if I don't have that C in, in my
secondary school, all the work that I've done, and everything, If
I don't get a C, there's no point me doing a retake in year – erm
– in college, I dunno. 'Cause she – 'cause my cousin she got a D.
And she retook it again and she got D again. So I think that
you've gotta have the basic knowledge. You've gotta work hard
to get – I think that they should – they should change the system
and make it like so you can get a C in foundation.

(Interview 24/11/00)

Complex identity work is going on here. For Hafsa, who is likely to get 'E'
and 'F' grades at best, this investment in dominant versions of success is as
worrying as it is understandable. In some ways, she is refusing to be seduced
into one of the commonest plot lines of the success-as-individual-progress
story. She does not see successive retakes at college as a solution to the
problem of low exam grades at school, and thus refuses the construction of
herself as someone who is learning slowly, but will get there in the end if
only she has enough patience. She wants the good grades now, in Year 11,
and is not prepared to believe that she will get them in college if she fails to
get them while at school. In her account, she is referring to the future, not to
the past, and to her projected opportunities once she has left school. The
backward-looking consolation version of success, which celebrates students'
achievements in comparison with those of their past, is of no use to her in
the project of envisaging a future. The forward-looking dominant version of
success *is* potentially of use to her in this project, but she is working with the
knowledge that this version does not readily make a successful position
available to her.

Hafsa is a 'sweet little girl' and her sense of herself draws heavily on her
position as a recipient of learning support. One of the explicit rationales of
learning support is that it exists to remediate and to 'fix'. Although this

rationale is contradicted by many of the practices of learning support, it remains intact as a way of legitimizing the identification of 'special needs students'. Hafsa is taking up one of these explicit legitimators: that 'special needs students' can have their needs 'met' and can thus be enabled to perform according to national 'expectations' in public exams. To produce herself as 'sweet little girl' she must, to some extent, take up the promise that she can be 'fixed'. For Hafsa, believing in the promise means investing in the possibility of examination success, despite considerable evidence in practice exams that this version of success is not available to her. Continued belief in the prospect of exam success also means continued belief in the promise that hard work at school will bring that success and the material rewards associated with it. Hafsa does not have the incentive nor the microcultural location that will enable her to produce herself as oppositional, so she is invested in remaining positive towards the schooling enterprise. And in Year 11, a positive orientation towards school necessarily means an investment of some kind in the dominant story in which hard work leads to examination success which leads to material reward.

Perhaps the last word on the subject should go to Chantelle. As a 'big bad girl', her orientation towards exam success is much less stable than Hafsa's. Where Hafsa will make every effort to read herself into the dominant discourse of examination success, Chantelle has less to lose in exposing the contradiction between the two discourses: between whether it is normative success or individual progress that really counts. In exposing this contradiction, the consolation discourse is likewise exposed as a deficit discourse, only making sense as the poor relation of the dominant discourse, however benevolent the intentions of the teachers who deploy it. Following a science test in which her mark of 12 per cent – an outright failure in the terms of the dominant discourse – was read back to her as a measure of individual improvement, her response was to name and describe the contradiction. The well-intentioned attempts by the class teacher (and by me) to construct a measure of success for her could not work.

Chantelle does not want to go so far as to reject the educational enterprise itself, but within the discursive field of the examination, there do not appear to be any readings that would be both available and desirable to her. She cannot read herself into the dominant discourse: to do this she would have to suspend disbelief in her examination results to date, and she would be obliged to take up the offers of learning support that so threaten her construction of herself as 'big bad girl'. And she will not read herself into the deficit discourse of success, because she knows that, in the end, it does not count, and will bring few rewards, material or otherwise. She wants what appears to be available to so many of her friends: a successful position in the dominant discourse, which would bring the prospect of examination success without the loss of her anti-teacher microcultural status. It is as if the two discourses around examination success pull away from each other, and the contradictory space between them is a void, with nothing positive to fill it. The obvious candidate to fill this empty space is the word 'failure'. But, as I argued in Chapter 4, this is a word that has been made unsayable, and so the space remains empty. For Chantelle, this void seems to have become part of her sense of herself.

> *Chantelle*: And you know what Miss? You know what, tape recorder? What'm I gonna get in the mocks? You've guessed it. Zero. *Zero*. Forget threes. We're talking zero. I've been here five years, and we're talking zero.
>
> *SB*: Chantelle, I don't really know what to say to you. Um – let me just think a minute . . . [pause] – I think it's that I don't know – I mean I'm not sure I know what you mean when you say we're talking zero. I mean, I've seen your exam results – some of your test results – and I don't – you didn't actually *get* any zeros. I mean, I know the results weren't good, but I don't think – I don't remember any actual zeros. So I'm kind of wondering what you mean. Yeah?
>
> *Chantelle*: . . . Well, you can call it 12 per cent, yeah, you can call it 12 per cent if you like, but inside, it's a big fat zero. I mean 12 per cent – it's a zero, whatever you call it, it's a zero, and that's what's inside of me. Zero, zero, zero.
>
> (Interview 10/11/00)

This chapter has considered the examination as a site of the production of intellectual subordination. It has looked at the examination as event and as discursive production, in relation to prevailing policy, micropolitics and microcultural practices. I have suggested that the examination plays a crucial part in securing students' consent for the processes of intellectual subordination, winning from them their consent to a dominant version of success from which they have little to gain. This chapter has also considered the examination process as productive of two distinct versions of academic success. In the dominant, future-oriented model, students are positioned as desirous of examination success according to normative benchmarks because of the future opportunities successful performance opens up. In the consolation version, students are encouraged to look back and compare present achievements with those of the past. This version may appear to have something to offer, and to be kinder and more humane than the dominant one, but it works to inscribe students as needy, and has nothing to say to them about the futures to which they can aspire. It is a deficit discourse of academic success, and it works both to close down certain options for certain students, and to reinscribe the borders of 'special educational needs'.

Note

1 Bentham designed the Panopticon as the ultimate prison, in which the warders occupied a central tower from which prisoners were perpetually visible in their cells. This enabled a perpetual surveillance that regulated prisoners through their awareness that they were always potentially visible, though they would never know whether or not they were actually being watched. Foucault's theory of panopticism is derived from this.

CHAPTER EIGHT

'Success' and the autistic spectrum: the 'really disabled discourse'

The dominant discourse of success at Newbrook constructs the subject 'student' according to her curricular/examination performance measured against national norms. The consolation discourse constructs the subject 'student' according to her performance measured against her previous personal record. Both discourses can be understood as mainstream: they operate to define 'normal' success, and to make contingent, consolation versions of success available to those who find themselves in and around the borders at which 'learning difficulties' blend into 'normality'.

This chapter looks in detail at the experiences of two autistic students,[1] Cassandra and Josie, and at the discourses through which they are produced as distinct versions of the subject 'special needs student'. Their experiences indicate the existence of a third, 'really disabled' version of success which is deployed in relation to a small number of students at Newbrook. This version of success is located within the charity/tragedy discourse widely written about in disability theory, which positions disabled people as the objectified recipients of pity. In this chapter, I explore how and why Cassandra's placement at Newbrook could be narrated as 'successful' while Josie's could not.

Disability and success: the third discourse

Increasingly, Newbrook is providing for groups of students who have not, in the past, been considered able to benefit from mainstream schooling. Cassandra and Josie are amongst this group. A distinct discourse of success operates in relation to these students. This discourse apparently floats free of academic progress. It is a discourse that simultaneously *allows* students to be different by valuing non-academic (or non-credentialized) success, and *reinscribes* them as different by exempting them from requirements relating to academic performance. This discourse produces what is in many ways the most progressive and humane of the formal versions of success in circulation at Newbrook. But because it is applied only in relation to a group who have historically been marginalized and oppressed, one of its functions is to police the borders of a binary division between 'able' and 'disabled'.

Cassandra and Josie did not have an assured place within this third discourse. As students with an autistic spectrum disorder, and not an intellectual impairment, there was room for contestation over whether they could be regarded as *really* disabled. Their placements at Newbrook were closely tied to perceptions of success. If Cassandra and Josie made progress according to the 'really disabled' discourse, then the school and, in particular, its learning support department, would be able also to claim success. If they did not make progress, then the school would be understood as failing. There were, accordingly, very intense feelings about these students and their success, and many members of staff worked long and hard to support both of them. In particular, elaborate individual education plans were written for Josie and Cassandra. SMART targets were put in place to try to ensure their progress according to a rational linear model. But it is hard, and, I would suggest, inappropriate, to attempt to evaluate the success of autistic students in a wholly rational and linear way.

Cassandra: a successful placement?

Cassandra is a young woman from a Greek Cypriot family. Her primary schooling and her first year of secondary schooling took place in a local special school. She entered Newbrook in Year 8 (at the age of 12), and remained there until the end of her compulsory schooling. I first met Cassandra when I began working at Newbrook, during her second term in Year 9. I very much enjoyed working with her, and was considerably invested in her success and her continuing placement at Newbrook. I had previous experience with autistic young people, having earlier in my career worked at a special school in which autistic children and young people were a large minority group. They had been the children and young people in whom I was most interested, and with whom I was perceived (and perceived myself) to have the most 'success'. Within days of my arrival at Newbrook, I had read the 'autistic signpost' (Jordan and Jones 1999) and was responding to Cassandra accordingly, as someone I would like and be able to work with productively. My reading of Cassandra is thus produced through a relationship in which I was more closely involved in her 'progress' and more invested in her 'success' than was perhaps the case with most of the other participants in this study.

Cassandra is a gentle, timid young woman. Despite being tall and well-built, she tends to be positioned as a 'sweet little girl'. She 'does autism' in ways that are likely to be read as endearing and charming, and are likely to evoke tender feelings in other people. The aspects of social life that often frighten and bewilder autistic people – such as changes in routine, apparent rule-breaking and perceived unkindness – frighten and bewilder Cassandra. Her response is to cry quietly, with her fists jammed into her eyes in the attempt to stop tears running down her cheeks. Like many autistic people, she speaks in an untypical and stylized way. In her case, it has meant adopting a high-pitched, childlike voice, together with frequent reversals of noun and verb order. She has a fixated interest in cartoons, and, during her time in Year 11, would spend entire lessons drawing Pokemon characters. She was thus inscribed into traditional discourses of hyperfemininity in which she could be read as a vulnerable and rather charming 'child' in need of help.

> I go to lunch. There's a huge crowd in the corridor, which I fully intend to ignore by going through the hall. But Cassandra comes up to me, with her mouth turned down at the corners. She tells me she is 'feeling sad'. I ask why. She can't get to the till to buy her lunch token. She asks if I will take her with me. I do. The crowd of Year 11 girls is almost impenetrable. There is no way Cassandra could have managed it on her own. We hold hands, and I make my way through, Cassandra behind me. I'm not sufficiently high in status for the young women of the crowd to melt away as I pass through. But I'm high enough for individuals to allow me to push them aside. And Cassandra is 'special' enough for them not to protest at her coming with me. I ask someone why the crowding is so bad. There are new staff on duty, who haven't got the hang of the system. We get to the till. There is a little corner behind it, where I install Cassandra while I buy her token. Again, there are no protests from any of the waiting young women in front of whom we have pushed. I don't think they would have been nice enough to let Cassandra through on her own, but Cassandra, who they know is vulnerable, plus me in my authorized position as her protector, evoke their 'niceness' sufficiently to allow us this special privilege. Cassandra rewards me with one of her beaming smiles.
>
> (Fieldnotes 21/3/00)

In many ways, this extract can be read as an instance of very good practice around disability. Cassandra has been correctly read as 'different', and because of that difference, we 'normies' (Institute for the Study of the Neuro-Typical 1999) have modified our own actions so that the environment becomes more accommodating and less disabling for Cassandra. The situation (of the corridor being unwontedly crowded and a lunch token not being as readily available as expected) is one that could reasonably be expected to threaten the composure of an autistic student. The fact that Cassandra seeks help and verbalizes her distress, rather than panicking, speaks well for the progress she has made at Newbrook, and for the work that has been done with her. The other students' contingent willingness to make way for Cassandra indicates both their understanding of her difference, and points to the work that still needs to be done if they are to recognize and act on this understanding without prompting. While there is undoubtedly much truth in this reading, there is more besides.

The recognition of Cassandra as different in this instance goes beyond the notion of 'any old difference' to imply a binary. There are many students in the school who find jostling the crowds unpleasant, and would prefer to be exempted from it. But they are not deemed worthy of special recognition. Somehow, Cassandra has crossed the line between 'different but normal' and 'really different'. And it is perhaps impossible for that recognition not to contain remnants of the charity/tragedy discourse, when what we are asking the other students to do is to suspend parts of their usual struggle for power in order to show special consideration for Cassandra. It is certainly possible, and very attractive, to understand the students in this extract as being 'nice'. Their actions do contain an element of just that: unselfish niceness, and the ability to consider someone else's needs. But doing 'nice girl' involves more in the way of identity work than is suggested by unselfishness, however problematized that notion becomes (Francis 1997, 1998). It also involves, in this instance, a measure of distancing oneself from the identification with disability. Cassandra is not just positioned as different: she is positioned as 'not-like-us', and such an act is charged with power.

Many of the girls in the crowd that day had their own investments in doing 'bad girl', or at least in distancing themselves from the sensible/selfless model of young woman student. Such young women are unlikely to be afraid of me, so it is highly unlikely that they made way for Cassandra out of fear of authority. What, then, was going on? In the student microcultures that operate in Year 11, it has become unacceptable for anyone to be seen deliberately to frighten Cassandra. She has become so established as 'not-like-us' that acts of meanness towards her have been ruled out. This could be said to have the much-desired effect of helping all members of the school community to understand and value diversity, to accept people for who they are, and to act towards them accordingly. And Cassandra is not just *positioned* as vulnerable: she *is* genuinely vulnerable, inasmuch as the social world operates according to rules that do not make sense to her. But the effect seems to be to reify the students' (and adults') notions of what counts as *real* disability. Far from enabling everyone to benefit from a wider notion of what constitutes personhood, the discursive field that constitutes Cassandra as 'not-like-us' appears to demand that 'normal' students distance themselves from her. This is especially true of the Year 11 'special needs students', who are concerned to mark out the distinctions that constitute Cassandra as 'not-like-us'.

> *Suleika*: Like, Ms Russell she's never helping people, and Cassandra, I don't want to be mean, don't get this wrong, but Cassandra she can't do nothing if Miss doesn't tell her what to do, and Miss never goes over to her, and Cassandra, like every lesson, she's just sitting there [pause]. She's just sitting there, and she

isn't doing nothing, and Miss doesn't even notice, she doesn't
even see . . . And like Cassandra as well, she's just sitting there,
and, don't get this wrong, it's like some people they say, 'Oh,
it's only Cassandra, it doesn't matter, she won't get no GCSE's anyway'. But that ain't fair, and when it was Ms Corby, Ms Corby
was all the time, 'Are you OK Cassandra, do you understand,
Cassandra?' and Cassandra she could do it, like she wasn't just
sitting there, and you should've seen this – what did she make
– what was it?

Amina: Oh, I know, I remember that – it was like this thing for a
uniform, like a coat what you wear and it hasn't got no sleeves,
and it was all red –

Suleika: Yeah, right, and she made this coat thing, and it was really
good, you should've seen it Miss, it wasn't like it was just good
for Cassandra, it was really *good* –

Amina: And now, she don't make nothing no more, and she – erm – it's
not like it's her fault, she doesn't understand what to do, how
can *she* understand what to do? And Miss she doesn't even
care, just as long as Cassandra's not bothering her, she doesn't
even care if she knows what to do, and I don't think that ain't
even fair.

(Interview 9/12/99)

It appears that Suleika and Amina's principal intention in this extract is
to demonstrate what they see as the inadequacy of a new teacher. Within
the discursive field that constitutes meanness to Cassandra as unacceptable,
this teacher's actions have crossed the boundary between ordinary, run-
of-the-mill teacherly neglect, and absolute inadmissibility. The two young
women are illustrating their own grievances against the teacher by referring
to Cassandra. This teacher has often left them 'just sitting there', and they
resent this. But the teacher's actions in leaving Cassandra 'just sitting there'
are qualitatively different in their account. It is reprehensible of the teacher
to leave Suleika and Amina 'just sitting there'. But for her to leave Cassandra
in this way is, in their account, an act of cruelty. The depth to which this
teacher has apparently sunk is illustrated by her lack of caring towards this
most vulnerable of their classmates.

What Suleika and Amina leave out of their account is that Cassandra
herself always enjoys being left alone: she appears to be at her happiest when
she is allowed to draw cartoon characters in her pocket notebook. But they
are concerned to monitor her learning. They adopt a caretaking role in
relation to Cassandra, in which they can express outrage at the teacher's
neglect of her curricular progress. They are able to make judgements about
that progress themselves: Suleika's surprise at Cassandra making a garment
that was really *good* (as opposed to just good for Cassandra) contained an
element of motherly pride as well as surprised approbation of both Cassandra and the facilitating ex-teacher. This effectively establishes a distance between themselves and her. As they perform this piece of identity work, they

are reinscribing the borders between themselves and the 'really different' Cassandra.

It is not only the students who customarily position Cassandra as 'really different'. Indeed, the textiles teacher incurred Suleika's and Amina's disapproval for her failure to recognize Cassandra's difference and give her special treatment. The public setting of the examination hall is a place where teachers (including myself) can be seen to treat Cassandra very differently from her peers.

> In the chemistry exam . . . Cassandra is fiddling with her hair. I check she has carried out the starting instructions, which she has. I leave her. Madge draws my attention to the fact that she is still fiddling with her hair. I know perfectly well that she will continue to fiddle until her hair is done to her satisfaction, but I feel obliged to be seen to be talking to her again, as if I can make her start the chemistry paper . . . Cassandra finishes in about half an hour. She puts her pen down, and leans back in her chair, looking pleased with herself. Martin comes over to me, and asks if we should be doing anything about her. I know there's nothing we can do, but I agree to go over and have a word. As if I have a privileged expertise that enables me to talk to Cassandra, and that stops any other member of staff from doing so. Cassandra is pleased with the work she has done, and has no intention of doing any more. She knows it is the rule that she remains in the hall until the end, and is not bothered by it. I give her some paper to draw on. It will give her something to do, and keep the other teachers' attention away from her, so long as they don't look too closely.
>
> (Fieldnotes 6/12/99)

Cassandra's atypical way of doing the exam causes consternation among the teachers in the hall. There is a limited repertoire of ways in which to do student during an examination, and Cassandra's activities do not fall within this agreed repertoire. If any other student was seen to play with her hair, or to finish the paper in less than half of the time available, any one of the invigilating teachers would have intervened. But the teachers are reluctant to intervene directly with Cassandra, and, I think, with good reason. She has a well-known reputation for becoming distressed when faced with demands that do not make sense to her. None of the teachers wants to distress her, and risk an upsetting scene in the middle of an exam. Neither do they want to make (or be seen to make) her cry. So they bring their concerns to me, as someone who might be expected to know how to make those demands in a way that Cassandra will understand, or who might be able to reassure them that Cassandra is acting quite normally 'for Cassandra'. In reality, I do not know how to make the demands of an exam make sense to Cassandra, and I do not think it is possible to do so. But I want to be seen to be 'doing something' to remedy the situation, both in terms of my own credibility, and to 'protect' Cassandra from possible interventions. Like the students in the corridor, I both modified my actions to take account of Cassandra's difference, and effectively kept intact a reified notion of that difference as 'really different'.

Overall, Cassandra's placement in Newbrook as its first ever autistic student has been deemed to be 'successful'. The dominant stories that are told about Cassandra cast her as someone who has made progress at the school, and whose needs Newbrook has been able to meet. Where concerns are raised, they are in relation to her academic progress, but this is usually judged to be of secondary importance to the opportunities she has had to 'socialize' with mainstream students.

> I try to start Cassandra off, but she's busy sorting money out, and I know she will insist on finishing this task before she will consent to do any of the past paper. I would stay and talk to her about what she's doing, but it's hard when others are clamouring for help. In this class, there's always someone waiting, stuck, and asking for attention . . . I go around, always meaning to come back to Cassandra, but not managing it . . . By the end of the lesson, I still haven't managed to return to Cassandra, and, typically, she has done none of the past paper. I feel the need to be apologetic about this to Don. He replies that Cassandra is able to do the work, and, if he sits next to her, she gets it done. I apologize again. That's what I'm supposed to be doing in these lessons. I have a very unpolitically correct thought. I don't think the abstractions of maths GCSE can be made accessible to Cassandra. In which case, why do we make her go through the motions? Why can't she do something that we *can* make accessible? But that goes against many of the principles of inclusion and the National Curriculum, which is supposed to be about equal entitlement. Equal provision doesn't – and shouldn't – mean identical provision. But where does differentiation blend into low expectations, blend into some people being given an inferior, watered-down version of what others are getting?
>
> (Fieldnotes 16/2/00)

Counter-hegemonic stories about the ways in which conventional academic success cannot be made available to Cassandra are seldom told, except, as here, in the privacy of the classroom, between two unpromoted teachers. Don's insistence that Cassandra can do the work only if a teacher sits with her not only positions me as failing in my duty, but also positions Cassandra as incapable of the meaning-making that will lead to independent work. The tacit understanding that what goes on within the formal world of the curriculum is meaningless for Cassandra is an understanding that cannot make it into any of the public stories about her. It would challenge too many of the basic foundations upon which the notion of progression according to an equally available curriculum is constructed.

The maths curriculum (like most of Newbrook's curricula) does not appear to make sense to Cassandra. She cannot make the linear progress which is the only kind of progress that a linear, developmentally based curriculum can make admissible. For Cassandra, yet another discourse about success has to be invoked. Where the dominant version is about GCSE A*–C grades, and the SEN version is about individual (curricular) progress at individual rates, another discourse has to be deployed in relation to Cassandra. Her 'special needs' must be differentiated from those of the other 'special needs students' and the discourse of individual progress similarly differentiated. Where ordinary 'special needs students' are recuperated into a discourse in which they do make academic progress, but supposedly not as fast as the dominant majority group, Cassandra does not have to be seen to make individual curricular progress. For her, it is enough to succeed on what one colleague called 'the social side'.

> *Sarah*: I haven't given up on Cassandra, but I've more, I've more or less taking her, you know, trying to teach her social rather than science now, because she understands, she's very limited as understanding's very limited but I think it's important that she gets relationships with adults. So I talk to her, and when she's doing a practical, I try and pair her up with someone who knows what they're doing, so that they can guide her, but I go over and I talk to her, and I ask her how she's doing. So I try and be a little bit more social with Cassandra. But it was really nice like when you came in and you did the experiment with her. 'Cause it took the pressure off – that class, there's just so many that need help, it took the pressure off me a bit, and let me go off with the other, the other students. 'Cause she is a *real* – she *is* someone who needs, who needs [pause], well she really needs, she really needs somebody following her round the school, basically, in every lesson sort of.
>
> (Interview 6/4/00)

Again, this teacher's position can be understood as modification of practice to take account of and value diversity. But she is also positioning Cassandra as someone who, unlike the other 'special needs students', is *really* different. In some ways, the discourses deployed in relation to Cassandra are those I would want to support. Sarah has decided that relationships are an arena in which Cassandra can be helped to make meaningful progress, and in which she can be given an enjoyably successful experience. I would want to agree with her in this analysis. I would want to deploy differing notions of what could count as success, and not depend on the dominant curricular-success-is-the-only-recognizable-success notion.

But the problem is that, of all the students in Year 11, Cassandra is the only one in relation to whom this more flexible account of what counts as success is applied. Cassandra's presence does not appear to enable different versions of success to circulate to the benefit of all students. To the contrary, her presence establishes the borders of normal success and of normality and, in many ways, strengthens and preserves them. Newbrook has to understand Cassandra as successful, because she is in many ways a diligent and hardworking student: or, at least, she is one who does not act in ways that can be configured as challenging. An earnest, well-meaning student has to be read as successful in order to preserve the story that hard work brings success. But the version of success that is ascribed to Cassandra both allows her difference, and at the same time reinscribes her distance from the norm.

Josie: an unsuccessful placement?

Josie is a girl from an African Caribbean family. She entered Newbrook at the start of Year 7 with a long history behind her of what had, for a long time, been considered as very difficult behaviour and attributed to family problems: class and race, as well as disability were key determinants of the stories that could be told of her as a young child. It was not until she was 9 years old and in Year 5 that she was identified as autistic. Her primary education had been spent in a number of mainstream schools, at which she never remained long enough for a thorough investigation of her difficulties to be carried out. Since moving in with her aunt, her home life has been more settled.

When Josie entered Newbrook, very little information was given to staff about her disability. Her statutory statement of SEN had not been completed, and she arrived with what is known as a 'note in lieu': an interim device intended to give some background information but which has no standing in law. Her completed statement was received during the course of her first term. The head of the pastoral faculty, Pam, initially decided not to divulge the contents of the 'note in lieu' to staff, in order to give Josie a fresh start.

Josie is a big, boisterous and energetic girl. She seldom sits still for more than a few moments. The aspects of the social world that typically frighten and bewilder autistic people frighten and bewilder Josie, in the way they do Cassandra. But where Cassandra responds in ways that evoke 'maternal' feelings in those around her, Josie panics and tends to lash out. She usually shouts, often using abusive language, and sometimes hits and kicks, or runs away. Although she is not intentionally aggressive, her actions tend to be perceived as threatening, and are more likely to evoke anger than tenderness. Like Cassandra, Josie speaks in a stylized way. She uses the vocabulary and inflection of rap music, which also serves to position her (albeit problematically) within discourses of big, threatening, African Caribbean girl.

Within a few days of the beginning of term, Pam's decision to withhold information about Josie was being questioned. Those members of staff who taught her were astonished that a new Year 7 student could have such a disruptive effect on their classes, at a point in the year when the new intake are customarily at their most subdued. During a learning support meeting early in the term, we were told of Josie's diagnosis, and this information was passed on to the rest of the staff. Heads of faculty were soon involved, as Josie's effect on lessons was such that subject teachers quickly began to refer her to their heads of faculty to take disciplinary action. Josie became the frequent subject of staffroom conversation and formal meetings. About four weeks into the term, I was asked to lead a staff meeting to give information about Asperger Syndrome, and to suggest practical strategies. Later in the year, I was asked to work an additional half-day each week to support her and the teachers who taught her. So, as had happened with Cassandra, I became invested in Josie's success at Newbrook, and my own credibility with my colleagues was linked to my ability to work productively with her.

Students whose effect on classes is often disruptive tend to be identified as having 'emotional and behavioural difficulties' (EBD), or as 'disaffected' and at risk of social exclusion. The dominant official discourse at Newbrook is that EBD students, and those who are disaffected, need to be enabled to become responsible for their own behaviour through positive expectations. These expectations in turn are, so the story goes, reinforced by clear target-setting based on reasoned discussion of their actions. Pam's decision to with-hold information about Josie drew directly on this discourse. Josie was to be allowed to make good at her new school, not hampered by low expectations because of previous 'behavioural' problems. In effect, Pam was initially read-ing her, despite her formal diagnosis, as 'bad, not mad' (Slee 1995). Josie trod a much finer line than Cassandra when it came to being positioned as recognisably disabled. As a big, athletic, African Caribbean girl, she was likely to be read as naughty, not as vulnerable. She towered over most of the Year 7 girls, and over many of the teachers. Her temper tantrums were frightening: although I knew quite well they were the outward sign of panic and not of aggression, I could find myself feeling afraid when they suddenly erupted. Many of the students found her very frightening, and others responded to her with anger, reading an intentionality into her perceived violence and aggression. But perhaps what was most damaging was the day-to-day, unremit-ting sense of profound annoyance and apparent powerlessness which Josie's mode of operation tended to evoke in those around her.

> After break it is humanities. Josie arrives late as usual. She sits down next to me, in her appointed place, but moves her chair as far away from me as possible. The others are already doing their work on their 'Castles' books. Josie hasn't brought hers. I give her a piece of paper, but it is not the kind she wants. She creases it up, and says she cannot use it because it is too creased. She goes to get some more. She biffs people hard on the head as she moves around the class. Most of the girls try to ignore her. A few say 'ow', some cringe, and Fredra whirls around as if to hit back, then thinks better of it. Josie returns with some paper. She does not want to do anything related to castles. She wants to draw a picture of Marie. I try to persuade her to copy a castles picture. She makes four false starts, each time crumpling the piece of paper. I feel bad about the waste. She decides she hasn't got the right colours, and grabs Marie's felt-tips. Marie tries to take them back, but Josie at first holds onto them, then throws them to the floor. I give her 'first warning'. The others on the table know what is coming next, and hurriedly put their pens into their pencil cases, to hide them. Marie moves onto another table. Josie takes Juliet's entire pencil case, laughing loudly. She opens it, and throws the pens, one-at-a-time, to the floor. Juliet looks at me in desperation. I tell Josie she must give the pencil case back, or it will be 'second warning'.
>
> (Fieldnotes 31/3/00)

Josie presents much more of a challenge to good governance than Cassandra. Cassandra evokes feelings of tenderness, and members of staff typically find ourselves wanting to protect and look after her. By contrast, members of staff find ourselves drawn into another kind of protection discourse around Josie. We want to protect other students from her. She was simultaneously positioned both as 'in danger' and 'dangerous'. At the same time, most of us felt as confused and unable to understand her mode of making sense of the world as she must feel in relation to ours. This profound confusion and complex discursive positioning led often to an immobilization of other people around her. Her position as someone 'really different' implied that we should treat her with the tenderness that we showed to Cassandra. But this was extraordinarily difficult in the face of her often disturbing effects on virtually everyone with whom she came into contact.

> Josie and I have agreed that I will not sit next to her so long as she gets on with her work, but if she does not get on, then I will sit with her on her table ... When Josie gets really outrageous – wandering around the room, and playing with someone else's pencil case, I go over, and tell her to sit down and go on with her work, which she does. I could probably get away with sitting with her, but I decide not to try it. I rationalize that I might wreck Martin's lesson if I try. But really, I think I'm taking the route of least resistance.
>
> (Fieldnotes 24/3/00)

The governmental procedures that are invoked in relation to 'special needs students' are in many ways hyper-rational ones. The Code of Practice appears to construct a techno-rationalist reality in which struggles of any kind can be objectively qualified and quantified, and a solution found. If only we get the targets right, and the provision right, then the 'special needs student' will make the kind of linear progression that rational, developmental models demand. And so difficulties in learning are measured, mapped and evaluated and remedial measures put in place to alleviate the effects of those difficulties. But those of us in Newbrook who carry out those governmental procedures and operationalize those remedial measures do not do so in a hyper-rational way. We respond, as one person to another, in a relationship that is always changing and developing, and, in Josie's case, is characterized by heightened emotions in response to the difficulties she presents. In deciding that Josie is to receive classroom support, her own preferences have been overridden. This is apparently necessary, as the procedures of identifying her support 'needs' and the means by which those 'needs' are to be met are presented as rational choice-making exercises in which costs and benefits are objectively weighed up. As an autistic student this process does not make sense to her. But does it make sense at all?

> I tell Josie that I am there to help keep her on task, and that if she doesn't want me to sit with her, she must show me she doesn't need me by getting on with her work. I use the example of the first humanities lesson, when I worked mainly with Sunna and Fozia, to illustrate what I'm saying. She doesn't want me in the same room. I say this isn't an option. Now, I'm thinking about all the disability theorists who might

argue that so-called 'normal' children don't have to prove themselves in order to be left alone, so why should someone who's been labelled disabled have to do so? And the orthodoxy (which often is merely lip-service) that young people have choices and options in how their 'special needs' are to be met. In this instance, I'm taking away most of Josie's choices. But how is an autistic student to make those choices, when the nature of her impairment makes the rational, choice-making exercise something of a mystery to her, and one of the things she can't really do?

(Fieldnotes 24/3/00)

Perhaps one of the discourses that needs interrogating here is the one that constructs 'special educational needs' according to a hyper-rational framework. What was really at issue with Josie was not her autism, but the fact that she does autism in a way that renders the network of social relationships around her, including relationships of power, unviable. My first thought, that Josie was unable because of her autism to take part in the rational decision-making process at which she was apparently the centre, told only a fraction of the story. What was going on was much more than a rational decision-making process: it was a complex negotiation, and what (understandably, I think) was at the centre of it was whether the other members of the school community would be able to coexist with Josie.

Versions of rights, entitlements and equal opportunities discourses were used in weighing up the tenability of Josie's placement (Corbett 1998a). These were posited in opposition to each other. On the one hand was placed Josie's entitlement to a place in a mainstream school, and the obligations of the school to provide an environment in which she could learn effectively. On the other hand was placed all the other students' rights to a schooling experience in which their learning would not be disrupted by Josie, and in which they need not fear her constant low-level and occasional high-level abuse. These discourses were very much configured in terms of curricular entitlements, as the other students' right to learn. Newbrook's assessment procedures appeared to rule out discussion of what seemed to me to be at the heart of the difficulties associated with Josie – the realm of the non-rational.

I sit behind the screen to watch what group B are doing. They're arguing. Nell is trying, desperately, to chair, but she can't be heard above the noise. Josie is shouting at the top of her voice, and the others have to shout to be heard above her . . . She wants to be a mad man in the café. Marie incorporates her into the drama, making reference to, 'That mad man over there, I don't like him'. The group want to move the drama on, past the café scene. Josie now insists on being the bus driver. She yells, 'I wanna be what I wanna be'. They can't get on without her shouting at them. I really don't know whether to try to intervene – it's a fieldwork day, not a work day, and I so want to see what happens when I don't try to play Superwoman. But can I let her wreck the lesson? She is particularly going for Jessica . . . Catherine [the teacher] takes Josie out for a moment. When Josie comes back, she looks for Marie, then announces to everyone, 'I'm gonna be the friend, right, so you can't boss me around' . . .

Eventually the two groups get back together. Group B show theirs first. Juliet and Dilshad start off on their own playing 'Nadia' and the stranger. They are very credible. They are soon interrupted by Josie, first in the role of bus driver, shouting out the destinations, then in the role of mad man in the café. She dominates the space so that it is difficult to act around her. I feel like she's not so much being included within a learning experience so much as preventing everyone else from learning. The position of knowledge creator is not one she can take up – and I don't think it's just because she has been positioned as having SEN. I don't know how she could really be included in what the teacher is trying to achieve. The best we could hope for, probably, is that she doesn't disrupt. But would that be inclusion? They get as far as the end of the café scene. Then Jessica, not wanting to prolong the agony, says 'It's finished'. This doesn't please Josie, who had wanted to improvise the next scene, in which she would have played the friend. She calls Jessica 'stupid idiot', and lunges towards her. Jessica is saved by the bell, as Josie picks up her bag and belts out of the room, without waiting to be dismissed.

(Fieldnotes 21/3/00)

When I wrote these fieldnotes, I noted that they were written 'after a bad day with Josie'. My own annoyance and frustration with Josie as a social actor, and my own sense of not knowing what to do, are writ large within them. What I intimate is a problem about the way in which Josie's presence inhibits the curricular experience of the other students is also produced through and by my difficult feelings towards her on that particular day. This is not to say that there are not very real problems about what Josie's presence prescribes and proscribes for the students in the drama lesson. It is very hard to see how she could be included in a lesson that is concerned, amongst other things, with complexity in human relationships and complexity in how those relationships are enacted. Perhaps this is a case of curricular fundamentalism (Slee, 1998), together with an understanding of equal opportunities that does not work in practice. This is a lesson that cannot be made accessible to Josie, but equal opportunities appear to demand that the teacher differentiate it so that Josie can access it. Perhaps this is an impossibility. But it is an impossibility produced both by a curricular framework that is inadequate for the purpose, and by a set of procedural expectations that operate as if the complex feeling and embodied responses that Josie evokes can be reduced to the anodyne rhetoric of IEP targets set and met.

The annual review of Josie's SEN statement took place just before the summer half-term holiday. Her continued placement was always in doubt: officially because she had not made sufficient progress in terms of her IEP, and unofficially because she was ungovernable and because people's goodwill towards someone who enacted her difference in demanding ways had been exhausted. Two days before her review was scheduled, she was part of a 'serious incident'. She had been in a fight with another girl who then involved some friends, one of whom made fun of Josie. Josie panicked, and began to hit and kick the girl, shouting that she would kill her. The girl (who was known to have her own struggles in constructing a viable set of social relations at Newbrook) ran off, and Josie made to follow her but was forcibly detained by three male teachers. The teachers took her into the school office (the nearest room available) where she caused considerable damage to property before the three men and myself as a witness could corral her behind a desk. Eventually Josie's uncle arrived to take her home. She was not allowed back on the premises.

At her annual review, Josie's placement was formally terminated, and a placement in segregated special provision recommended. Mine was the only report at her annual review to comment positively on her time at Newbrook. I explicitly referred, in my report, to liking Josie, and to enjoying working with her. There was an overall truth to this, although it was far from an accurate representation of the emotional roller-coaster that had been my working relationship with Josie (Jordan and Jones 1999). None of the other reports made reference to personal feelings, but underlying all the rational comments about lack of progress and deleterious effects on other students' learning lurked a strong subtext of dislike and despair. That subtext spoke of wanting Josie to go elsewhere: of wanting her to become somebody else's perplexing, worrying and seemingly insurmountable problem.

Whose diversity can be valued?

Could there have been another way? Along with the relief that accompanied Josie's departure was a feeling that everyone involved had failed. It would be easy to slip into a critique of Newbrook, and to suggest that it is the failure of mainstream schools adequately to value diversity that is the problem here. But that apparent failure to value diversity has to be interrogated in the context of the schooling system in the UK. It is very difficult to see a way in which Newbrook, itself under an unsustainable techno-rationalist regime of surveillance, could have offered anything very different to Josie.

The social model of disability recommends valuing the 'difference' that is inherent within autistic individuals, while also enabling them to develop strategies to help them manage a non-autistic and autistic-unfriendly world. For Josie, the autistic-unfriendliness of Newbrook lay less in the intentions of individuals, and more at the heart of its mission. As a successful school, it has to make dominant versions of success available and desirable to as many of its students as it possibly can. And those versions of success are underwritten by, and reinscribe, the hierarchical, competitive and linear model of rationality which itself shores up the inconsistencies and inhumanities of global capitalism. Newbrook, like other schools, has to work a fundamentally inhumane system in the most humane way it can. It also has to present the complex and often deeply emotional processes of learning as if they were a single, simply understood, unitary process. The presence of both Josie and

Cassandra flagged up some of the fundamental contradictions inherent in such an endeavour.

Cassandra does her autism in a way that can leave at least some of these contradictions intact. We (the staff) could feel that we were doing something compassionate and humane in relation to her. And she made a version of progress, albeit not the dominant one, which allowed us to think that she was learning to manage her autism and learning to exist in a non-autistic world. As caring people doing a difficult job, the staff needed to feel this. And as young women with formal and microcultural struggles of their own, the other students needed to feel this too. But Josie's mode of doing autism left none of the contradictions undisturbed. In the challenges she presented to both staff and students, none of us could feel that we were doing any-thing remotely humane in relation to her. She appeared to make no progress of any sort, and, indeed, appeared to be 'getting worse'. It is difficult to envisage how other students – 11- and 12-year-olds themselves faced with the demands of finding a path through dominant versions of success and an unfamiliar microcultural world – could have constructed viable social rela-tions with someone to whom their versions of rationality make little sense.

> I overhear Maggie [a PE teacher] telling Lorraine [her head of faculty] about how rude Josie was to her at breaktime. Lorraine pulls me into the conversation. She clearly wants me to deal with the situation. Josie has built up an obsession in which Maggie is her enemy. Today at breaktime, she threatened to set her relations on to Maggie. This was said in a rude and aggressive way. I can well imagine. And it builds on a history of Josie sneering and being rude whenever she passes Maggie. In Maggie's account, it all stems from a time she told Josie off for pushing past her on the stairs. Lorraine is indignant, not so much at what Josie has said and done, but that the staff have been given no guidance, other than the staff meeting I led, about how to handle these kinds of situations. We go together to look for Josie. We can't find her. On the way to her form-room, we pass Cassandra, who's sitting outside the office wrapped up in a scarf. She's not well. Lorraine tells me that a supply teacher put her in the duty room yesterday. We share indignation at how anyone could be inhumane enough to put Cassandra into the duty room. She was in floods of tears apparently. Later, I think how similar Josie and Cassandra are. But no one feels sorry for the boisterous Josie when she gets sent to the duty teacher. She hasn't got the 'Ahh factor'.
>
> (Fieldnotes 17/3/00)

Cassandra's version of apparent success at Newbrook is configured both by current techno-rationalist imperatives and by the desire of the people – adults and students – who work at the school to recuperate some kind of humanity into the system. In many ways she came to represent the feared Other of rational discourses: the student who does not make linear progress. But, as that Other, a version of progress could be constructed around her, so that she could be valued in a non-dominant way for the progress she appeared to be making in her social relationships. She was also a vehicle around which a discourse of caring and compassion could be constructed. As someone who was not going to make anything approximating to the dominant version of progress, Newbrook's staff and students could relax our usual demands, and allow ourselves to look after someone who we had produced as vulnerable. In doing so, we did draw on the notion of valuing diversity, but we also drew on a long tradition of feeling pity and charity towards the childlike and not-quite-human figure of the irrational and therefore helpless 'defective'.

Josie's version of apparent failure was configured by those same techno-rationalist imperatives. Like Cassandra, she was the student who does not make rational, linear progress. But she was a student who cannot exist in mainstream schools today: she was a student who seemed to make no form of progress whatever. There were no reachable targets on her IEP, and staff had not been given a rulebook of strategies through which to manage her 'behaviour'. And, far from Josie's presence facilitating the deployment of a discourse of recuperated humanity, she found herself positioned as a very, very bad girl, a position nuanced by her African Caribbean background and her physical size and strength. She was so bad a girl that she could not be reasoned with, and this constructed her as outside of all the formal stories that can possibly be told about student badness at Newbrook.

So while Josie's 'failure' cannot be attributed to her 'inadequacy', neither is it quite fair to attribute blame to the staff and students at Newbrook. The problem is much more systemic than that. At the same time, Cassandra's apparent success needs to be unpacked. What actually went on in lessons for Cassandra was often not successful, except in that she presented no obstacles to good governance. Again, I would not want to argue that this was the 'fault' of the staff and students at Newbrook. I would want to suggest that the instances in which Cassandra's success was contingent, and Josie's non-existent are in fact pointers to how the schooling process could have been made more productive for all of Newbrook's students.

Don gives out a past paper. He's altered it to make it into a non-calculator version. He's angry that non-calculator papers have made a comeback, and he bristles with indignation on behalf of this, the Graduated Assessment group, who thus may be barred from achieving a grade. I'm determined to spend most of this lesson with Cassandra. At first, all goes according to plan. There's a tally graph, which she can do. I sit with her while she does it. Then there's a bar graph. By now, lots of people are asking, with the usual note of desperation, for help. I can't resist it any longer. I check that Cassandra knows what to do, then go to Esin. By the time I get back, Cassandra has drawn a few Buzz Lightyears, but no bar graph. I admire the drawings, then bring her attention back to the bar graph. She's quite happy to do it. There's concern that, in the exams, she will spend the time drawing, or, as it's usually put, 'doing nothing'. Except in art. I manage to spend most of the lesson working with Cassandra, although I do spend some time with other students. Most of the work is beyond them. I'm sure inclusive education is not supposed to mean everyone being given the opportunity to do the same work, irrespective of whether they can learn from it. I'm feeling irritated by a morning spent trying to 'make the curriculum accessible' when it manifestly isn't.

(Fieldnotes 22/3/00)

It is becoming common to talk about the need to 'value diversity' in schools and elsewhere. But one of the problems with 'valuing diversity' arguments as they are often deployed, is that 'diversity' is located within particular groups or individuals. The standards agenda demands a certain homogeneity in its construction of academically successful students. It implies that one curriculum can be made to fit everyone, and that, with the correct teaching, every student's 'needs' can be correctly assessed, measured and, if necessary, remediated. Students and teachers in schools struggle with the daily reality that this implication is profoundly flawed, and that many students experience no success within it. None of the young women in Don's Year 11 group can use the maths non-calculator curriculum to produce themselves as successful. Newbrook tries to reconcile the dilemma of a prescriptive set of curricular demands on the one hand and its commitment to equal opportunities and attainment for all on the other, by identifying a few students as 'really different' and then appearing to value the diversity they bring.

But this diversity can be valued only for as long as it leaves intact the common-sense contradictions upon which Newbrook publicly constructs its values and its explicit sense of purpose. Very few students can be allowed to be diverse, if that diversity implies inability to access dominant versions of success, according to either dominant or consolation discourses of progression. This means there is a real problem with diversity. If only specific students and groups of students are valued for diversity, while everyone else is valued for what essentially is a form of conformity with the hyper-rational rules of the standards agenda, then diversity operates as yet another binary. It becomes another way of distancing a group from the norm, and a device for establishing and reifying boundaries.

Cassandra and Josie are profoundly affected by this. Their 'difference' cannot be understood in neutral terms. When difference, or particular versions of difference, are permitted to only a few, then that difference has to be understood in terms of social relations of domination and subordination. These social relations cannot be explored through an unpoliticized call to value diversity. For the placements of Cassandra and Josie to have really worked for them and for the other students in the school, something radical would had to have happened around understandings of diversity. Everyone would have to have been recognized as different, and ways of interrogating those multiple differences in terms of the social relations they construct and are constructed by would have needed to have been in place. These are things that curricular fundamentalism and the demands of the standards agenda do not make possible. Credentialization, and the later material rewards associated with it, mean that differences that significantly impact on a student's ability to perform according to dominant norms cannot be understood as neutral differences.

'Normalization' discourses and practices are much critiqued within the disability movement, but it is hard to find the spaces within the techno-rationalist standards agenda where Cassandra and Josie could have been helped to live in a non-autistic world without an emphasis on normalization. Their task was one of having to find ways to exist both inside and outside of a non-autistic walled garden to which rationality, or the understanding of rational discourses, holds the key. Other students could come and go with more or less facility, and more or less success. But Cassandra and Josie were simultaneously trapped both inside and outside the wall, according to how they were positioned in discourses that made no sense to them.

Does feminist post-structuralism provide another account of how things could have been? An account that, unlike the valuing diversity argument, can illuminate the unequal relations of power that produced Cassandra and Josie as disabled students, and can point to more radical practices? Kenway et al. (1994: 197) argue that 'feminist work for change must be predicated on an expectation of tension, ambiguity, instability, contestation and resistance'. The formal discursive world at Newbrook is rather short of space for these qualities, predicated as it is on the expectation of consensus, clear and consistent goals, linear 'improvement' and SMART targets. The expectations for which Kenway and her colleagues argue certainly exist in Newbrook's microcultural spaces. If they had been brought to bear in the official accounts of Cassandra and Josie, then space for interrogating the unequal relations that characterized the experiences of these two students might have been constructed.

But there is still a basic problem. When they come to suggest practices arising from a feminist post-structuralist pedagogy, Kenway et al. (1994: 201) contend that, 'one fundamental purpose for a feminist pedagogy for girls must be their production both as informed and critical readers of their life worlds and as informed and visionary agents for a better world'. The degree to which Cassandra and Josie are going to be informed and critical readers of their life worlds is always going to be limited. It is configured through a triad of impairments that severely restrict their ability to understand themselves in relationship to the social world, to understand themselves as actors in that world, and to generalize meaning from experience (Jordan 1999; Jordan and Jones 1999). Whether or not we call this a 'different' way of understanding the world or an 'impaired' one, we need to take on board that the ability to produce oneself as a critical reader of one's own social world, like all abilities, is not equally distributed.

Cassandra and Josie assuredly resist and take up positions in discourse. But reading too much intentionality into this is damaging and unrealistic: it would be unhelpful and inaccurate to read Cassandra as actively taking up a position as a 'sweet little girl', or Josie as actively taking up a position in 'big bad girl' discourses. It is these students' misreading or non-reading of the social world that produces them as vulnerable, often renders their actions contextually inappropriate, and identifies them according to a binary difference. The challenge for feminist post-structuralist theory is to construct a pedagogy for girls and young women that produces them as differentially able readers of their social world, without pathologizing those who are less able, or virtually unable, to construct such readings.

This chapter has discussed Newbrook's 'really disabled' discourse of success. The discourse shares common ground with the 'sweet little girl' position available to some of Newbrook's 'special needs students', and Cassandra could be positioned and recognized fairly unproblematically within both. But the 'really disabled discourse' cannot work alongside the 'big bad girl' positioning, and so Josie presented more of a discursive conundrum for all of us. We could feel we were doing something humane in relation to Cassandra, and she could be perceived to make social progress, holding in place a notion of valuing diversity. Josie could not be understood to be making progress in any recognizable way, she met no targets, and her placement was considered to be a failure. She troubled the valuing diversity arguments, since hers was a diversity that could not be valued: it was *too* diverse. I have argued here that the valuing diversity argument itself works to police a binary divide, between the majority group who are valued for their ability to succeed according to the linear curriculum of the standards agenda, and a small minority who are valued for something different.

Note

1 Opinion is divided about the use of 'people first' language – i.e. 'person with a disability' as opposed to 'disabled person'. Many have argued that disabilities are a constituent part of people's identities, not add-ons. It would not, for example, make any kind of sense to describe a gay man as a 'person with gay-ness'. Following this line of argument, I describe Cassandra and Josie as 'autistic', though the autistic signpost (Jordan and Jones 1999) does not say everything there is to say about them.

CHAPTER NINE

Conclusion: school effects sustainable change and the redistribution of 'success' – rethinking inclusive education

In September 2000, when I was in the middle of writing up my PhD thesis, a new headteacher started at Newbrook. This new head, Ms Foster, brought with her some (now quite distant) experience of teaching in special education. She consequently positioned herself as someone with expertise in the teaching of 'special needs students' and she has kept up with developments in the field. A few weeks into the term, at the end of a teaching day and as we sat waiting for a staff meeting to begin, my head of department took the opportunity to introduce me to Ms Foster. He explained that I was a part-time teacher, doing a PhD for the greater part of the week. She asked me what my research was about. One eye on the clock, and feeling somewhat under pressure, I answered that I was looking at 'special needs in mainstream schools'. With a knowing, professional-to-professional look of insider solidarity, she remarked, 'Oh yes, partnership teaching never quite works, does it?' I nodded vaguely, not quite knowing how to respond, and she moved to sit elsewhere, murmuring that I must come and talk to her about my PhD some time.

Why was I so singularly unable to give a meaningful account of my research to someone who had good reason on many levels to be interested in it? The possible explanations of my inability, like the research itself, are located in policy, micropolitics and identity work. In educational policy, what counts as legitimate research, and especially what counts as legitimate *practitioner* research, is work that can confirm, and can operationalize, the standards agenda (Reynolds 1998; Tooley 1998; Atkinson 2000). In micropolitical terms, Ms Foster occupied a position of considerable seniority relative to myself. But as a new headteacher, one of her most important managerial tasks was to secure the support of the staff and win our consent to her direction. As a junior member of the teaching staff, I did not have institutional power on my side, and it was in my interests to secure the good opinion of the new headteacher. It made micropolitical sense, then, for us to collude in positioning each other as allies. These conditions were also the context of our identity work in this exchange. Ms Foster needed to produce herself as 'good headteacher'. In this instance, the subject 'good headteacher' is one who shows an informed interest in current theories of special needs pedagogy, and who demonstrates her interest through a remark about what works in practice. I wanted to produce myself as a version of 'good teacher', but the subject 'good teacher' in which I am invested is not easily recognized within schools today, since it is grounded in notions of sustained critique which are hard to maintain in the present climate. And, framing the conversation, was an ever-present politically and locally produced shortage of time. I gave an inadequate description of my research topic because my perception was that a more accurate one would require discussion of complexities for which time could not be made available.

What do I wish I had said to Ms Foster? Given as much time as I would have wanted, and the interest of someone who is able to exert considerable influence on the direction of Newbrook School, what account of my research would I have wanted to present? I would not have wanted to make concrete recommendations, 'tips for teachers' style. The conversation I would have had, in ideal circumstances, would have led towards the three discursive changes – noted in the Introduction – in the way 'achievement' in general and 'special needs' in particular, can be thought about at Newbrook. The first of these is the shift from an emphasis on 'school effectiveness' to one of 'school effects', in which the understanding of schooling outcomes would be situated within a politics 'which acknowledges the different, diverse and hybrid identities students bring to schools' (Lingard et al. 1998: 85). The second discursive shift would foreground notions of sustainable change in place of notions of continuous improvement. The third move would replace the liberal pluralist concept of diversity with the more explicitly egalitarian concept of redistribution: where 'diversity' has become a way to hold hierarchies of achievement in place, 'redistribution' can, by contrast, enable an engagement with the ways in which schools take part in the production of winners and losers in the games of global capital.

How would I have explained to Ms Foster the need for such discursive changes? The perceptions of one of my Year 7 research participants would make a good starting point for such a conversation.

> *Shazia*: Why do you want to know what we think, Miss? I mean, 'cause
> we don't know nothing, we're just all the stupid girls, we don't

know nothing to say, there's lots of girls in my class, they know what to think, you should talk to them.

(Interview 12/3/00)

Shazia's observation, already cited in Chapter 5, is worth a second outing here. This book is concerned with the perceptions and views of what she calls 'all the stupid girls': its argument is that the identity work of these students takes place within a policy, micropolitical and microcultural context that positions them as intellectually subordinate. Shazia's surprise that I wanted to talk to her points to the many ways in which such students are produced as 'knowing nothing', since their knowledge does not appear to count within dominant discourses of success. This book argues that those dominant discourses of success are produced and reproduced locally but always in relation to wider societal discourses. It suggests that current rhetoric and reforms associated with 'inclusive education' have, in the main, acted to complexify, rather than transform, the subordination of those school students to whom dominant versions of academic attainment are inaccessible. The focus of the book is those resultant complexities.

The starting point of this research was my own dissatisfaction, as a learning support teacher, with the discursive practices through which the students with whom I work are marginalized by a system which presents itself as egalitarian in intent. As a teacher in the English state school system, I was contractually obliged to implement the standards agenda. As a learning support teacher in a comprehensive school, I was required to work around the edges of that agenda. School micropolitics required me to make complicated accommodations on the behalf of students who stand to jeopardize both the school's perception of itself as a successful school, and its performance in local league tables. My intention in this research was to use my position as insider to examine, through my own contradictory investments, the discursive resources available to some of the 'special needs students' in one girls' secondary school. I wanted to join in, as far as I could, with the sense-making of those students, and to learn about how they used those discursive resources in producing themselves as 'special needs students'. I wanted to think with the girls and young women who, in Shazia's account, do not 'know what to think', and to see if, together, we could make some kind of social, political and theoretical sense of their student identity work.

In essence, this book tells three principal stories, each of which I will retell very briefly here. First, there is the story of the contradictory space that exists in the intersection between the standards agenda and the historically, socially and politically produced drive towards 'inclusion'. This is the policy story. Second, there is the story of the interpersonal contexts and power relations that are produced in that intersection, when policy on paper finds its way into school life. This is the micropolitical story. Third, there is the story of what students do with those contexts and relations. This last is the story of how those specific relations of power interact with other locally and systemically constructed indices of difference to produce identity resources, and of the multiple ways in which students use those resources in constructing their sense of themselves as school students. It is the story of student identity work and it can make sense only in the context of the first two stories. It is also the story that makes sense *of* those first two stories, since it illuminates and explicates them, and, perhaps above all else, disrupts any notion that any of them can paint a complete, linear or simple picture of reality.

The policy story is framed by the normative terms of the standards agenda, which positions school students as, amongst other things, units of production, to which schools can and must 'add value'. The means used to determine added value is the proportion of students reaching 'the expected standard for their age' (DfEE 1999b). For secondary comprehensive schools such as Newbrook, this benchmark standard is the proportion of Year 11 students attaining five GCSE passes at grades A*–C. The standards agenda is enforced through a battery of coercive and co-optive measures, including inspections whose results are made public, league tables of schools according to their students' exam results, and, perhaps most significantly, through the targets on which first David Blunkett, and now his successor, Estelle Morris, have staked their reputations. Alongside the standards agenda runs the drive for the 'inclusion' of certain groups of children and young people within mainstream education. In the policy story, 'inclusion' has increasingly come to connote 'social inclusion', in line with some of New Labour's other policy priorities (Blunkett 2001). As I argued in Chapter 3, the meanings of 'inclusive education' are open to many interpretations. One commonly found assertion is that inclusive education should enable the removal of 'barriers to learning and participation'. This book argues that the normative, competitive and unsustainable standards agenda is itself central in the production of some very intransigent 'barriers to learning and participation'. I have suggested that the standards agenda positions students to whom normative versions of success are not accessible as marginal, thus producing the conditions of exclusion within a system that claims to be moving towards inclusion.

Chapters 3 and 4 looked at the interrelationships of policy and practice at Newbrook School. Chapter 3 considered the construction of successful schooling as narrated in the policy story, while in Chapter 4 I suggested that the policy story elides failure in ways that can be unhelpful, especially to those students who experience failure in all but name. To explicate and elucidate the policy story, I told it in tandem with the micropolitical story. Newbrook produces itself as a successful school. Central to this production is its success in local league tables of schools, in which its 16-year-old leavers routinely 'out-perform' the leavers of other schools. Or do they? The reality, as always, is more complex. To position itself as 'successful', Newbrook needs to be 'continuously improving': league tables now show a school's improvement, year-by-year, in terms of its examination results. To maintain its position as market leader in which Newbrook's staff are, for very understandable reasons, invested, Newbrook has to enable an ever-increasing proportion of its students to score the coveted five A*–C grades. Its target for this year is that 60 per cent of its students will do so. This leaves 40 per cent who will not. Amongst these are many of the 'special needs students', for whom such an aspiration is out of reach.

So, while it is an 'effective' school, Newbrook has often contradictory effects for specific students and groups of students, which need to be written back into the stories it can tell itself of itself. In particular for this book, I have argued that one of its effects has been to complexify, rather than to ameliorate, the intellectual subordination of its 'special needs students'. Similarly, Newbrook's 'continuous improvement' contains costs that need to be uncovered. This is certainly not to suggest that prior to New Labour's education reforms the schooling system was perfect: to the contrary, change was much needed. But the current regime – of SMART targets that seek to make normative levels of 'performance' necessary and desirable to all students, including those to whom they are inaccessible – cannot be sustained over time. The 'hotting up' of the schooling climate may indeed have brought about improvements for many students (and teachers), but it is having deleterious consequences as well. These stories, too, need to be written back in, through paying attention to the complexities of change. Most importantly, ways of understanding these complexities – their costs as well as their benefits – need to be made available to everyone involved. A discursive move from 'continuous improvement' to 'sustainable change' could make such understandings possible.

Newbrook's sense of itself as an institution is also characterized by its attention to equal opportunities issues. A version of an equal opportunities discourse is used to legitimize its investment in examination results, and works also to make normative versions of success desirable. This discourse is premised on the notion that it is academic success, evidenced in good exam results, that will enable Newbrook's students, many of them from materially disadvantaged backgrounds, to overcome such disadvantage. The discourse operates together with the standards agenda, and with the simultaneously surveillant and 'can-do' culture of new managerialism, to produce the subjects 'successful teacher' and 'successful student'. The presence at Newbrook of 'special needs students' enables these discourses to work, as their presence provides a reason, extraneous to the school, for the existence of the 40 per cent of students who have not made the normative grade. But that presence also works, in a contradictory way, as proof that the dominant and legitimizing discourses of success are fictions. For this reason, as well as for reasons of benevolent humanity and good management, 'special needs students' cannot publicly be positioned as failing. Newbrook's students and teachers are addressed, and address each other, as though success were attainable for all. A public admission of failure would be a criticism of the normative and competitive nature of the standards agenda, and an admission that the standards agenda is essentially inegalitarian and unsustainable. For Newbrook's staff, invested as we are in egalitarian and humanitarian understandings of our work, such an admission is, if not unthinkable, certainly unsayable.

Chapters 5 to 8 examine how the subject 'special needs student' of policy and school micropolitics is produced by and produces student microcultures. These chapters look at how this subject is variously taken up by different students and groups of students. It is the students who I have called 'intellectually subordinated' who live the political and micropolitical contradictions outlined above. The can-do culture of school effectiveness sets them up to want and expect the choices associated with examination success, and to believe that they will have those choices so long as they work hard and are effectively taught. But the daily reality of their lived experience, and the microcultural complexities of that experience, demonstrate to them the impossibility of ever being, or becoming, 'successful' young women.

In Chapters 5 and 6, I suggested that it is possible to make three (necessarily provisional) distinctions in the way that 'special needs students' are positioned at Newbrook. Such students tend to take up positions as 'sweet little girls', 'big bad girls' and 'lazy girls'. Each of the three positions is thoroughly gendered, and is, in addition, nuanced by 'race', social class, sexuality, religion, physical appearance and command of the English language as well as by perceived academic ability. What all three positions have in common is reference to a deficit discourse. Where they account at all for their academic ability, all of these girls and young women talk about themselves as 'stupid', 'thick' or 'dumb': the language of 'special educational needs' appears to have no relevance or usefulness for them.

To explore the production of this deficit discourse, it is necessary to look at the imbrication of macro and micro-discourses, and to stitch the policy, micropolitical and identity work stories together again. Chapter 7 looked at the examination, and practices around the examination, as a site of the production of this deficit discourse. I suggested that three separate and hierarchized versions of academic achievement co-exist in Newbrook. The dominant version of success relates to national benchmarks as enshrined in policy. But there has to be another version, in order for Newbrook to make sense of and for those students who are not going to be able to achieve according to this normative version. The answer is a deficit – consolation – version of academic success, where it is individual progress that is measured and counted as success. This version may look (and in many ways is) more humane than the dominant one. But the fact that it is deployed only in relation to students who are failing in normative terms means that it works mainly to shore up, and not to challenge or unsettle, the dominant discourse.

The consolation version of success is one of individual, not purely normative, academic progress. But it does not account for all of Newbrook's students. Chapter 8 identified a further version, that of the 'really disabled student', in which it is personal and 'social', not academic, progress that is valued, measured and acclaimed. At present there is a small number of students at Newbrook in relation to whom this version of success is invoked: local and national policy changes mean this number is steadily creeping up as students who would until very recently have been educated in special schools are now being placed in Newbrook. Chapter 8 considered the 'inclusion' experiences of two autistic students. The placement of Cassandra was narrated as a success. Cassandra was able to occupy a version of the 'sweet little girl' position, nuanced by her successful insertion into the 'really disabled' version of success. By contrast, Josie's placement was considered to have been unsuccessful, and was abruptly and prematurely terminated. At a discursive level, Josie tended to be positioned as a 'big bad girl', but such a position cannot coexist with the 'really disabled' discourse at Newbrook. Staff and students were able to position themselves as humane and bene-volent in relation to the often puzzling but manifestly needy Cassandra. But both staff and student members of Newbrook felt puzzled by Josie and also frightened of her. She did not produce herself as vulnerable, and there was very little space for anyone to take up a position of power in face-to-face relation with her.

I suggested in Chapter 8 that Josie's and Cassandra's experiences highlight some of the inadequacies of liberal pluralist arguments about 'valuing diver-sity'. The standards agenda, in which Newbrook's dominant discourse of success is embedded, values a bottom-line homogeneity. This homogeneity forms the bedrock of curricular and managerial policies through which students experience schooling and make sense of themselves as students. Newbrook tries to reconcile the dilemma of a prescriptive set of curricular demands on the one hand, and its commitment to equal opportunities on the other, by identifying a handful of students as *really* different, in most cases in relation to their prior assessment and calibration as 'disabled'. Valuing Cassandra's diversity in this context acted also to leave the homogeneity of the standards agenda in place. When only specific students and groups of students are valued for diversity, while everyone else is valued for what is essentially homogeneity and conformity, then 'diversity' operates as another binary. It becomes yet another way of marking out and distancing those who are identified as 'different' from the norm. I suggest that 'valuing diversity' will not be a productive concept to take forward into the inclusion debates. Rather, we need to look at the implications of 'difference' for all students, and to use language that will enable us to pay attention to the enduring reproduction of inequalities. Difference cannot be understood as neutral, and the shift towards 'redistribution' as an organizing concept will better enable us to address the redressing of social and material imbalances.

The case studies of Cassandra and Josie presented me with a theoretical problem, in that they demonstrated the limits of feminist post-structural theory in explaining the subjectivity of two young women who do not make sense of the world in ways that make sense to me. Notwithstanding (or perhaps in addition to) this current theoretical limitation, I would want to argue very strongly for the unique contribution a feminist post-structural approach can make to the understanding of intellectual subordination in classroom contexts. A feminist post-structural analysis, with its attention to the complexities of the politics of difference together with its commitment to egalitarian change, can enable the kinds of nuanced understandings often missing in 'inclusive education' rhetoric, and certainly absent from the stand-ards agenda. Such an approach makes it possible to uncover the layers of meaning embedded in the social and political processes of intellectual sub-ordination, and compels detailed attention to the production of meaning and practice by individuals, groups, institutions and systems. This kind of contextualized and multilayered understanding will be crucial in moving the debate on.

Other questions remain. There is the set of questions around naming, which I raised in the introductory chapter. For the purposes of the book, I have worked with the concept of intellectual subordination. As a means of describing the social and political processes through which a distinct group of school students are inscribed into relations of subordination, this name has served its purpose. But I remain doubtful about it on two counts. First, I developed the concept without the knowledge or consent of the participants. I felt I had to do so, since the meanings associated with the inability to make academic progress within the normative range are so negative that I could not discuss them openly with the students. But naming an oppression to which one is not personally subject is politically dubious at the very least, and I would not want to pretend otherwise. I would have wanted things to have been different: I would have wanted a piece of terminology to have arisen from discussion with the students. No such piece of language emerged, and I did the best I could, while recognizing that the solution with which I worked was not an ideal one.

My other reservation about the concept of intellectual subordination is that it does not adequately represent, or allow for the interrogation of, the material reality of differential learning ability. This is a very difficult question, and one I would like to explore further. Throughout the book, I have perhaps evaded a thorough engagement with it. Arguing for a material base for 'learning difficulty' (and here, the term 'intellectual subordination' is inadequate) is a political minefield, and could easily be co-opted into some very reactionary discourses. Yet I would want to argue that differential learning ability does indeed exist. Much of it is socially and politically produced, but there is a materiality too. The meanings and practices associated with 'learning difficulty', and the apparatuses through which individuals are measured and their ability calibrated as distance from the norm, are undoubtedly social constructions, produced by and embedded in a set of social interests. I would want to hold onto this argument, while asserting that there also exist a group of people who are potentially made vulnerable because of their intrinsic intellectual limitation. I have not found a way to say this, or to engage with it, in ways that do not connote lack, or inferiority, or, on my part, something politically much worse.

Bearing these questions and reservations in mind, I want to return to my imaginary conversation with Ms Foster, and to the three discursive shifts outlined at the beginning of this chapter. While it is important not to overstate the case in terms of the difference schools and teachers are able to make – they do, after all, occupy an unenviable position in the chain of surveillance and regulation that links government policy with student experience – I would not want to fall into the trap of positioning them as completely without agency. The discursive (and other) resources available to schools are assuredly produced in the context of macropolitical conditions, but this does not mean they are determined by them.

In current terms, Newbrook is an 'effective school'. But if it were to apply an analysis of school effects to its understandings of its purpose, other questions might be highlighted. Who is enabled to be successful and on whose terms? And indeed, what is to count as 'success', and what does 'success' count for in the wider political and socio-economic context? As a 'successful school' within the parameters produced by the standards agenda, Newbrook asks itself many questions about how it can continuously improve students' overall examination performance. Such a line of questioning is intensely problematic. Any form of social change is complex, and will have unexpected and often contradictory effects. I have already argued that 'improvements' associated with the standards agenda can be costly. Further changes in the policy and practice of inclusive education – even, or perhaps especially, those changes that seem to be egalitarian in intent and consequence – will need to be interrogated in similar ways. The notion of sustainable egalitarian change draws our attention to the fact that some people may benefit from change, in ways that are relatively easy to see. For others, the benefits may not be immediately noticeable, or may be embedded in a complex network of costs as well as benefits. And some people may lose out, or appear to lose out, or experience themselves as losing out, particularly those who benefit disproportionately from the status quo. Sustainable change necessarily involves redistribution of different kinds, from the 'rich' – in terms of material wealth, or, in this case, perceived academic success – to the 'poor'.

Redistribution can be painful, but the consequences of leaving inequalities intact, or allowing them to intensify, are worse. One of the many problems with the school improvement discourse is its implication that change is unitary and simple, that it benefits everybody in the same kind of way, and that it can take place incrementally, year-on-year. We need, urgently, to look at the costs of such arguments. On a purely economic level, research shows that girls leaving school without examination qualifications can expect to earn, on average, one-sixth of the earnings of degree-level educated men, and that they are three times more likely to face long periods of unemployment (NACETT 2000). Surely, the question that must arise from this is not about how schools can produce larger numbers of students who attain normative levels or better in competitive examinations, leaving those to whom those levels are inaccessible further and further behind. Rather, the question that must be asked, in schools as well as outside of them, is about how schools are complicit in such widenings of economic and social inequalities, often contrary to the intentions and values of those working in them. The discursive shifts from school effectiveness to school effects, from continuous improvement to sustainable egalitarian change, and from diversity to redistribution allow such a question to be posed.

In the introduction, I asked myself whether I was letting down the students with whom I worked, and said that this book is the story of how I tried to answer that question. The story is about multiplicitous (though not infinite) meanings: it is a story in which actions and events may have many meanings, but in which the availability of those meanings is bounded by the discourses and discursive practices in play, and by the power relations through which they are constructed. It is a story of girls and young women making sense of themselves as school students in ways that are extraordinarily nuanced and complex, and which are deeply personalized at the same time as being politically situated and implicated. The story, and this book, show that the processes of intellectual subordination are located in discourses and discursive practices at systemic, institutional and interpersonal levels: indeed, these discourses and discursive practices *are* the micropolitics of inclusive education. Both the challenge and the pleasure of the story lie in its indication that these processes are not amenable to simple causal explanations, or to linear and reductive prescriptions for change. Inclusive education is, and will be, a complex and contested social practice. A sustained intellectual and practical engagement with the micropolitics of difference will be vital to its continuing development.

References

Ainscow, M. (1999) *Understanding the Development of Inclusive Schools*. London: Falmer.

Allan, J. (1996) Foucault and special educational needs: a 'box of tools' for analysing children's experiences of mainstreaming, *Disability and Society*, 11(6): 219–34.

Allan, J. (1999) *Actively Seeking Inclusion: Pupils with Special Needs in Mainstream Schools*. London: Falmer.

Alton-Lee, A., Rietveld, C., Klenner, L. et al. (2000) Inclusive practice within the lived cultures of school communities: research case studies in teaching, learning and inclusion, *International Journal of Inclusive Education*, 4(3): 179–210.

Apple, M. (1995) *Education and Power*. New York: Routledge.

Apple, M. (1996) *Cultural Politics and Education*. Buckingham: Open University Press.

Armstrong, F. (1999) Inclusion, curriculum and the struggle for space in school, *International Journal of Inclusive Education*, 3(1): 75–87.

Arnot, M. and Barton, L. (eds) (1992) *Voicing Concerns: Sociological Perspectives on Contemporary Educational Reforms*. Wallingford: Triangle Books.

Atkinson, E. (2000) In defence of ideas, or why 'what works' is not enough, *British Journal of Sociology of Education*, 21(3): 317–30.

Bailey, T. and Furby, D. (1987) 'Kevin': including pupils with disabilities, in T. Booth and W. Swann (eds) *Including Pupils with Disabilities*. Milton Keynes: Open University Press.

Ball, S. (1987) *The Micro-Politics of the School: Towards a Theory of School Organization*. London: Routledge.

Ball, S. (1990) Discipline and chaos: the New Right and discourses of derision, in S. Ball (ed.) *Politics and Policy-Making in Education: Explorations in Policy Sociology*. London: Routledge.

Barber, M. (2000) High expectations and standards for all – no matter what, *Times Educational Supplement*, 7 July.

Barton, L. (1993) Labels, markets and inclusive education, in J. Visser and G. Upton (eds) *Special Education in Britain after Warnock*. London: David Fulton.

Barton, L. (1998) Developing an emancipatory research agenda: possibilities and dilemmas, in L. Barton and P. Clough (eds) *Articulating with Difficulty: Research Voices in Inclusive Education*. London: Paul Chapman.

Barton, L. and Clough, P. (1995) Conclusion: many urgent voices, in P. Clough and L. Barton (eds) *Making Difficulties: Research and the Construction of Special Educational Needs*. London: Paul Chapman.

Barton, L. and Slee, R. (1999) Competition, selection and inclusive education: some observations, *International Journal of Inclusive Education*, 3(1): 3–12.

Beck, U. (2000) Living your own life in a runaway world: individualization, globalization and politics, in W. Hutton and A. Giddens (eds) *On the Edge: Living with Global Capitalism*. London: Jonathan Cape.

Bell, L. (1998) Public and private meanings in diaries: researching family and childcare, in J. Ribbens and R. Edwards (eds) *Feminist Dilemmas in Qualitative Research*. London: Sage.

Benjamin, S. (2001) The micropolitics of 'special educational needs' in a comprehensive girls' school. Unpublished PhD thesis, Institute of Education, University of London.

Bhatti, G. (1999) *Asian Children at Home and at School*. London: Routledge.

Bines, H. (1986) *Redefining Remedial Education*. London: Croom Helm.

Bines, H. (1989) Developing a special professionalism: perspectives and practices in teacher training, in C. Roaf and H. Bines (eds) *Needs, Rights and Opportunities*. Lewes: Falmer.

Bines, H. (1995) Risk, routine and reward: confronting personal and social constructs in research on special educational needs, in P. Clough and L. Barton (eds) *Making Difficulties: Research and the Construction of Special Educational Needs*. London: Paul Chapman.

Bines, H. (2000) Inclusive standards? Current developments in policy for special educational needs in England and Wales, *Oxford Review of Education*, 26(1): 21–33.

Blunkett, D. (2000a) *Opportunity for All: Skills for the New Economy. Initial Response to the National Skills Task Force Final Report, 27th June 2000*. London: DfEE.

Blunkett, D. (2000b) Raising aspirations in the 21st century: the North of England speech on the future of education, 6 January 2000, DfEE.

Blunkett, D. (2001) Education into employability: the role of the DfEE in the economy. Speech to the Institute of Economic Affairs, London, 24 January 2001.

Boler, M. (1999) *Feeling Power: Emotions and Education*. London: Routledge.

Boli, J. and Thomas, G. M. (1997) World culture in the world polity, *American Sociological Review*, 62(2): 171–90.

Bomford, J. (2001) Woodhead joins attack on exam standards, *Times Educational Supplement*, 24 August.

Bordo, S. (1993a) Feminism, Foucault and the politics of the body, in C. Ramazanoglu (ed.) *Up against Foucault: Explorations of Some Tensions between Foucault and Feminism*. London: Routledge.

Bordo, S. (1993b) *Unbearable Weight: Feminism, Western Culture and the Body*. Berkeley, CA: University of California Press.

Boswell, T. and Chase-Dunn, C. (2000) *The Spiral of Capitalism and Socialism*. London: Lynne Riener.

Bourdieu, P. (1984) *Distinction: A Social Critique of the Judgement of Taste*. London: Routledge and Kegan Paul.

Boyden, J. (1990) Childhood and the policy makers: a comparative perspective on the globalization of childhood, in A. James and A. Prout (eds) *Constructing and Reconstructing Childhood: Contemporary Issues in the Sociological Study of Childhood*. Basingstoke: Falmer.

Bullen, E., Kenway, J. and Hey, V. (2000) New Labour, social exclusion and educational risk management: the case of 'gymslip mums', *British Educational Research Journal*, 26(4): 441–56.

Butler, J. (1990) *Gender Trouble: Feminism and the Subversion of Identity*. London: Routledge.

Carrington, S. (1999) Inclusion needs a different school culture, *International Journal of Inclusive Education*, 3(3): 257–68.

Cherland, M. R. (1994) *Private Practices: Girls Reading Fiction and Creating Identity*. London: Taylor & Francis.

Chitty, C. (1999) The comprehensive ideal, in C. Chitty and J. Dunford (eds) *State Schools: New Labour and the Conservative Legacy*. London: Woburn Press.

Clark, C., Dyson, A., Millward, A. and Robson, S. (1999) Theories of inclusion, theories of schools: deconstructing and reconstructing the 'inclusive school', *British Educational Research Journal*, 25(2): 157–77.

Clough, P. (1998) Differently articulate? Some indices of disturbed/disturbing voices, in L. Barton and P. Clough (eds) *Articulating with Difficulty: Research Voices in Inclusive Education*. London: Paul Chapman.

Clough, P. and Barton, L. (1995) Introduction: self and the research act, in P. Clough and L. Barton (eds) *Making Difficulties: Research and the Construction of Special Educational Needs*. London: Paul Chapman.

Coffey, A. and Delamont, S. (2000) *Feminism and the Classroom Teacher: Research, Praxis and Pedagogy*. London: Routledge/Falmer.

Cohen, P. and Bains, H. S. (eds) (1988) *Multi-Racist Britain*. London: Macmillan.

Cole, T. (1989) *Apart or A Part? Integration and the Growth of British Special Education*. Milton Keynes: Open University Press.

Connell, R. W. (1995) *Masculinities*. Cambridge: Polity.

Connolly, P. (1998) *Racism, Gender Identities and Young Children: Social Relations in a Multi-Ethnic, Inner-City Primary School*. London: Routledge.

Cooper, D. (1989) Positive images in Haringey: a struggle for identity, in C. Jones and P. Mahony (eds) *Learning Our Lines: Sexuality and Social Control in Education*. London: The Women's Press.

Corbett, J. (1996) *Bad-Mouthing: The Language of Special Needs*. Bristol: Falmer.

Corbett, J. (1998a) *Special Educational Needs in the Twentieth Century: A Cultural Analysis*. London: Cassell.

Corbett, J. (1998b) 'Voice' in emancipatory research: imaginative listening, in L. Barton and P. Clough (eds) *Articulating with Difficulty: Research Voices in Inclusive Education*. London: Paul Chapman.

Corbett, J. (1999) Inclusive education and school culture, *International Journal of Inclusive Education*, 3(1): 53–61.

Creese, A., Daniels, H., Hey, V. and Leonard, D. (2000) *Gender and Learning*. ESRC Research Project.

Davies, B. (1989) Frogs *and Snails and Feminist Tales: Preschool Children and Gender*. Sydney: Allen and Unwin.

Davies, B. (1994) *Poststructuralist Theory and Classroom Practice*. Geelong, Vic.: Deakin University Press.

Davies, B. (1997) The subject of poststructuralism: a reply to Alison Jones, *Gender and Education*, 9(3): 271–83.

Dehli, K. (1996) Between 'market' and 'state'? Engendering education change in the 1990s, *Discourse*, 17(3): 363–76.

DfEE (1994) *Code of Practice on the Identification and Assessment of Special Educational Needs*. London: DfEE.

DfEE (1997a) David Blunkett says jobs are at the heart of a people's Europe, DfEE press release 166/97, 27 June.

DfEE (1997b) *Excellence for All Children*. London: HMSO.

DfEE (1997c) *Excellence in Schools.* London: HMSO.

DfEE (1998) *Teachers: Meeting the Challenge of Change.* London: HMSO.

DfEE (1999a) *Excellence in Cities.* London: DfEE.

DfEE (1999b) *National Learning Targets for England for 2002.* Sudbury: DfEE.

DfEE (2000) *Gender and Achievement: Different Phases of Concern about Gender.* http://www.standards.dfee.gov.uk/genderandachievement/data_1.2.7.html (accessed 18 Dec. 2000).

DfES (2001) *Inclusive Education: Children with Special Educational Needs.* Statutory Guidance to Local Education Authorities, Health and Social Services in England. London: DfES.

Dunn, L. L. (1995) Free trade zones: issues and strategies, in G. Ashworth (ed.) *A Diplomacy of the Oppressed.* London: Zed Books.

Dyson, A. (1999) Inclusion and inclusions: theories and discourses in inclusive education, in H. Daniels and P. Garner (eds) *World Yearbook of Education 1999: Inclusive Education.* London: Kogan Page.

Edwards, R. and Ribbens, J. (1998) Living on the edges: public knowledge, private lives, personal experience, in J. Ribbens and R. Edwards (eds) *Feminist Dilemmas in Qualitative Research.* London: Sage.

Epstein, D. (1993) *Changing Classroom Cultures: Anti-Racism, Politics and Schools.* Stoke-on-Trent: Trentham.

Epstein, D. and Johnson, R. (1998) *Schooling Sexualities.* Buckingham: Open University Press.

Fine, M. (1994) Dis-tance and other stances: negotiations of power inside feminist research, in A. Gitlin (ed.) *Power and Method: Political Activism and Educational Research.* London: Routledge.

Fletcher-Campbell, F. (1994) *Still Joining Forces? A Follow-up Study of Links between Ordinary and Special Schools.* Slough: National Foundation for Educational Research.

Foucault, M. (1975) *Discipline and Punish: The Birth of the Prison.* London: Allen Lane.

Foucault, M. (1980) *Power/Knowledge: Selected Interviews and Other Writings 1972–1977 by Michel Foucault.* Hemel Hempstead: Harvester.

Foucault, M. (1988) Technologies of the self, in L. H. Martin, H. Gutman and P. H. Hutton (eds) *Technologies of the Self: A Seminar with Michel Foucault.* London: Tavistock.

Francis, B. (1997) Power plays: children's construction of gender and power in role-plays, *Gender and Education*, 9(2): 179–92.

Francis, B. (1998) *Power Play: Children's Construction of Gender, Power and Adult Work.* Stoke-on-Trent: Trentham.

Fulcher, G. (1995) Excommunicating the severely disabled: struggles, policy and researching, in P. Clough and L. Barton (eds) *Making Difficulties: Research and the Construction of Special Educational Needs.* London: Paul Chapman.

Gewirtz, S., Ball, S. and Bowe, R. (1995) *Markets, Choice and Equity in Education.* Buckingham: Open University Press.

Giddens, A. (1991) *Modernity and Self-Identity: Self and Society in the Late Modern Age.* Cambridge: Polity.

Gipps, C., Gross, H. and Goldstein, H. (1987) *Warnock's Eighteen Per Cent: Children with Special Needs in Primary Schools.* London: Falmer.

Goacher, B., Evans, J., Welton, J. and Wedell, K. (1988) *Policy and Provision for Special Educational Needs: Implementing the 1981 Education Act.* London: Cassell.

Goodley, D. (2001) 'Learning difficulties', the social model of disability and impairment: challenging epistemologies, *Disability and Society*, 16(2): 207–31.

Gordon, T., Holland, J. and Lahelma, E. (2000) *Making Spaces: Citizenship and Difference in Schools.* London: Macmillan.

Griffiths, M. and Troyna, B. (eds) (1995) *Antiracism, Culture and Social Justice in Education*. Stoke-on-Trent: Trentham.

Hall, S. (1990) Cultural identity and diaspora, in J. Rutherford (ed.) *Identity: Community, Culture, Difference*. London: Lawrence and Wishart.

Hall, S. (1992) The question of cultural identity, in S. Hall, D. Held and T. McGrew (eds) *Modernity and its Futures*. Buckingham: Open University Press/Polity.

Hamilton, D. (1998) The idols of the market place, in R. Slee, G. Weiner and S. Tomlinson (eds) *School Effectiveness for Whom? Challenges to the School Effectiveness and School Improvement Movements*. London: Falmer.

Haseler, S. (2000) *The Super-Rich: The Unjust New World of Global Capitalism*. London: Macmillan.

Hatcher, R. (1995) Racism and children's cultures, in M. Griffiths and B. Troyna (eds) *Antiracism, Culture and Social Justice in Education*. Stoke-on-Trent: Trentham.

Haw, K. (1998) *Educating Muslim Girls: Shifting Discourses*. Buckingham: Open University Press.

Henry, J. (2001) Board hits back over maths GCSE, *Times Educational Supplement*, 31 August.

Hey, V. (1996) 'A game of two halves' – a critique of some complexities: between hegemonic and counter-hegemonic discourses concerning marketisation and education, *Discourse*, 17(3): 351–62.

Hey, V. (1997) *The Company She Keeps: An Ethnography of Girls' Friendship*. Buckingham: Open University Press.

Hill, J. (1995) Entering the unknown: case-study analysis in special schools, in P. Clough and L. Barton (eds) *Making Difficulties: Research and the Construction of Special Educational Needs*. London: Paul Chapman.

Holland, J. and Ramazanoglu, C. (1995) Accounting for sexuality, living sexual politics: can feminist research be valid?, in J. Holland, M. Blair and S. Sheldon (eds) *Debates and Issues in Feminist Research and Pedagogy*. Buckingham: Open University Press.

Hulley, B., Hulley, T., Parsons, G., Madden, S. and Swann, W. (1987) 'Samantha', in T. Booth and W. Swann (eds) *Including Pupils with Disabilities*. Milton Keynes: Open University Press.

Hunt, P. and Frankenburg, R. (1990) It's a small world: Disneyland, the family and the multiple re-representations of American childhood, in A. James and A. Prout (eds) *Constructing and Reconstructing Childhood: Contemporary Issues in the Sociological Study of Childhood*. Basingstoke: Falmer.

Hurt, J. S. (1988) *Outside the Mainstream: A History of Special Education*. London: B. T. Batsford.

ILEA (1983a) *Race, Sex and Class*. London: ILEA.

ILEA (1983b) *Race, Sex and Class 2: Multi-ethnic Education in Schools*. London: ILEA.

ILEA (1983c) *Race, Sex and Class 3: A Policy for Equality – Race*. London: ILEA.

ILEA (1983d) *Race, Sex and Class 4: Anti-racist Statement and Guidelines*. London: ILEA.

ILEA (1983e) *Race, Sex and Class 5: Multi-ethnic Education in Further, Higher and Community Education*. London: ILEA.

ILEA (1985) *Race, Sex and Class 6: A Policy for Equality – Sex*. London: ILEA.

Institute for the Study of the Neuro-Typical (1999) *What is NT?*, ISNT@grrltalk.net. http://isnt.autistics.org/index.html (accessed 8 Feb. 2001).

Johnson, R. (1991) My New Right education, in Cultural Studies Birmingham Group 2, *Education Limited: Schooling, Training and the New Right since 1979*. London: Unwin Hyman.

Johnson, R. (1997) Contested borders, contingent lives: an introduction, in D. L. Steinberg, D. Epstein and R. Johnson (eds) *Border Patrols: Policing the Boundaries of Heterosexuality*. London: Cassell.

Jones, C. and Mahony, P. (eds) (1989) *Learning our Lines: Sexuality and Social Control in Education*. London: The Women's Press.

Jordan, R. (1999) *Autistic Spectrum Disorders: An Introductory Handbook for Practitioners*. London: David Fulton.

Jordan, R. and Jones, G. (1999) *Meeting the Needs of Children with Autistic Spectrum Disorders*. London: David Fulton.

Kehily, M. J. and Nayak, A. (1996) 'The Christmas Kiss': sexuality, storytelling and schooling, *Curriculum Studies*, 4(2): 211–28.

Kelly, L., Regan, L. and Burton, S. (1995) Defending the indefensible? Quantitative methods and feminist research, in J. Holland, M. Blair and S. Sheldon (eds) *Debates and Issues in Feminist Research and Pedagogy*. Buckingham: Open University Press.

Kenway, J. (ed.) (1995) *Marketing Education: Some Critical Issues*. Geelong, Vic.: Deakin University Press.

Kenway, J. and Epstein, D. (1996) Introduction: the marketisation of school education: feminist studies and perspectives, *Discourse*, 17(3): 301–14.

Kenway, J. and Willis, S. (1990) Self-esteem and the schooling of girls: an introduction, in J. Kenway and S. Willis (eds) *Hearts and Minds: Self-esteem and the Schooling of Girls*. London: Falmer.

Kenway, J., Willis, S., Blackmore, J. and Rennie, L. (1994) Making 'hope practical' rather than 'despair convincing': feminist post-structuralism, gender reform and educational change, *British Journal of Sociology of Education*, 15(2): 187–210.

Kenway, J., Willis, S., Blackmore, J. and Rennie, L. (1997) *Answering Back: Girls, Boys and Feminism in Schools*. St Leonards, NSW: Allen & Unwin.

Kirk, G. (1995) Women resist ecological destruction, in G. Ashworth (ed.) *A Diplomacy of the Oppressed*. London: Zed Books.

Kugelmass, J. W. (2001) Collaboration and compromise in creating and sustaining an inclusive school, *International Journal of Inclusive Education*, 5(1): 47–65.

Lauder, H., Jamieson, I. and Wikely, F. (1998) Models of effective schools: limits and capabilities, in R. Slee, G. Weiner and S. Tomlinson (eds) *School Effectiveness for Whom? Challenges to the School Effectiveness and School Improvement Movements*. London: Falmer.

Levitas, R. (1998) *The Inclusive Society? Social Exclusion and New Labour*. London: Macmillan.

Lingard, B., Ladwig, J. and Luke, A. (1998) School effects in postmodern conditions, in R. Slee, G. Weiner and S. Tomlinson (eds) *School Effectiveness for Whom? Challenges to the School Effectiveness and School Improvement Movements*. London: Falmer.

Lloyd, C. (2000) Excellence for all children – false promises! The failure of current policy for inclusive education and implications for schooling in the 21st century, *International Journal of Inclusive Education*, 4(2): 133–51.

Lowe, R. (1997) *Schooling and Social Change 1964–1990*. London: Routledge.

Lucey, H. (2000) Identity work in social democracies. Paper given at Education and Social Democracies Conference, Institute of Education, University of London, 3–5 July.

Lunt, I. and Evans, J. (1994) Dilemmas in special educational needs: some effects of local management of schools, in S. Riddell and S. Brown (eds) *Special Educational Needs Policy in the 1990s: Warnock in the Marketplace*. London: Routledge.

Lunt, I. and Norwich, B. (1999) *Can Effective Schools be Inclusive Schools?* London: Institute of Education, University of London.

Martin, J. R. (1985) *Reclaiming a Conversation: The Ideal of the Educated Woman*. New Haven, CT: Yale University Press.

Marx, K. and Engels, F. ([1845–6] 1975) *The German Ideology*. Southampton: Lawrence and Wishart.

Mauthner, M. and Hey, V. (1999) Researching girls: a post-structuralist approach, *Educational and Child Psychology*, 16(2): 67–84.

Mirza, H. S. (1992) *Young, Female and Black*. London: Routledge.

Mirza, M. (1995) Some ethical dilemmas in field work: feminist and antiracist methodologies, in M. Griffiths and B. Troyna (eds) *Antiracism, Culture and Social Justice in Education*. Stoke-on-Trent: Trentham.

Modelski, G. and Thompson, W. R. (1996) *Leading Sectors and World Powers: The Co-Evolution of Global Economics and Politics*. Columbia, SC: University of South Carolina Press.

Morley, L. and Rassool, N. (1999) *School Effectiveness: Fracturing the Discourse*. London: Falmer.

Morris, J. (1995) Personal and political: a feminist perspective on researching physical disability, in J. Holland, M. Blair and S. Sheldon (eds) *Debates and Issues in Feminist Research and Pedagogy*. Buckingham: Open University Press.

Mort, F. (1994) Essentialism revisited? Identity politics and late twentieth-century discourses of homosexuality, in J. Weeks (ed.) *The Lesser Evil and the Greater Good*. London: Rivers Oram Press.

NACETT (2000) *Aiming Higher: NACETT's Report on the National Learning Targets for England and Advice on Targets beyond 2002*. Sudbury: National Advisory Council for Education and Training Targets.

Norwich, B. (1990) How an entitlement can become a restraint, in H. Daniels and J. Ware (eds) *Special Educational Needs and the National Curriculum: The Impact of the Education Reform Act*. London: Kogan Page.

Norwich, B. (1993) Has 'special educational needs' outlived its usefulness? in J. Visser and G. Upton (eds) *Special Education in Britain after Warnock*. London: David Fulton.

Paechter, C. (1998) *Educating the Other: Gender, Power and Schooling*. London: Falmer.

Pateman, C. (1988) *The Sexual Contract*. Cambridge: Polity.

Peters, S. (1995) Disability baggage: changing the educational research terrain, in P. Clough and L. Barton (eds) *Making Difficulties: Research and the Construction of Special Educational Needs*. London: Paul Chapman.

Rea, J. and Weiner, G. (1998) Cultures of blame and redemption – when empowerment becomes control: practitioners' views of the effective schools movement, in R. Slee, G. Weiner and S. Tomlinson (eds) *School Effectiveness for Whom? Challenges to the School Effectiveness and School Improvement Movements*. London: Falmer.

Reay, D. (1998) Micropolitics in the 1990s: staff relationships in secondary schooling, *Journal of Education Policy*, 13(2): 179–96.

Raey, D. and Lucey, H. (2000) Children, school choice and social differences, *Educational Studies*, 26(1): 83–100.

Renshaw, P. (1990) Self-esteem research and equity programs for girls: a reassessment, in J. Kenway and S. Willis (eds) *Hearts and Minds: Self-esteem and the Schooling of Girls*. London: Falmer.

Reynolds, D. (1998) *Teacher Effectiveness: Better Teachers, Better Schools – the TTA Annual Lecture 1998*. London: Teacher Training Agency.

Riddell, S., Adler, M., Mordaunt, E. and Farmakopoulou, N. (2000) Special educational needs and competing policy frameworks in England and Scotland, *Journal of Education Policy*, 15(6): 621–35.

Robinson, W. I. (1996) *Promoting Polyarchy: Globalization, U.S. Intervention and Hegemony*. New York: Cambridge University Press.

Rustin, M. (1999) Equal opportunities and social exclusion in New Labour. Paper presented to the Critical Politics Conference, London School of Economics, 27 April.

Rustin, M. (2000) The New Labour ethic and the spirit of capitalism, *Soundings*, 14: 111–26.

Sennett, R. (1998) *The Corrosion of Character: The Personal Consequences of Work in the New Capitalism*. New York and London: W.W. Norton.

Shiva, V. (2000) The world on the edge, in W. Hutton and A. Giddens (eds) *On the Edge: Living with Global Capitalism*. London: Jonathan Cape.

Skeggs, B. (1994) Situating the production of feminist ethnography, in M. Maynard and J. Purvis (eds) *Researching Women's Lives from a Feminist Perspective*. London: Taylor & Francis.

Skeggs, B. (1997) *Formations of Class and Gender*. London: Sage.

Skeggs, B. (1998) Seeing differently: ethnography and educational power, *Australian Educational Researcher*, 26(1): 33–53.

Skelton, C. (1998) Feminism and research into masculinities and schooling, *Gender and Education*, 10(2): 217–27.

Skidmore, D. (1999a) Divergent discourses of learning difficulty, *British Educational Research Journal*, 25(5): 651–63.

Skidmore, D. (1999b) Relationships between contrasting discourses of learning difficulty, *European Journal of Special Needs Education*, 14(1): 12–20.

Slee, R. (1995) *Changing Theories and Practices of Discipline*. London: Falmer.

Slee, R. (1997) Imported or important theory? Sociological interrogations of disablement and special education, *British Journal of Sociology of Education*, 18(3): 407–19.

Slee, R. (1998) High reliability organizations and liability students: the politics of recognition, in R. Slee, G. Weiner and S. Tomlinson (eds) *School Effectiveness for Whom? Challenges to the School Effectiveness and School Improvement Movements*. London: Falmer.

Smith, J. (1999) Our mission: inclusion not exclusion, *Managing Schools Today*, 9(2): 35–6.

Stanley, L. and Wise, S. (1993) *Breaking Out Again*. London: Routledge.

St Pierre, E. A. (2000) Poststructural feminism in education: an overview, *Qualitative Studies in Education*, 13(5): 477–515.

Swain, J. (1995) Constructing participatory research: in principle and in practice, in P. Clough and L. Barton (eds) *Making Difficulties: Research and the Construction of Special Educational Needs*. London: Paul Chapman.

Taylor, P. J. (1996) *The Way the Modern World Works: World Hegemony to World Impasse*. New York: John Wiley.

Thomas, G. and Loxley, A. (2001) *Deconstructing Special Education and Constructing Inclusion*. Buckingham: Open University Press.

Thomas, G., Walker, D. and Webb, J. (1998) *The Making of the Inclusive School*. London: Routledge.

Tomlinson, S. (1982) *A Sociology of Special Education*. London: Routledge and Kegan Paul.

Tomlinson, S. (ed.) (1994) *Educational Reform and its Consequences*. London: Rivers Oram Press.

Tooley, J. (1998) *Educational Research: A Review*. London: Office for Standards in Education.

Urwin, C. (1985) Constructing motherhood: the persuasion of natural development, in C. Steedman, C. Urwin and V. Walkerdine (eds) *Language, Gender and Childhood*. London: Routledge and Kegan Paul.

Vlachou, A. (1995) Images and the construction of identities in a research context, in P. Clough and L. Barton (eds) *Making Difficulties: Research and the Construction of Special Educational Needs*. London: Paul Chapman.

Walkerdine, V. (1988) *The Mastery of Reason*. London: Routledge and Kegan Paul.

Walkerdine, V. (1989) Femininity as performance, *Oxford Review of Education*, 15(3): 267–79.

Walkerdine, V. (1990) *Schoolgirl Fictions*. London: Verso.

Walkerdine, V. (1997) *Daddy's Girl: Young Girls and Popular Culture*. London: Macmillan.

Walkerdine, V. and Girls into Mathematics Unit (1989) *Counting Girls Out: Girls into Mathematics*. London: Virago.

Walkerdine, V. and Lucey, H. (1989) *Democracy in the Kitchen: Regulating Mothers and Socialising Daughters*. London: The Women's Press.

Warnock, M. (1978) *The Concept of Educational Need: The Charles Gittins Memorial Lecture*. Dyfed: Gomer Press.

Weedon, C. (1997) *Feminist Politics and Poststructuralist Theory*. Oxford: Blackwell.

Welton, J., Wedell, K. and Vorhaus, G. (1990) Meeting special educational needs: the 1981 Act and its implications, in H. Daniels and J. Ware (eds) *Special Educational Needs and the National Curriculum: The Impact of the Education Reform Act*. London: Kogan Page.

Wilson, J. (2000) Doing justice to inclusion, *European Journal of Special Needs Education*, 15(3): 297–304.

Wright, C., Weekes, D. and McGlaughlin, A. (2000) *'Race', Class and Gender in Exclusion from School*. London: Falmer.

Zollers, N. J., Ramanthan, A. K. and Yu, M. (1999) The relationship between school culture and inclusion: how an inclusive culture supports inclusive education, *Qualitative Studies in Education*, 12(2): 157–74.

ɟ

Index

SPECIAL EDUCATIONAL NEEDS, INCLUSION AND DIVERSITY: A TEXTBOOK

Norah Frederickson and Tony Cline

This book has the potential to become *the* textbook on special educational needs. Written specifically with the requirements of student teachers, trainee educational psychologists, SENCOs and SEN Specialist Teachers in mind, it provides a comprehensive and detailed discussion of the major issues in special education. Whilst recognizing the complex and difficult nature of many special educational needs, the authors place a firm emphasis on inclusion and suggest practical strategies enabling professionals to maximize inclusion at the same time as recognizing and supporting diversity.

Key features:

- takes full account of linguistic, cultural and ethnic diversity unlike many other texts in the field
- addresses the new SEN Code of Practice and is completely up to date
- recognizes current concerns over literacy and numeracy and devotes two chapters to these areas of need
- offers comprehensive and detailed coverage of major issues in special educational needs in one volume
- accessibly written with the needs of the student and practitioner in mind.

Contents

Part 1: Principles and concepts – Children, families, schools and the wider community: an integrated approach – Concepts of special educational needs – Inclusion – Special educational needs: understanding pathways of development – Part 2: Assessment in context – Identification and assessment – Reducing bias in methods of assessment – Curriculum-based assessment – Learning environments – Part 3: Areas of need – Learning difficulties – Language – Literacy – Mathematics – Hearing impairment – Emotional and behavioural difficulties – Social skills – References – Index.

528pp   0 335 20402 3 (Paperback)   0 335 20973 4 (Hardback)

INCLUDING PARENTS?
EDUCATION, CITIZENSHIP AND PARENTAL AGENCY

Carol Vincent

- How do parents and professionals experience their involvement with locally-based education groups?
- Who joins local groups and who gets involved in campaigns?
- What do their experiences of 'including' themselves tell us about public participation and citizenship today?

Carol Vincent focuses upon the neglected topic of lay activity in relation to education. She describes the experiences and motivations of parents involved in a variety of grass-roots groups, organizing around educational issues, and examines their problems and successes. She explores how parents' relationships with educational institutions cast light on the broader issues of public participation and how citizenship is experienced today by different social class and ethnic groups.

Contents

Parents and education: consumers, partners or citizens? – Being a 'good' parent – Seeking advice: the special education advice centre (SEAC) – Education for motherhood? – Parents, collective action and education – An alienating system? – Conclusion – including parents? – References – Index.

176pp   0 335 20442 2 (Paperback)   0 335 20443 0 (Hardback)

DECONSTRUCTING SPECIAL EDUCATION AND CONSTRUCTING INCLUSION

Gary Thomas and Andrew Loxley

Deconstructing Special Education and Constructing Inclusion is a sophisticated, multidisciplinary critique of special education that leaves virtually no intellectual stone unturned. It is a must read for anyone interested in the role and significance of inclusive pedagogy in the new struggle for an inclusive society.

Professor Tom Skrtic, University of Kansas

In this book the authors look behind special education to its supposed intellectual foundations. They find a knowledge jumble constructed of bits and pieces from Piagetian, psychoanalytic, psychometric and behavioural theoretical models. They examine the consequences of these models' influence for professional and popular thinking about learning difficulty. In turn, they explore and critique the results of this dominance for our views about children who are different and for the development of special education and its associated professions. In the light of this critique, they suggest that much of the 'knowledge' of special education is misconceived, and they proceed to advance a powerful rationale for inclusion out of ideas about stakeholding, social justice and human rights. Concluding that inclusion owes more to political theory than to psychology or sociology, the authors suggest that a rethink is needed about the ways in which we come by educational knowledge. This is important reading for students of education, and for teachers, advisers and educational psychologists.

Contents

160pp   0 335 20448 1 (Paperback)   0 335 20449 X (Hardback)

STRUGGLES FOR INCLUSIVE EDUCATION
AN ETHNOGRAPHIC STUDY

Anastasia D. Vlachou

This is a lucid, authoritative and original study of teachers' views and attitudes towards the integration into mainstream schooling of a particular group of children defined as having special educational needs. It offers one of the clearest and most comprehensive analyses of the socio-political mechanisms by which the 'special' are socially constructed and excluded from the normal education system that has so far been produced.

Sally Tomlinson,
Professor of Educational Policy at Goldsmiths College,
University of London

In its detailed analysis of primary school teachers' and pupils' attitudes towards integration, this book locates the question of inclusive education within the wider educational context. The wealth of original interview material sheds new light on the reality of everyday life in an educational setting, and shows us the nature and intensity of the struggles experienced by both teachers and pupils in their efforts to promote more inclusive school practices. The author's sensitive investigation of the relationship between teachers' contradictory views of the 'special' and their integration, and the wider social structures in which teachers work, adds to our understanding of the inevitable difficulties in promoting inclusive educational practices within a system which functions via exclusive mechanisms.

The book will be of interest to students of education, sociology and disability as well as teachers and policy-makers involved in inclusive education. The original methodologies adopted when working with the children will also appeal to students of attitudinal, disability and educational research.

Contents

Introduction – Part 1: Setting the theoretical scene – Disability, normality and special needs: political concepts and controversies – Towards a better understanding of attitudes – Part 2: Teachers' perspectives – Teachers and the changing culture of teaching – Teachers' attitudes towards integration (with reference to pupils with Down's Syndrome) – Part 3: Children's perspectives – Integration: the children's point of view – Disabled children and children's culture – Conclusion – Appendices – References – Index.

208pp   0 335 19763 9 (Paperback)   0 335 19764 7 (Hardback)